# NORTH NORFOLK
# FISHERMEN

# NORTH NORFOLK
# FISHERMEN

## FRAN WEATHERHEAD

*Sadly, since this book has been in preparation, former lifeboat cox'n and fisherman Richard Davies and fisherman Ralph Kirk have both died.*

*Frontispiece:*

Above: Billy (W.H.) Davies fishing from the skiff *Rory James*. Cromer, 2007.

Below: Kitty Lee at her family crab stall. Cromer, 2000.

First published 2011

The History Press
The Mill, Brimscombe Port
Stroud, Gloucestershire, GL5 2QG
www.thehistorypress.co.uk

© Fran Weatherhead, 2011

The right of Fran Weatherhead to be identified as the Author
of this work has been asserted in accordance with the
Copyrights, Designs and Patents Act 1988.

British Library Cataloguing in Publication Data.
A catalogue record for this book is available from the British Library.

ISBN 978 0 7524 5798 7

Typesetting and origination by The History Press
Printed in Great Britain
Manufacturing managed by Jellyfish Print Solutions Ltd

# CONTENTS

# ACKNOWLEDGEMENTS

I would like to thank the many people who have helped me during the preparation for this book. Most of all I am indebted to the fishermen, who have given their time with humour, good grace and patience when I have made my interviews, recordings and films. Some have taken me out on fishing trips, others have searched out personal photographs or have read my manuscript. The following are sincerely thanked: John Balls, John Balls (Sn), Steve Barrett, Joyce Blythe, Alan Cooper, Bob Cox, George Cox, Willy Cox MBE, Richard Davies, John Davies, Billy (W.T.) Davies, John Dowsing, Marjorie Dowsing, John Jonas, Billy Gaff, Dennis Gaff, Ralph Kirk, Ivan Large, Donny Lawrence, John Lee, Kitty Lee, David Leeder, Richard Little, Lewis and Mabel Harrison, Bennett Middleton, Roger Seago, John Webster, Lenny and Anne West. Amongst others who have kindly provided information are Andy Davies, Billy (W.H.) Davies, Dean Ellis, Andy Pardon, Keith Shaul, Andy Webster, Andy Williamson and John Worthington.

I am extremely grateful to boat-builders Alan Goodchild and David Hewitt for explaining their work to me; also to Mike Emery, Richard Harvey and David Barker who supplied additional information. Thank you, too, to Paul Williment and David Bywater who took the time to explain the work carried out on their premises. I am very indebted to Mat Mander, Clerk and Chief Fisheries Officer of Eastern Sea Fisheries and to Ady Woods, Fisheries Officer, for reading my manuscript and kindly making suggestions; also to Alistair Murphy of Cromer Museum, Ms Emma Davison of Time and Tide Museum, Great Yarmouth, and to staff at Sheringham Museum for providing assistance and information. Some photographs are reproduced courtesy of *Eastern Daily Press*, Norwich and Norfolk County Library and Information Service; others are the author's or generously supplied by individuals credited in the captions.

Final words of gratitude should go to Emily Locke, Miranda Love, Amy Rigg, Marc Williams and others at The History Press who have steered me through the publishing process, to my partner Andy Boyce who provided the line-drawings and helped in many ways, and to Jenny Griffin, Jim and Brenda Hare and other friends who have been generally supportive and kept me afloat.

# PREFACE

The fishing industry discussed in this book covers a 30-mile area of the North Norfolk coast from Wells at one end to villages south-east of Cromer at the other. This coincides with the geographically distinct area of the Cromer Ridge, a glacial feature which makes this part of the coast particularly picturesque. It includes the small towns of Cromer, Sheringham and Wells, with interspersed villages. The area also coincides with the membership of the North Norfolk Fishermen's Society, of which I am secretary. This has meant I have come to know the fishermen in the immediate region. Being aware of changes in the fishing industry, some of which have happened quite quickly in the region, as well as of the possible threats to its survival, my instincts as an archaeologist have impelled me to record traditional knowledge before it is lost. Over the last eight years I have recorded interviews and photographed and filmed aspects of fishing life at sea and on land. Fishermen are particularly difficult to 'catch' as they work unusual, fluctuating hours, but many have been very kind in taking the time to talk to me about their work, and in taking me fishing. This book is a distillation of some of that material.

Fishing from North Norfolk is characteristically small-scale, mainly done from beach-launched boats. These days, the fishermen are mostly potting for crabs and lobsters. Harbour-boats going from Wells and Morston work on a larger scale. I have discussed Wells because it makes for an interesting comparison with the towns and villages to the east. Wells has traditional links eastwards because some of its fishermen once came from there and its boats had once been not too dissimilar from beach boats.

In this small stretch of the English coast, I have tried to show how fishing has changed within living memory and what has stayed the same. I have concentrated on Cromer, a present-day centre for potting. Much of the gear in the region is still hand-made, and it is only in recent years that some gadgetry (for example GPS) has been taken up and fibreglass boats have replaced wooden boats. There was once much more diversity in the fishing. Besides potting, there was herring-catching, whelking, lining, trawling, bait-digging, cockling and shrimping, now all mainly gone by the wayside. I have included the mussel fishery at Stiffkey to the east of Wells where there is a revival of a tradition which was almost lost. Mussel-fishermen have connections with crabbing and other forms of fishing, as either they or their fathers had once done it.

Where possible I have used the fishermen's own words. Their accounts read with refreshing clarity, humour and unusual terms, besides revealing something of their personalities and attitudes to their work.

John Balls cutting up bait on a crabbing trip from Cromer, his son Michael at the tiller. 2003.

# CHAPTER 1

# INTRODUCTION

It is a memorable experience to be down on Cromer beach at first light. One moment it is pitch dark, then as the first rays of light sweep across the sky, the fishermen's pick-up trucks rumble down the cobbled Gangway and pull up on the prom. Quietly talking among themselves, they load boxes of bait onto the boats and get things ready. Within a few minutes they have scrambled onto the boats; with a few puffs of black smoke from the tractors, the boats trundle off down the beach on their carriages. The skippers instinctively time the launchings, looking for gaps or 'levels' between the waves. Ropes are cast off, the boats slide off their carriages, and they quickly steam off into the distance, plunging through the waves. The catamaran is the only boat to be launched stern first. She is turned round, the engine grunting and murmuring; in seconds she is away too. To be on one of these boats and see the twinkling lights of the town recede into the distance and the beautiful colours of dawn emerge over the horizon is a moving experience. This is not lost on the fishermen, but they have a hard morning's work to start. On one occasion with John Balls on an old wooden crab boat in 2003, we took an extra person who jumped over to another boat when it was brought up alongside. Transferring crew like this had once been commonplace; as John pointed out, 'You won't see *that* often now!'

As we steam off, the fishermen whack their arms across their chests to keep warm. The business of preparing the bait begins before the crab grounds are reached. This is not a pleasant job as it is sometimes still frozen; large, somewhat revolting, pieces of cod are ripped apart by hand or cut by knife. My vantage point is from the edge of a box of stinking bait in the bows, sometimes disappearing behind a wall of pots which gets higher as hauling proceeds and the pots are to be moved somewhere else. There is little space on a crab boat and, with ropes going over at speed, it is potentially danger-ous. On the catamaran and on John Balls's skiff, one could have a quick warm-up in the wheelhouse, but not for long as the skippers constantly move in and out giving a quick flip to the wheel or a scan of the GPS screen.

It is a very long morning's work, five to seven hours at sea. As each shank of pots is reached, the winches whirr and moan as pot after pot is pulled up, emptied, rebaited and chucked back overboard. The rhythm is repeated again and again. Dan buoy – anchor – pot, pot, pot – anchor – dan buoy. Haul and shoot, haul and shoot; then steam off to another dan buoy and do it again. The tow ropes which link the pots coil round and are kept in order as pots come onto the boat. The fishermen seem to know every inch of the sea – my untutored eye only gets a rough idea of our location by looking at the distant coastline. Other fishing boats whisk by, while sometimes we get near a large vessel steaming past; one is called the *Dealer* which causes a few laughs. I see one or two seals, but am told porpoises, dolphins, and even the occasional whale or puffin have been seen. After a few hours it's time for a quick cup of flask coffee, then back to work. Eventually, all the shanks have been visited and the boat is splashed clean with buckets of sea water. Boxes of crabs are restacked, and lobsters have their claws tied with elastic bands and covered with wet sacking. We steam home at a steady pace, leaving a foamy trail in our wake. Undulating cliff tops and villages pass by until Cromer's pretty seafront, now in full sunshine, hoves into view. It is too early for much activity – just a few dog-walkers patrol the beach.

A tractor and trailer take the boat up the beach, bumping over the ridges of shingle. Within minutes, boxes of crabs and lobsters are loaded onto pick-ups and driven away. A few hours later, the cooking and dressing completed, the shellfish is out on sale in local shops and stalls. The fishermen might also deliver a few box-loads further afield. They can snatch a few hours sleep in the afternoon but in the evening there is preparation to do for the next day's trip. Such is a typical day, not much changed over the last few years, except that the boats are now mostly one-man skiffs. Fishing goes on often six days a week, throughout the crabbing season. 'It's a young man's game' they say, but some fishermen not in the first flush of youth are still crabbing.

# The Region

Fishing developed along the North Norfolk coast where water gouged deep cuts or 'gaps' in the cliffs and boats could be moved down to the beaches. All along the coast in towns and villages this access has been made easier in modern times by concrete and wooden ramps. Long steeped in fishing tradition, the coastal settlements only took off as tourist destinations when they were reached by the railways in the late nineteenth century. Although transportation of crabs and lobsters to Norwich and London had been established well before this time – in 1724 Daniel Defoe noted Cromer lobsters were reaching London – the railways made access to markets in London and other cities easier. The emergence of local ice-merchants, as listed in nineteenth-century street directories, is presumably connected with storage and transportation of fish.

Cromer, Sheringham and, to a lesser extent, the smaller adjacent villages, have long been famous for the excellent taste and high meat content of their crabs. Cromer is practically synonymous with crabs, although Defoe in his time highlighted Cromer as famous for 'good lobsters' which were caught in 'great numbers'. Cromer was also known for its abundance of fish according to nineteenth-century accounts.

Along the North Norfolk coast, from Sea Palling to just east of Cromer, the beaches are fairly flat and sandy. There are areas of flinty rock offshore, which provide

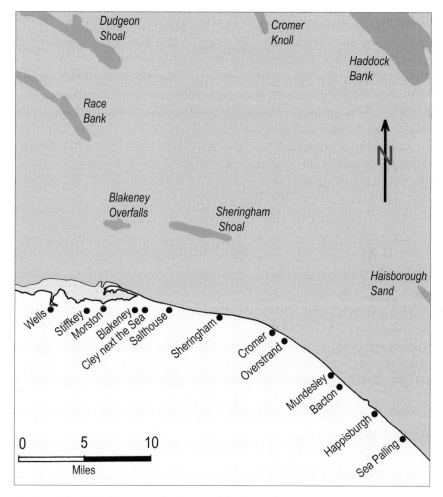

Section of the Norfolk coast, with features of the North Sea.

good habitats for crabs and lobsters. Rocks are noticeable at low-tide off East and West Runton and Cromer, for instance forming the horseshoe-shaped 'Tongue' off Cromer. Sheringham was once the most important fishing station in this section of coast, but now, Cromer with just over a dozen fishing boats far outstrips Sheringham. Sheringham has become like Mundesley and other coastal villages, which support at most two or three full-time boats. Some villages are even reduced to one or none. To the south-east, old photographs show fishing activity at Bacton, Happisburgh and Sea Palling. Nowadays commercial fishing has either stopped at these and other south-easterly fishing stations, such as at Happisburgh, where erosion has had a hand, or lingers on, as at Bacton. Sometimes the fishermen have moved: Michael and Andy Williamson on *Julie's Dawn* and *Early Rose* fished from Cart Gap near Sea Palling until Andy moved to go from Mundesley. In recent decades in this section of coast, there has been a development of more part-time fishing.

Going west from Sheringham one reaches Weybourne, where the beaches become steep, shelving pebbles. This continues to Cley and Salthouse, where land reclaimed from the sea in the seventeenth century lies behind. The marshes here are nature reserves, havens for migrating birds. Three fishing boats now go from Weybourne, Cley has just one or two boats, Salthouse none. From all these places – Sea Palling to Salthouse and Cley – wherever boats could be got off from the beach, fishing has been until recent times much the same. Usually working no more than 1 to 4 miles from the shore, that is, within the inshore waters of 6 miles, fishermen have supplemented potting with herring and mackerel-catching, long-lining for whitefish, whelking, and occasionally shrimping, where the ground is sandy. Since these options have largely gone by the wayside, crabbing is now the mainstay.

Further west there are the harbours of Blakeney, Morston and Wells. All are prone to encroaching marine and river silt. For centuries Blakeney and Wells were busy ports, as also Cley until choked by silt. They supported healthy oyster industries in the nineteenth century, which lasted at Blakeney until 1935 when the last oyster smack finished. Blakeney and Morston have now become the haunts of yachts and other pleasure-craft, including some which take visitors to see the seal colonies. But a handful of fishing boats still go on long potting trips from Morston. Wells's heyday was when it became the national centre for whelking, after supplanting Sheringham. When the industry collapsed, potting became the mainstay as elsewhere along the coast. Vessels involved with building wind farms have recently brought new life to the town, but the fishing industry is still healthy: eleven boats of 7–13m, which work up to 40 miles offshore. Shipping and visiting fishing boats have tailed off at Wells, after an increase in the 1970s–80s.

On either side of Wells, from Stiffkey to Brancaster and beyond, there are large stretches of marshland and nature reserves cut by creeks and tidal estuaries. From the adjacent villages, cockles, mussels and winkles have traditionally been gathered at low tide. Of these, only musseling continues on a commercial basis.

The fishing industry has long given character and colour to all these towns and villages along the Norfolk coast. Even though somewhat diminished and under threat, the industry is much valued by local authorities for its tourist appeal. With the exception of Wells, it is relatively small-scale, but shellfish sales are nevertheless worth many millions of pounds to the local economy. In terms of labour, besides fishermen there are scores of people who process and market the shellfish behind the scenes.

# Families

As in many other fishing ports in Britain, fishing runs in families in North Norfolk. Some claim seven or eight generations of fishermen, with branches of the family spread up and down the coast. One can see tombstones in old churchyards with carvings of sailing fishing-boats, or lifeboats, and family names going back three or four generations, and yet know their descendants are still fishing today. The Davieses,

Bob and George Cox, a quiet moment as they steam out to sea. (Via B. Cox)

Wests, Coxes and Coopers have long been 'big' in the region, and there are many more. Nicknames have helped to distinguish those sharing the same surname, but fewer fishermen use them today.

There was once little doubt that one or more sons would take over from their fathers. Often they had been taken to sea as soon as they were able to walk, while by the time they were schoolboys they would be helping on the boats in their holidays. As a youngster, John Balls helped his uncle on the last hand-hauling boat, the *Charles Perkins*: 'If you were big enough to get in the boat, you were big enough to work!' Richard Davies, former lifeboat cox'n and recently retired from a lifetime of fishing, recalled when he told his father he wanted to work on a farm or go in the navy, his father retorted:

'Good, the Cromer navy!' I was seasick for two years, every day, and hated being at sea for one year. I wanted to die, I remember lying in the bottom of the boat – the swell, the old bait! – no freezers then – I wanted to *die*. And the old man would say 'Die when you get home'. After that it was habit-forming, and if it was a fine day I'd not worry about it. 'Shrimp' (Davies) was the same.

Occasionally, outsiders unconnected with fishing have taken it up. Dennis Gaff, now retired but with son Billy following him, started as a painter and decorator. Dennis 'took' to the sea, learning his skills from Henry 'Shrimp' Davies. He was fishing full-time by age sixteen. John 'John'o' Lee also came from 'outside', marrying Shrimp's daughter Kitty. More recently, the occasional young man has come from fishing else-where, such as from trawling or line-fishing when these declined at Lowestoft, or from Grimsby. The influx of new blood is to be welcomed as many of the sons from fishing families are not carrying on from their fathers, preferring jobs with regular money and normal hours, or careers based on qualifications. Others have gone into the navy, such as two of the four Balls boys who had all at some time fished with their father. The trend to move out has occurred as fishermen have become better off and more opportunities have opened up. As Richard Davies has said, it was a smaller world when he was young. Some fishermen even discourage their sons from follow-ing them. They feel that fishing has become harder, including being beset by rules and regulations which were not there in their younger days. Witness a slogan, 'DEFRA sucks, but they ain't fishermens friends' on a Wells vehicle! As Norfolk's fishermen get older, getting new recruits into the industry is a serious concern.

In the past, crew members often moved from vessel to vessel, then got their own boats. Fishermen also moved themselves and their boats to different fishing sta-tions along the coast. The Cox brothers went back and forth between Cromer and Mundesley to do different types of fishing. Others like the Davieses and John Jonas, from Cromer, have worked out of Wells. Short moves also occur when sea defences or promenades have to be repaired, so swelling the boat numbers elsewhere for a time. At Cromer, four or five boats from East Runton have recently joined the resident fleet when it became difficult to launch from their own beach.

# The fishermen

Many traditional communities, such as of trawlermen, miners and dockers, have disappeared when the livelihoods which sustained them went to the wall. Fishing communities have struggled on, in Norfolk as elsewhere in Britain. Although families still 'look out' for each other if someone is in trouble, older fishermen will say families no longer socialise together like they used to and the fishermen, themselves, gather less on the beach or cliff-top just to chat. Even step-dancing, which once entertained the community in local pubs, notably by the Davies family, was only carried on in recent years by one fisherman, Richard Davies.

When it comes to character, fishermen as a breed are instinctively at home at sea, and seem ever keen to get out there. On land, North Norfolk fishermen become independently-minded businessmen; they do not market their catch co-operatively as in some places in Britain. They are skilled craftsmen, inventively making gear accord-ing to 'needs must' and economy (Chapter 5), while some become mechanics if they service their own boats and tractors. Because like other fishermen their lives are marked by unpredictability, whether due to the weather, the catches or the markets, planning ahead even a few days can be difficult. Flexibility and adaptability become second nature. Most noticeable to the outsider is their refreshingly anarchic outlook on life and not liking to be hemmed in by rules and regulations. In spite of their no-nonsense attitude and toughness, coming from lives spent in hard, demanding, and sometimes dangerous work, there is frequently a leavening of in-jokes and wit.

The wives pitch into the family firm, often taking over the paperwork and running the fish shop if they have one. Insights into family life and the work undertaken by fishermen's wives cannot be bettered than by referring to Katherine Lee's first-hand account in *Crabs and Shannocks*.

Over the years there have been many tragedies of both shipping and fishing boats off the Norfolk coast, part of which was once called the 'Devil's Throat'. The sea bed is reputedly strewn with wrecks. Many of the fishermen have given exemplary service on the lifeboats, with outstanding figures such as Cromer's Henry Blogg and Henry 'Shrimp' Davies. The Davieses have provided several generations of cox'ns. Several fishermen have had life-threatening experiences. When asked about the dangers of fishing, Norfolk's fishermen do not dwell on the subject and tend to brush it off with understatement or even humour. Donny Lawrence:

> Biggest laugh one year we got was when I was working with Jack Davies and John Jonas, and it turned up rough. As we were steaming back home, just 50–70 yards off the beach, I got the bucket to wash all the boards down. And John said to me, 'What the bloody hell do you think *you're* doing!' – I said just washing the boat down. He said, 'There's enough bloody water coming over without you chucking gallons of water about!' It *did* get a bit rough coming in to Cromer – the other fishermen were all standing on the beach waiting for us so they could help get us up.

When a boat was late returning, it was customary for a knot of concerned fishermen to look out for it from the cliff top or the beach. Ralph Kirk:

> There was no radios when I first went. To attract attention you shout. When we broke down with 'Tuna', we tied an oilskin on an oar and held that up. That's all you had, no flares, no radio, no nothing. Someone would come and see if you were alright, and give you a tow in. We didn't even know what a lifejacket was. When I was with Dennis in the early 70s and it was blowing up rough, and the lifeboat threw us a couple of lifejackets – that was the first I saw one other than when I was in the navy! You prayed the good Lord would keep an eye on you. But years ago – not like now – if it was bad, you stayed on the beach.

Probably arising from the dangers at sea, fishermen are notoriously superstitious. Even now, several have told me that whistling is banned (don't whistle up a wind!)

and nothing new can start on a Friday. The first time I went on a fishing trip, it could not be on a Friday. Even new boats could not be launched on a Friday. Green was a colour to be avoided. Retired Bob Cox:

> But we had to put up with green when we got synthetic materials (twine); usually it was orange, blue or black. Dad would not have a white handled knife on the boat, that's a belief probably passed down. He detested things upside down. He'd not want the lid off the engine – you mustn't tempt providence. Boxes in the boat always had to be the right way up. I'm not worried by mentioning pigs and rabbits – but father was. I'd not start anything on Friday. I don't know why, perhaps it's something in the Bible. When I was herring-catching on the drifters, it was Friday 13th, we were setting away from Yarmouth, everyone was uptight about it but the owner wanted us to go. These tubes in the engine blew, so we turned round and go back in – we put it down to Friday 13th!

Religion once played a big part too, especially in Sheringham where there were a good many Bible-thumpers. The Sabbath was observed everywhere, until the Coxes started fishing on Sundays.

Poverty was a factor for some fishermen before the latter half of the twentieth century when general living standards rose. A wonderful portrait of life in Sheringham between the wars is given in May Ayres's book *Memoirs of a Shannock*. Some of the poorer fishermen in Sheringham had to hire their boats from entrepreneur Harry Johnson, thereby becoming 'tied' to him to sell their catch or give him a cut. He also made loans to have engines installed. Later, 'Downtide' West hired out boats and marketed their catch. One fisherman pointed out that marketing was not always an easy matter for fishermen until they got their own phones and vehicles. The hardship was brought home to me when Richard Little (still fishing) recalled when fishing had been bad in winter, his father had come home to their cottage one day with 15s for the week to keep a wife and four children.

Fishermen's clothing marks them out. Photographs from thirty or so years ago might show a dozen or so fishermen on the beach all looking exactly the same in their flat caps and 'slops' with 'roppers', or neckerchiefs. The buttonless smocks, or slops, are still worn, being most practical, but the ubiquitous baseball hat has made occasional inroads. At Sheringham there was once a tradition of wearing hand-knitted 'ganseys' (local word for guernseys). Old ones were worn on the boat, new ones were for the rest of the time. Sheringham wives knitted them for their husbands and for other fishermen. Others along the coast wore mainly factory-made ganseys, unless they married a Sheringham girl or commissioned one. Mrs West is still making them for retired fisherman Lenny West, who even now would never be seen without one. Patterns were not written down, so women learnt by word of mouth or from looking at old ganseys. Church was a good place to eye up someone's new gansey and get ideas for your own, but the overall design became unique to a particular fisherman.

Lenny remembers as a youngster he had to be quiet while his grandmother concentrated as she 'set up the pattern' for the first two rows. The gansey was tightly knitted in one piece and had very fine stitches. Some women might knit in a group on the beach, but in the evening only lamp-light was available. Receiving 4–9s a gansey, Lenny's grandmother had knitted for a firm in Yarmouth which sold them to fishermen along the coast.

The wives once made all the clothing for their husbands, from flannel drawers and shirts to cotton trousers (tanned with the slops in the tan tub), boot-stockings and oilskins. The tradition of wearing smart tailor-made suits for formal occasions still endures. They might also wear smart navy guernseys. The suits were beautifully made in heavy serge, and sometimes they were passed down the family – one present-day fisherman is 'wearer number four'. In Cromer, they were made until the 1970s by Mayes the tailors in a basement in Garden Street. The trousers have a flap opening and a small slit by the ankle. David Leeder's suit made in 1964 cost him £16, which was 1½ weeks' wages. It would have cost a little more with a velvet collar. Bell-bottom trousers, worn by fishermen after the First World War, made a brief comeback in the 1960s–70s when the style became fashionable.

## Other work

Most fishermen I have spoken to have spent all their working lives fishing. Most have enjoyed it – with the rider, 'But we knew no different!' Occasionally, some of the older ones like Dennis Gaff or the Cox brothers did a spell of trawling from Lowestoft or herring-drifting from Yarmouth. Others have served in the navy or merchant navy, especially during the war.

They often took up additional work to make ends meet. Earlier in the twentieth century in the tourist towns they hired out rooms, beach tents, deck-chairs, and even swimming costumes and towels to tourists. This would be done mainly after crabbing finished in June. Taking holiday-makers on boat trips lasted past the middle of the century, until health and safety stepped in. With 'tripping seats' added, a boat could pack in over a dozen people. Boats run by former fishermen still take visitors out to see the seals from Morston and Blakeney.

Winter was a time to look for work. Mid-century, in Sheringham, some like 'Teapot' West had picked stones off the beach. Barrow-loads of stones were dragged to where the former Grand Hotel stood near the golf links. Only small blue stones were needed, which were sent by train to the Staffordshire potteries. Many fishermen in the region did sprout-picking or bait-digging, while others like David Leeder in the 1960s–70s worked with engineering firms repairing walls and revetments along the coast. Others worked on laying gas pipelines or constructing oil rigs in the North Sea.

If one refers to official reports on fishing it is no surprise to note that the numbers of working fishermen along the Norfolk coast have decreased over the years.

Richard Davies, well-known Cromer fisherman and former lifeboat cox'n.

The quoted figures of 100 crab boats in Sheringham and 120 fishermen (about fifty boats) in Cromer in 1875 seem incredible now. For a Parliamentary Enquiry in 1913, official figures record the number had gone down to twenty-five boats at Cromer, about seventy-five at Sheringham as some had moved to Grimsby and Yorkshire. By 1966, a MAFF report states there were only thirty beach boats for the region between Mundesley and Salthouse. At present there are about thirty-four boats if this stretch extends to Morston, and eleven bigger boats going from the harbour at Wells. The industry is surviving, but manpower for the future will be the problem. There are threats like offshore dredging, and possibly wind farms, the long-term effects of which are unknown, although it has been suggested that they may create protected grounds for shellfish larvae and therefore be beneficial. Other threats are erosion and loss of the beaches. A major problem is going to be the cost of maintaining sea defences and the groynes which keep the beaches in place. A brace of rock armour has been put in to protect Sheringham's seafront, and artificial reefs now help to secure the area around Sea Palling. Some fishermen are gloomy about the future of fishing in the area: 'In twenty years it will all be gone!' Others are more hopeful, like Willy Cox, who has told me, 'There will *always* be fishermen at Cromer!' It will be a sad day if the industry becomes just a heritage 'experience' while the real thing is allowed to slip away.

The next two chapters discuss the fishing boats which have made harvesting the seas off Norfolk possible and have sustained so many livelihoods. This is followed by two chapters on crab-fishing, recent changes, and the associated fishing gear. Other chapters cover the mainly lost fishing activities at Cromer, along the North Norfolk coast and at Wells: long-lining, herring-catching, whelking, trawling, bait-digging, shrimping, cockling, while the last chapter looks at a small comeback of the mussel industry in Blakeney Harbour.

# CHAPTER 2

# BOATS AND BEACHING

Until the 1990s, a line of traditional wooden crab boats, similar except for variations in colour, could be seen parked at the top of the beach at Cromer. This was also the situation at Sheringham and villages along the North Norfolk coast. These boats were the famous wooden double-ended 'crabbers', symmetrically pointed at head and stern. They have given a distinctive character to Norfolk's beaches, delighting holiday-makers who have watched them come ashore or set up picnics in their shade. Now, different sorts of boat have appeared on the beach, mainly one-man skiffs. This is a response by today's fishermen to a lack of available crewmen as fewer youngsters join the industry, and to new technology which has become available.

The newer types of boat have meant a few changes from the old ways. Norfolk's fishermen have always adapted their fishing to changing circumstances, but it is only comparatively recently that the boats themselves have changed. Today, there is only one working traditional wooden crab boat along the whole of the North Norfolk coast, the splendid *Mary Ann* owned by John Jonas of Cromer. Sadly, another wooden boat at Overstrand, the *Star*, has recently been withdrawn from service as the owner has died. She had long been seen among the picturesque array of boats and fishing gear near the holiday-makers' café. Even the period of the GRP (glass reinforced plastic) double-ender, which superseded the wooden type and was commonly used by fishermen in the 1970s–90s, has finished bar one boat. But the traditional crab boat, in wood or glass-fibre, has not entirely disappeared. Some have been restored as pleasure boats and can be seen in leisurely pursuits in the creeks around Morston and Burnham. 'Gone soft', as fisherman John Balls put it, when his old boat retired to Morston.

Fishermen have regarded the crabbers as particularly suitable for North Norfolk's beaches. Most beaches are pebbly near the cliffs with wide stretches of sand lower down, and the majority are fairly flat. The rows of small breakers which push against the boat as it comes ashore are divided by the pointed shape of the stern. The boat is not so easily broached or knocked aside as would a flat-sterned boat. The beaches change at Sheringham and going westwards from Weybourne to Cley, where they are shelving and pebbly. Yet here too fishermen have managed to launch their crab boats. In South Norfolk and Suffolk the tradition has been flat-sterned boats, the change-over beginning beyond Sea Palling.

Fishermen explain that coming ashore, they 'get on the seas and run on it'. The particular shape of the boat has meant that it could then be laid athwart on the shore-line, with the bilge to the breakers and the low side of the boat to the shore. A familiar sight until recently was a crew member sitting on the gunwale dangling his feet in the water, as it gently bobbed up and down. A tractor would be coming down the beach to haul it out of the water and up the beach. On the occasions of getting the tractor himself, the fisherman placed the boat just right so that it could be left on its own for a few minutes, while he ran up the beach for the tractor – although I have heard of a boat wandering off! In earlier times, if conditions were right, the boat would be left athwart to 'knock up' the beach with the incoming tide. This would save the effort of manhandling it up the beach. The shape of the boat helped nudge it up the beach and not be dragged back to sea.

As is traditional among fishing communities, Norfolk fishing boats are named after wives and children, or have lyrical or religious names like *Ever Hopeful, Our Provider* or *Laus Deus*. The names are usually retained when boats are sold between fishermen because to change them is regarded as unlucky. Sometimes a fisherman will replace his boat and keep the same name in the family, so two *Don't Knows* have been owned by the Cox family. Registration numbers are marked on the boats, and abbreviations of where the boat is registered, such as YH for Great Yarmouth. Nowadays, the one-man skiffs are predominantly white with the tops red or blue, but the main body of the earlier wooden crab boats was usually black, later also white, with the top two or three planks in combinations of white, blue or red, sometimes with thin coloured stripes. In times gone by, the black was due to the boats being tarred. A tendency towards one colour or another for the top planks ran in families, or in different branches of the same family, such as red or blue for different branches of the Davies family. All-white boats did not show up well at sea, hence a couple which started out white were later repainted.

## Earlier boats

The traditional Norfolk fishing boat has been around for over 200 years. Beach scenes on early to mid-nineteenth-century prints and watercolours show double-ended sailing vessels. Probably the earliest detailed representations of the double-ended shape are by marine artist E.W. Cooke, in 1828. This basic type with clinker construction falls within the North European boat-building tradition which goes back to antiquity. This clinker construction was better for beach landing than carvel construction, as it made the boats strong yet have some 'give'. Historian E.W. White describes early ones as 16ft long, 6½ft wide. The Science Museum in London has a collection of models of fishing boats from around the country made by local boat builders, amongst them a model of a crabber, *c*.1870, built in Sheringham. The original sailing boat which it copied was bigger than White's description: recorded as 19ft long, 7ft broad, 3ft deep.

It was clinker-built in oak and believed to represent a type used along the North Norfolk coast at the time. There were no gunwales, and as with later wooden crab boats, it has no rowlocks or thole pins, but oar ('orrock') holes cut in the top planks.

The oar holes on Norfolk's crab boats stopped the oars being dislodged in rough seas, but they also allowed them to be carried up the beach by the oars, as the early crabbers were fairly small and light. The oars, which were passed through the six orrock holes, were grasped by the fishermen, who walked the boat up the beach. This is seen on late nineteenth-century photographs. To lighten the weight, the sail, mast and catch were taken out first, sometimes to be seen lying on the beach on old photographs. As most boats came ashore and were ready to be moved at about the same time, fishermen joined together in small teams to help move each other's boats.

On early crab boats, the stern and stem posts were slightly rounded, and like on Yorkshire cobles, there was a long, downward-projecting, curved rudder. The mast was well forward, at the back of the fore thwart (seat), so as to be out of the way of those working in the boat. The sail was a dipping lug type. The features can be seen on models, such as two built in 1912 and 1936 by Sheringham boat-builders Robert and James Emery, respectively. The earlier model is in Sheringham Museum; the later *Y35 Welkshell* was on temporary display. Made in lacquered wood, it is particularly beautiful, resting in its own mausoleum-style case. The sail was taken down while fishing, and moved out of the way of the crew working in the stern. Its large surface-area helped to maximise speed. Sheringham Museum records a mast 18ft high, the foot of the sail as long as the boat[1].

The sailing-and-rowing crabber was in regular use two or three generations before today's fishermen. It is said Cromer once had about fifty, Sheringham twice as many in the early twentieth century, bringing to mind the major role fishing then played in the region. Older fishermen recall their earliest days fishing on these boats. Retired Sheringham fisherman Lenny 'Teapot' West told me his first boat, the *Laus Deus* was an early crabber, with a curved rudder and without floorboards, except in the stern where the man who hauled stood and a foresheet in the bows. The boats were not sharp enough to be well down in the water and with a sail on there was a tendency for them to go over, so bags of shingle were taken on board as ballast:

> There was only a parting board in the middle so you could move the bags of ballast from one side to the other when you were sailing. Once you've got enough weight of crabs in it, you would shoot the stones overboard. There were no lockers; we put the crabs in the bottom of the boat.

Lenny's father had used *Laus Deus* for everything, but Lenny used it up to the 1960s for lining trips: it was carried up and down the beach to lay the lines, row home and go out again later to haul them. Two men rowed from the main thwart, another man rowed from the fore thwart. The rowers would push their feet against a small transverse plank at the bottom of the boat. Another old-style crabber used in the region

Model in Cromer Museum of the sailing crab boat *Viking*, which was worked until the 1960s. A fisherman adjusted the sail by the rope from the clew, which passed through an orrock hole via a hole in the stern post. The course was directed by a man at the tiller.

was the *Viking*, owned by Donald and Harry Cox, which was worked off Cromer and Happisburgh in the 1950s. There is a model of it, made by Donald, in Cromer Museum.

Lenny West, who comes from seven generations of fishermen, stressed that Sheringham had long been self-sufficient in making everything needed for its fishing industry, including the sails. His grandfather had repaired sails but at that time there would have been three or four people earning a living making them. One was 'Old' Grimes. In Cromer, Richard Davies believed Mayes the tailors, where some of the older fishermen had had their suits made, started out as a sail-maker. John Worthington, retired fisherman at Overstrand, told me fisherman Walter Seago of Trimingham had made sails for some of the last sailing crabbers for the Cromer region probably up to fifty years ago. John's mother had obtained the calico, Mr Seago cut it out and stitched it. The sails had to be tanned after the first year to make them durable. Other sails may have come from Jeckell's factory at Wroxham.

Bob Cox, now retired, who fished from Cromer and Mundesley, recalled when some fishermen acquired motor boats they still kept their sailing-rowing boats. They would be used for 'odd jobs' like being rowed a short distance offshore to collect their moorings, or for lining as Lenny West had done. Bob went shrimping from Mundesley on his father's small crabber *Don't Know*. He, like Lenny, is among the last fishermen who can recall carrying the boat in the traditional manner. It was lifted completely if four people were available, otherwise two would lift and one would push from behind. The oars went through the orrocks to rest on the bottom of the boat or on a thwart, and the fishermen held them in the crook of the arms as they walked the boat up the beach. Bob also recalls doing what must have once been standard all along the coast: carrying the catch and fishing gear up the beach by hand-barrow, or if back from herring-catching, 'running' the nets out of the boat onto a herring-net stool which was carried up the beach with another fisherman.

Even with the coming of engines, boats sometimes put up a sail. Bob Cox's father, with fourteen-year-old Bob accompanying him, sailed to the whelk grounds during the period of petrol-rationing just after the last war. Similarly, Richard Davies remembers his father Jack, with a 'pop-pop' engine on the *White Rose*, sailing to whelk grounds. Richard, in the 1970s, had a boat built with a sail, which he put up when coming home from fishing trips. A 16ft sailing crabber fitted with an outboard engine was worked up to four years ago. This was *My Dream*, used single-handed for occasional shrimping from Happisburgh. Today, John Jonas's *Mary Ann* has the distinction of being not only the last working wooden crab boat in the whole of North Norfolk, but one built with a sail. This was comparatively late, in 1972. She was originally built as a pleasure-boat, so is slightly lighter in construction than other crab boats. John last used the sail during a race at carnival-time in Cromer twenty-five years ago, but not when fishing. There is an attachment for the mast on the fore thwart, and a hole in the stern post and hooks on the gunwales for attaching the ropes from the sail. The sail is still kept, rolled up in storage, though mice have had a nibble at it.

Before crab boats with inboard engines became widespread, some of the smaller crabbers had small outboard engines added. These were used well into the 1960s, and as mentioned above the boat from Happisburgh was using one even later. The engines were taken off and removed together with the catch and fishing gear before carrying the boat up the beach. Bob Cox recalls when shrimping or trawling in a rowing crab boat with an engine, two or three bags of sand were kept in the stern to keep the propeller submerged. Although built relatively late, in 1961–62, the sailing-rowing crab boat *Little Swallow*, now in Cromer Museum, has features of early crabbers, including curved rudder and ballast 'parting' board slotted between mid and aft thwarts. This too had an outboard motor. It was owned by Richard Davies, and used as a pleasure boat for taking tourists on sea trips, and for herring-catching.

Other types of boat were hovellers, skiffs and cobles[2]. Like the crabbers, hovellers were double-ended, but they were bigger when they first appeared in the nineteenth century, although crabbers were later to catch them up in size. They were originally salvage vessels, but when used for fishing they outstripped crab boats in being able to go further to sea, work more gear and take more crew. Small removable 'cuddies' in the bows gave the crew some protection. They could work throughout the year, so as well as crabbing they would be mackerel-trawling, herring-catching, lining, and whelking, especially the latter which at Sheringham had once been a major industry. Working from dawn to dusk or even longer, Sheringham hovellers fished several miles offshore behind Sheringham Shoal. Some went as far as Grimsby, cod-fishing. They were six-oared, rowing-sailing boats to begin with; engines were put in from about the time of the First World War. Henry 'Joyful' West records twenty 22ft motorised 'whelkers' between the wars at Sheringham. They gradually became bigger and sturdier, especially the whelkers used from the harbour at Wells. The 30ft *William Edward* was worked for nearly fifty years, whelking into the 1980s. Hovellers at Cromer were known well into the twentieth century. Retired fisherman Dennis Gaff remembers three standing on the Gangway, at a time when fishermen sometimes worked two boats. One was the 24ft *QJ and J* built in 1915 worked by Henry Blogg, which is soon to come back lovingly restored to be put on display at Cromer. Others were the *Puffing Billy* and *Admiral Jellicoe*. The last hoveller was the *Ace*, worked post-war by 'Shrimp' Davies, 'Buster' Grout and Bob Davies. She was used for herring-catching off Yarmouth.

The coble was a type used in Norfolk in the nineteenth century. They were smaller than the traditional Yorkshire coble and built at Sheringham. Today's coble, with its deep forefoot, in-turning top strakes and flat sloping stern, is associated with Yorkshire's flatter beaches, where they are beached stern first before being hauled ashore. One or two cobles have been worked from Cromer, Sheringham and Bacton in recent years, but I am told by one owner that his coble, which had come down from Yorkshire, was difficult to manage on the beach at low water.

Wooden skiffs were in use up to the mid-twentieth century, before the war with sails. They had been common all along the coast, often used by part-time fishermen or youngsters – before John Balls was old enough to take up fishing his skiff was 'for messing about in'. They were also used for commercial fishing, one was Ivan Large's single-ended small rowing boat at Salthouse (which will be seen later).

To return to the crab boats, motorisation was taken up in the 1920s–30s. The boats became bigger and heavier, and additional strakes raised their height. The six orrock holes were reduced to four. Whereas in the nineteenth century crabbers could

A 'company' of fishermen skeeting Kelly Harrison's boat, *Carnival Queen*, down Cromer beach. Early 1960s. (Via Richard Davies)

lie unsupported on the sand, as they became bigger, especially with motorisation, wedge-shaped wooden 'stools' had to be placed under the belly of the boat. It was no longer possible for fishermen to carry their boats, so a method was introduced to move them using 'skeets'. These were devices consisting of metal rollers held in stout wooden frames. Two men would support the boat, while two others, sometimes willing youngsters or other fishermen, would run backwards and forwards with the skeets, putting one under the keel at the front of the boat and picking up another at the stern when the boat was pushed over it. There was an art in getting the skeets under the boat at just the right time, particularly going down the beach. Retired fisherman Dennis Gaff:

> The skeets were the same as now. But you looked after them – not like now! You'd oil and grease them, so you could take the boat down as fast as you could walk. There'd be 'Shrimp' and me walking backwards laying the skeets, and two or three others pushing the boat. Two would have arms through orrock holes. The boat'd run itself on the greased rollers.

For launching or 'shoving in' the crab boats, they could not be taken out to deep water as nowadays with the aid of tractors, but had to be rowed out until the engine took over. In bad weather fishermen co-operated in teams, or 'companies', to get the boats launched one at a time. Willy Cox, who is the last fisherman on Cromer beach who had been involved in 'manhandling' boats, described the launching. After skeeting a boat down the beach to the water's edge, a company would push it in a little further every time a 'level' or small wave came until the boat was able to float. If, say, a company of eight men worked three boats, the first boat was launched with one

Launch of Richard Davies's *JJ and F*, other fishermen going to help. Cromer, late 1970s. (Ben Gedge)

Transferring crew from boat in foreground to other boats waiting a short distance away. Cromer. (Via Richard Davies)

or two men who would jump in and pull on the oars to keep it straight to the waves – else possible disaster. Others in the company would stride into the water to help, sometimes almost to the tops of their thigh boots. Each time a boat was launched the last skeet which had become submerged had to be pulled out and thrown back up the beach. Once the boat was a little way off, another boat with one or two men in it was 'shoved in'. When eventually the last, 'finishing', boat was launched there would still be four to six men on the beach to do this. The finishing boat would then go out to the boats waiting at sea with these men, and transfer them.

Retired Ralph Kirk pointed out that to avoid hitting the bottom, the rudder was inside the boat when launched, then shipped to the outside. Later, the rudder was outside in a raised position, to be dropped down by pulling a rod out from a hole in the pintle.

It was fairly easy to get the boats skeeted down the beach, but extra power was needed to get them up, especially if the water was a long way out. At Cromer there were two mechanical winches with coiled cables (or 'wire') on either side of the Gangway. One was owned by Bob Cox's father and later taken to Mundesley. Block-and-tackles were used, with rings for the wire set into the slipways. Dennis Gaff, whose memory goes back a long way among the fishing fraternity at Cromer, remembers winches being used up to the 1940s, but they had become redundant by the time he started fishing in 1949. The winch at East Runton, thought to have been salvaged from an old sailing barge, has not been used within memory of the older fishermen I asked. When boats came in at low water, Dennis recalled:

When I was a boy, down there (on the beach) they'd leave them knocking up on 'the flats' (flat sand) athwart, the tide'd bring them up. They'd go home and have breakfast, and if the tide was right, they'd just winch them round at high-water time, and pull up a couple of lengths and leave them there on the skeets at just above the high-water mark. You didn't winch them to where you have them now, right to the Gangway, because you couldn't *get* them up there, and you'd have had to skeet them down again (further next day). You had plenty of room on the beach, the whole length of the beach to put them.

Two fishermen worked the winch, which had a pawl that stopped it flying back when they stopped hauling. At Sheringham, mechanical winches were replaced by electrical ones; one is still used today.

Another method was to have horses pull the boats up the beach. In nineteenth-century Cromer, horses had moved bathing machines, and later the Davies family used them to take beach tents and deckchairs down to the beach which they hired out. For moving the boats, horses were shared among the fishermen, and continued to be used by some fishermen after tractors were introduced after the last war. Horses had initially to be fetched from a farm in Metton, but later they were kept in fields on Runton Road. Usually a young lad was sent to fetch the horse and ride him back when a boat was due in. Bob Cox remembers fetching Charlie in his school holidays, 'He'd lead me a merry chase round the field before I could put a collar and bridle on. I was expressly told always to lead him down the Gangway, and once I decided to ride him down he slithered down the cobbles on his backside!' His family used a single horse to pull the boat up the beach with ropes while laying skeets; two people supported the boat on either side, while one led the horse up to high water mark. Older fishermen remember the Davieses used two horses. Horses may also have helped

'Yacker' Harrison on caterpillar tractor waiting to pull *Why Worry* ashore, which will be 'skeeted' up the beach. Skeet visible, far left. Cromer, 1960s. (R. Iredale)

Richard Davies's *Little Swallow* pulled up the beach on skeets, with the help of would-be fishermen. A skeet is visible in front of the boat. Cromer, 1970s. (*Eastern Daily Press*)

move boats at East Runton, according to fisherman Roger Seago, as some fishermen kept horses to move their beach huts.

After the Second World War, Cromer's fishermen came by two American ex-military half-tracks, the Davies's costing just £5. Another two were acquired for East Runton. Designed for going over rough terrain, these were ideal for moving beach huts about, also for getting boats up the beach. They would lumber up the beach, while fishermen ran backwards and forwards skeeting the boat. Ralph Kirk: 'It was so low-geared, you could get off it and let it go on its own. It gave you time to keep running the skeets, unless the bloke missed one, and you had to run like hell to stop the half-track otherwise the boat would plough into the beach!' Before ending up with wheeled tractors, caterpillar tractors, or 'crawlers', made an appearance. These were not a total success as the tracks were liable to come off. All these vehicles had to be shared at first. The boats were pulled up with ropes, skeeting all the while. They were left on skeets at the top of the beach supported by stools, not spread out along the middle as before; and older fishermen will say that, unlike today, they did not unload the catch immediately, but went off to have their breakfasts first.

Another advance was when the fishermen started to use wheeled carriages. These could be pulled by tractor with the boat lashed on, and used in launching. At Cromer, Allen's garage and a local blacksmith made them. At first the carriages could not be backed into the sea as they did not have rigid tow bars. Bob Cox described how after casting off the securing rope from the tractor, the fishermen had to push the carriage into the water before 'shoving' the boat off. At East Runton, Roger Seago recalled launching had been 'a bit Heath Robinson' there, using a long pole to push the boat off. Companies of fishermen still helped to launch each other's boats using the shared tractors and carriages. When the boats returned, the sharing palaver was repeated as each company got one boat up the beach at a time, leaving the last ones on carriages to be first off the next day.

Since the 1960s–80s, fishermen have had their own tractors and carriages, and so independence. Field Marshalls, Fords and other ramshackle characters have had their fans among the holiday-makers, too. They are backed well into the water – halfway up the tractor's tyres! – so that the boat can easily leave the carriage. An advance was when a tractor driver, such as a retired fisherman, was employed. The boat no longer had to wait with a man 'backing to the shore on the oars', while his crewman parked the trac-tor, ran back down the beach and jumped in. Bob Cox told me that once boats would always have had their oars shipped when 'shoving off', unless it was exceptionally calm. If the boat went askew of the waves it could be straightened up and got 'out of a muddle'. A boat swamped with water is difficult to manoeuvre. John Jonas once had the misfortune to hit a sharp rock. With the boat filling up with water almost to the thwarts he managed to limp it round a breakwater and land on the sand on other side. Billy Gaff added if the tractor conks out in the water 'then you're in a muddle as well!'

Launching the fishing boats takes place at daybreak between 3a.m. and 5.30a.m., depending on tides and weather. Their return has been familiar to generations of hol-iday-makers as it happens when they are up and about. Several boats come in within a few minutes of each other from 9a.m. until mid-afternoon, depending on when they set out. The tradition of communal assistance is still alive, even with the modern skiffs. As soon as one boat is safely beached, the crew will go to help another boat coming in, so help is relayed along the beach.

In the last years of the traditional crab boats, skeets were only used at the water's edge as they were beached. The rudder was unshipped when safely grounded and the boat laid athwart. It was pulled round by the tractor with a rope through the stern. Two or three men on one side then pushed it upright before the tractor's winch pulled it along a skeet and onto the carriage. The boat would lift up for a moment then descend with one or two grunts onto the carriage and slither along it. It was roped on using the orrock holes, then with a few puffs of smoke and roars from the tractor, the boat would be taken to the top of the beach

Beaching the boat has long fascinated onlookers, but fishermen say this can be the most dangerous part of their day, especially when there is a heavy swell. There is always a fear that boats will overturn and fatally trap someone underneath. Bob Cox:

> Coming ashore when it's rough is not best of things any time. It's quite a steep beach at Mundesley. One day when we were crabbing, Dad said to us when we hit the beach get out! All three did. When the next wave came the boat went up like that and it came up the beach scooping sand and shingle over the gunwales. If one had stayed in, there'd have been that extra weight there and it would been over on top of us! We didn't query what he said, we just did it!

John Jonas beaching the last working wooden crab boat in Norfolk in traditional manner. Having been laid athwart, *Mary Ann* is to be pulled round by the tractor's winch and onto a carriage. Cromer, 2008.

Donny Lawrence and Tony Payne pushing a skeet under a boat as it is pulled onto a carriage. Cromer, 1997. (*Eastern Daily Press*)

One of the last working GRP double-enders, *Joanne Elizabeth*, being winched by tractor onto a carriage. Billy Gaff on tractor, Andy Pardon and 'Tozzy' Osbourne steady the boat. Cromer, 2003.

For experience of going from a different type of beach, I looked west to the steep, pebbly beaches of Salthouse, Weybourne and Cley. These have always had fewer fishermen going from them than Cromer and Sheringham. Nowadays, no one goes from Salthouse beach, and only one commercial fisherman is going from Cley, the others being part-timers. Weybourne beach with its huge ledges of shingle is not for the faint-hearted, but still used by three fishing boats. Crawler-tractors struggle and strain to pull them up.

Ivan Large is a retired fisherman living in Salthouse. Still involved with fishing, Ivan has been for many years chairman of North Norfolk and Wells fishing societies. From his house on higher ground he looks across the marshes, and keeps an eye on the comings and goings at sea. Ivan started his long fishing career back in the 1950s from Salthouse beach. Two boats went from Salthouse in those days. Ivan mainly fished with his brother-in-law George Cook, but occasionally from Cley with another brother-in-law. He and George kept a boat on the beach at Salthouse throughout the 1970s to 1990s, but by this time he was mostly fishing from Wells.

Ivan and George launched their boat just east of the end of a track which cuts across the marsh. The shingle bank which keeps the sea at bay was as high then as it is now. 'It was a horrible beach to launch from unless you got used to it. And hard work until you got used to it!' Referring to their first boat, a 12ft 6in single-ended rowing skiff, *Boy George*:

> That's why we had a lighter boat; with a heavy boat you can't launch off Salthouse beach like you can off Cromer or Sheringham. When you go into the water you float as soon as you hit it, you can't walk out in the water as it's too deep. To launch, we'd carry the boat down the beach, or roll it down on rollers. We had three rubber rollers. When one come out of the back of the boat you'd run round and put it in the front, like that. No skeets, not skeeted at the waters edge, just straight in. We'd push like hell and jump in when it was afloat.

Bringing the boat back up the beach, Ivan said, 'We'd carry it up on rollers. We lifted it up by hand, or if there was anyone working on the beach, or some of them angling off there, or holiday-makers, we'd give them a feed of crabs and they'd give us a hand.' In the early 1960s, Ivan's brother-in-law changed to a 16ft crab boat, another *Boy George*. He told me this was first rowed, and then fitted with a Seagull outboard engine:

> We thought we were in seventh heaven! We didn't carry the bigger boat; we'd take it down the beach on rollers like we did the small one. Then when we come up the beach we'd drag it straight up the beach, and not use rollers. Then we pulled it up with the motor car, with a rope. We supported it, one holding it either side holding it upright. I had an Austin 12 at the time. I've not heard of horses being used round here. But we got a winch later on; it wasn't used very much, as we found it easier to use the motor car.

When the outboard engine was added, it was raised on a hinge at the waters edge to avoid scraping it on the shingle. Ivan explained the dangers of returning to Salthouse beach:

> You're either afloat, or you aren't – there's no in between! You can't stay over the side like at Cromer (when athwart). As soon as the boat hits the beach you jump out and the boat comes in fast. We'd run like hell! Then in the 60s we got a little Massey Ferguson, a grey Fergie, to pull the boat up. And we made ourselves up a carriage at the same time we got the tractor. Two wheeled. We just had a rope on ours. We'd back it (the tractor) up to the top of the beach, same as the car. We didn't take it, or the car, over the beach because we wouldn't get it back again because you can't drive up the shingle – you'd have had it!

At least two people were necessary, and unlike Cromer where a 'company' of fishermen could be relied upon, at Salthouse assistance was more casual, but asked if they ever got stuck, Ivan replied, 'No, we never had any problems that way. But I've been turned over a couple of times on Salthouse beach coming ashore! A big swell knocked us, turned us upside down. But we weren't stuck underneath the boat.' He recalled that another fisherman had been trapped under a boat on Weybourne beach, but thankfully enough men had been available to lift it and get him out:

> Sometimes in summertime you can get a thunderstorm coming, which can turn the sea rough in five minutes. If you're up at Cley fishing, you'd go in to the beach, wait for the storm to go over. Then go back out, and come home again. I always say, you can always walk home, where you can't swim!

Fishing from Norfolk's beaches has been transformed since the mid-1990s with the introduction of one-man skiffs. The new type of boat is a godsend, but some fishermen remember with fondness their wooden crabbers. One told me, 'The old crab boats were *built* for the water, they sit well in it, not like these modern ones which bob about on top!'

The main reason for the changeover is that the new type of skiffs can be worked single-handed. There is no longer a pool of potential crew members to draw on, as the tradition of sons following fathers into fishing has finished. A big advantage is there is no crew to pay. GRP skiffs are also easier to repair than wooden boats, so getting back to sea and earning money are not held up. In earlier times, some fishermen had two boats, a second boat for winter-fishing while the main crabbing boat was repaired and painted. Another plus is that they are not so costly: advertised at just £6–7,000 for the basic boat.

The skiffs are slightly shorter (19–21ft) than the old crab boats, flatter bottomed and flat-sterned. With powerful outboard petrol engines, they are faster, achieving 12–14 knots. A firm in North Walsham, 'Tactile Boats', makes them – the basic shape is the same, although deck height and different aspects inside the boat vary according to customer's request. Not all carry oars, and masts are a thing of the past because as the fishermen no longer go herring-catching they have no need of masts to carry lights. (If lights are needed, they can be attached to an 'A'-frame gantry which one or two skiffs have.) New types of pot-haulers, labour-releasing 'slave-haulers', are fitted at the head of the boat rather than at the stern, and because there is no central thwart on which to cut up bait and empty pots, there is a removable baiting-up table. As before, when returning ashore, the skiff is turned round and pulled onto a carriage stern first. This can be done single-handed on mild days, and being lighter I am told they are easier to manage than a crab boat on one's own. At Sheringham, the winch is still used, but with rollers and buffs (buoys) instead of skeets over the shingle.

Billy Gaff maintains that the traditional crab boat cannot be bettered for getting off in a heavy swell, but that the skiffs are safer for running ashore in a swell. 'They can outrun a sea, weave in and out – it's the speed, there's more power to them.' Roger Seago added:

> You got that much speed you can get in front of the seas. In a crab boat you had to get on the seas and run on it – you couldn't overtake as you hadn't enough speed. We can now come ashore between the seas. But weather conditions limits how far you can go out in these skiffs. In old crab boats you could go out further in worse conditions. They're that much bigger and more stable.

Willy Cox pointed out that on the plus side, a skiff has no thwarts to climb over when gear is moved on the boat and the outboard motor releases space from the centre. Some fishermen work fewer pots on them. Fishing solo has its dangers, but fishermen today carry mobile phones. On the subject of training up new fishermen, Willy considered it is possible to have two men on board while a skipper trained someone up, but it was not ideal.

John Jonas of Cromer has bucked the GRP and skiff trend. His wooden crab boat *Mary Ann* is still fishing, and he has no plans to change her. It is more difficult for a crab boat to be worked solo, but still possible. John Lee did for a while in 2005 on *Our Provider*, before obtaining a skiff. When John Jonas's son Charlie and 'Black Jack' Emery stopped crewing in 2006, John adapted his boat so that he could carry on alone. I have seen John leave the tractor at the water's edge, jump in the boat, start the engine up, and from the stern bounce the boat on the waves until it is afloat and can set forth. Returning ashore, a large buff is taken out of the boat and placed under its belly. Acting like a strong balloon, it supports the boat as the tractor winches it onto the carriage. John has rearranged the working layout on the boat. He is continually moving up and down the boat, hauling pots from a slave-hauler at the head and shooting from the stern. A shank of pots is placed on a board down one side instead of being piled up in the foreroom.

John Davies's catamaran *Laura Ann* turning round after being launched stern first. Cromer, 2009.

Another adaptation to the times is to go bigger. Richard and John Davies both worked catamarans from Cromer, but after Richard retired there is only the larger *Laura Ann*. After working for a time from Wells harbour, they wanted to cut down 'commuting' time and overcome being tide dependent. A *big* boat was the thing, one which could be launched from the beach at Cromer and yet work the same grounds as from Wells. Eventually they found one – a catamaran made on the Isle of Wight – which they brought to Cromer by sea. After one or two excitements, they adjusted to the new type of boat, which included launching it stern first and turning it round at sea. They designed a new carriage, with plastic rollers for hauling the catamaran onto it.

The big cat caused a sensation at Cromer when she first arrived. She was a new type for the whole of the East Coast at the time. The *Laura Ann* is worked by three men, and can reach crabbing grounds up to 40 miles out instead of 4. John told me:

It was quite a gamble. But as soon as we got on board I knew it was what we wanted. So much stability, and easy to handle. And it's got a lot of deck space which is the main factor. Catamarans are now becoming popular, every time I look in the *Fishing News* – for beach boats and for harbour. I remember one day, the weather changed and it got swelly. This big wave hit us – and the boat didn't move! If it had been a crab boat we'd have been hanging on for dear life. Empty and light, it can go 18–19 knots, quite different from 6–7 in a crab boat!

Its wheelhouse has modern instruments, including GPS navigation. The positions of crab pots along the seabed and the boat's route show up on a screen.

*Impulsive,* one of the eight
modern skiffs at Cromer riding
the waves. 2009.

Another sensation for a time was John Balls's boat, which replaced his fourteen-year-old *Valerie Teresa.* This was the *Aurora,* a 21ft GRP skiff with a wheelhouse housing the latest gizmos, and a decked floor. For years John had worked with a selection of his four sons on a traditional crabber, but as they took up new careers, he wanted a powerful boat which could be worked solo. David Hewitt, who had made the *Valerie Teresa* (see Chapter 3), came up with an entirely new design for the Norfolk coast. Fitted with two outboard motors, the *Aurora* could do 15 knots on three-quarter throttle. Once used to 'a new way of thinking', launching stern first and hauling from the head of the boat, John admitted he wished *Aurora* had been around when he first started fishing. The Yamaha engines burned twice as much fuel as a crab boat's engine, but with the extra speed and more fishing to be done *Aurora* was a winner. She has now gone with John to new fishing grounds in Devon, but several of the new skiffs appearing on Cromer beach have wheelhouses and are looking more and more like her. Another non-traditional beach boat at Cromer is the *Reap,* originally from the South Coast, which has been successfully adapted to one-man fishing.

End notes:
1. Similarly, the *Mary Ann's* sail. The latter's mast is further for'ard.
2. There had also been the large sailing 'great boats' until the time of the First World War. They fished far and wide up and down the North Sea, returning occasionally to Cromer, Sheringham and Morston. They took crab boats on board, used to help with the fishing.

# CHAPTER 3

# YOU'D WINK ALONG IT BY EYE

There were once several firms building boats in North Norfolk. At Cromer I have not been able to identify any boat-building premises, although three individuals are listed as boat-builders in late nineteenth-century trade and street directories[1]. When it comes specifically to crab-boat building, Sheringham was the major centre well into the twentieth century. Three boatyards are known to have supplied crab boats for Cromer and all along the Norfolk coast.

An early boatyard at Sheringham was Leonard Lown's, from 1840. 'Johnny' Johnson took over the business from 1906–50, and produced, it is said, 130 boats in his working life. Cromer fisherman John Jonas owns one of Johnson's boats, the *Duncan*, originally built for a Sheringham fisherman in 1937. She was only retired from active service in the 1990s. Another boatyard, established by R.G. Boxall in the late nineteenth century, had a workshop where boats were built on two levels.

The Emery family's boatshed, a former net shed on Lifeboat Plain, was another 'double-decker'. The business was established in 1850 by the splendidly named Lewis 'Buffalo' Emery, a carpenter by profession and fisherman. He built the lifeboat *Henry Ramer Upcher*, and according to his grandson Reginald made a crab boat for himself then carried on making others for a living. The boatyard continued as a family business for four generations, lasting until 1981. The building is now a private house, but is still remembered as a bustling enterprise in its later history. This was after Reginald died, when his son Harold continued to restore and repair boats, but the boat-building side ended. The last repair work was on Henry 'Joyful' West's boat, but the last boat actually built was in 1957. This was the *Charles Mark* for R.H. Davies of Overstrand.

As with other traditional boatyards of the time, such as the coble- and wherry-builders, construction was without drawings or plans, but using eye, measurement and memory. The several operations to make a durable, efficient and seaworthy boat demanded that the builders be consummate craftsmen.

It is remarkable that in the main only hand tools were employed. At Emery's the electric drill made an appearance after the last war, but when Reg and Harry tried the electric saw, it was deemed unsuitable and rejected. At Johnson's, it was a case of hand tools all the time. All worked in what would be considered cramped and less than ideal circumstances today. At the Emery workshop, rare photographs show the boats almost filling the work areas. Reg's grandson Mike Emery told me when

*Above:* Planking-up stage of a whelker, with strategically placed props. Emery's workshop, Sheringham, 1930s. (H.H.Tansley, via Mike Emery)

*Right:* The whelker *Knot* under construction. Timbers, part of cuddy and one thwart in place. Emery's workshop, late 1930s. (H.H.Tansley, via M. Emery)

whelkers were built benches and anything superfluous were taken out; lighting pre-war would have been by oil lamp, and heating in winter non-existent. Whelkers were constructed downstairs while crab boats were taking shape upstairs, to be brought down by ramp when finished. Not all boats were crab boats; Mike suggests some might early on have been 'pinkers' and skiffs. Some customers were from outside the region. In all, Sheringham produced an extraordinary number of boats. Reg Emery recalled the firm built about twenty boats a year in the early days. Production was all the year round until the Second World War, after which business declined and they built boats in winter and hired out deck-chairs and beach huts in summer.

In the later days of the rowing and sailing crabbers, these were typically 18ft long, 7ft in the beam and 3ft deep. But with the introduction of engines at the time of the

First World War, the boats got bigger and were built stronger. The weight increased from less than a ton for pulling boats to 1.5 tons when early engines were put in, pushing them further down in the water. The boats were therefore built a few inches deeper. When Reg was interviewed for the BBC in 1953 he described the boats as about 19ft long, 7ft in the beam. The entry, where the boat cut through the water, and the aft were still characteristically 'fine'. By the time Harold Emery was interviewed twenty years later the length had increased to around 20ft and the boats were beamier at 8–8½ft. Beaminess was generally what the fishermen wanted so that more load could be carried. The later boats were described by retired fisherman Richard Davies as having more 'bluff', and being less flexible and less sharp at the bottom.

Later crab boats were boarded in at the bottom, but earlier ones had no boards, or only a few, which were removable. These were aft for standing on while hauling, a foresheet for stowing 'bits of gear and lobsters', and sometimes for standing on while baiting up. Larger double-ended boats used for whelking from Wells and Brancaster were fitted with small cuddies to give some protection during longer trips. The largest was the 30ft, 6-ton *William Edward* built for Cyril Grimes. Smaller whelkers, the *Knot* and *Isabel* (26ft long, 10ft 6in beam), are shown being built on photographs taken in Emery's workshop. The *Knot*, with other old boats, is now restored at Morston. Hovellers, which were bigger than early crabbers and fished further at sea, were also built at Sheringham. One used by the legendary lifeboat cox'n Henry Blogg from 1931–37, the *QJ and J*, was built in 1915. This is now being restored and due to be put on show in Cromer. The last two hovellers were constructed in the 1930s, according to boat-builder David Hewitt. Mike Emery showed me documents for a 16ft crabber costing £28 in 1909, and the whelker *William Edward* costing £450 in 1949; both big expenses compared to a working man's income at the time.

Reg Emery recorded the keel, deadwood, stem and stern post for the boats were made from the best English oak; all were hand-sawn and shaped by adze. Oak, being strong and durable, was suitable for these parts; at the keel it would have protected against chafing on the beach. He went to local woods to select the appropriate shape from a tree, avoiding wood with cross-grain. Mike thought the planks and 'timbers' (ribs) would have been obtained ready-sawn, probably coming from Taylor's of Wroxham. Final shaping would have been done by the firm.

There were eleven planks each side, ½in thick. As with typical clinker-boat construction, the planking-up was done before fixing the timbers. The planks were not oak all the way up as on late nineteenth-century crabbers, but larch with oak top planks, or elm top planks in the case of Johnny Johnson; these needed to be strong to take the wear and tear of ropes going over the sides and to incorporate the orrock holes.

To make the ends of the planks and the timbers pliable they had to be steamed before being bent into shape. This was by a long steam-box heated in the middle. It was described by Mike Emery, who as a boy visited his grandfather Reg in the shed. Steam from an old fashioned washing-copper, which was heated by a coal fire within a brick surround, was funneled into a case of wooden trunking containing the timbers. Wet sacks at the ends kept the steam from escaping. David Hewitt, who visited Emery's shed, told me that the planks were then pushed into position to make the hull and held with props from the floor and ceiling. A watercolour sketch by Horace Tuck of a boat being built probably in the 1920s shows this, but omitting the large wooden pegs used to secure the planking. Some of these pegs are now in Sheringham Museum, others David obtained from Emery and used himself. Many of the firm's tools and workbenches are now in Sheringham Town Museum.

Retired fisherman Bob Cox pointed out that when he first went to sea, 'The Sheringham boats did not have gunwales as such; the planks came up, and there was an iron band all the way round. The boats were more flexible then. They always had orrock holes because of the need to row when you first went in. Father had the *Morning Star* and *John Robert* built at Sheringham.' Later, when mechanical pot-haulers were added, boats were built with gunwales to take the extra strain, strengthened by three strips of bin iron.

Cromer fisherman John Jonas showed me the *Duncan*, made by Johnny Johnson. Over seventy years old, she is now resting in a field. John had fished in the *Duncan*, as had his father before him. He told me she was sharper for'ard than some crab boats which came later. The planks were not continuous; we could see one or two of the joins at the head and the stern. John thought no particular rule applied here, just what lengths had been available. Where the pots were hauled up, rounded strips of wood had been put under the plank edges to stop them catching on the pots. This being one of Johnson's boats, iron nails had held the planks together, but due to corrosion John had replaced them with copper ones, as used on most of Emery's boats. The *Duncan* now needs some attention, but John considers her restorable.

Various types of engine were put into crab boats, including special marine engines. At first diesel engines were too heavy for the sailing-rowing crabbers, and petrol/paraffin or petrol engines had to be fitted instead. Two of the early petrol marine engines were Belfast Barkers and Kermath. Others included Ford-based petrol engines marinised by Parsons, Morris Vedettes and Felthams. Boats had become bigger by then, and were built with engines in. In the 1970s there was a changeover to diesel engines, such as the Perkins 4107/8. The first boat going to diesel was J. Worthington's *Early Rose* at Overstrand. Running costs could now be reduced. Engines were sited between the central and aft thwarts, the 'V'-shape at the bottom of the boat accommodating the propeller shaft. To house the propeller and protect it from hitting the beach when launching and coming ashore, Robert Emery invented a new type of enlarged sternpost. This type became widespread in Norfolk and the whole East Coast.

With motor power, fishing became less weather-dependent and trips could be more regular. Open crab boats, which can take in quite a lot of water, had previously to be baled out by bucket or hand pump. Jack Davies had commented to his son Richard that there was no better pump in the world than a frightened man and a bucket! But with a bilge pump fitted powered by the engine, this was clearly another advance. Later, pot-haulers were also powered by the engine.

Another boat-building firm was Worfolk's in King's Lynn. Established in 1900 by Walter Worfolk, his two sons continued up to 1977. They built large fishing boats for the Wash, designed for the particular needs of fishing there, but they also built crab boats and whelkers in the 1950s. The latter were made after the father's death, and there may not have been that many. Referring to lists of boats in Cromer Museum and from talking to retired fishermen Bob Cox and Dennis Gaff, these included *Young Fisherman*, *Ever Hopeful*, *Why Worry*, *Carnival Queen* and *English Rose* for Cromer, Mundesley and East Runton fishermen. Like the Sheringham boat-builders, boats were built by eye and measurement. The King's Lynn museum display shows they first made a small model of the boat and worked from this to make a full-sized version, for the Wash boats at least.

The boat-building focus later changed from Sheringham to the Broads. When Johnson's yard closed in 1950, and Emery's finally closed in the 1980s, fishermen went to Maycraft of Potter Heigham. This became the main firm making traditional wooden crab boats. The first one built was for Dennis Gaff of Cromer in 1959, named the *William Robert* after his two young sons. Production lasted until 1985 when the last boat *Our Provider* was built for two other Cromer fishermen, John'o Lee and his son John. There are records in Cromer Museum of nearly thirty crab boats built by Maycraft for Cromer, Sheringham and villages along the coast, although fifty have been cited by Sinclair (1989). Crab-boat building fizzled out after Billy May retired, but the firm still survives, run by his engineer son Harry.

Today, there are probably only a handful of people who carry the skill to build a traditional wooden crab boat. I was very pleased to have been able to speak to two of them. One is Alan Goodchild, who owns a large marine services firm at Burgh Castle near Yarmouth, and the other is David Hewitt, who with his brother George owns a boatyard near Blakeney. David is the builder of the last Norfolk crab boat. I visited Alan Goodchild in his roomy office which looks out on a number of moored boats including a very fine wherry. Much of the information below comes from this interview, with some reference to a report written in 1990 by Kevin Roll, who served an apprenticeship at Maycraft. Although Alan is now involved with building and servicing a variety of modern boats and has built smaller wooden boats, he has not built another wooden crab boat since moving to his own premises. He referred with affection to his early days working for Maycraft, which he joined in 1972.

Seamanship is in Alan's family, and he started going to sea at a young age. He initially gained experience with a boat-building firm in Yarmouth, but after helping a fisherman friend fit an engine in a crab boat, he took up a job offered to him at Maycraft. The method was much the same as Emery's, as Alan said: 'The traditional way – the only way to get the crab boat shape,' the difference being that Maycraft used wooden profiles, or 'moulds', to obtain the hull shape. As we spoke he sketched beautifully precise diagrams without one unsteady line. Here was a skilled draughtsman as well as a master craftsman.

Billy May's early premises, a shed downstream of Potter Heigham bridge, was small by boat-building standards today. At the time Alan worked there, Maycraft was

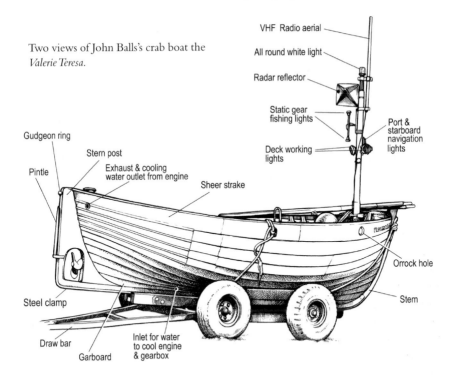

Two views of John Balls's crab boat the *Valerie Teresa*.

VHF Radio aerial

All round white light

Radar reflector

Static gear fishing lights

Port & starboard navigation lights

Deck working lights

Gudgeon ring

Stern post

Pintle

Exhaust & cooling water outlet from engine

Sheer strake

Orrock hole

Steel clamp

Stem

Draw bar

Inlet for water to cool engine & gearbox

Garboard

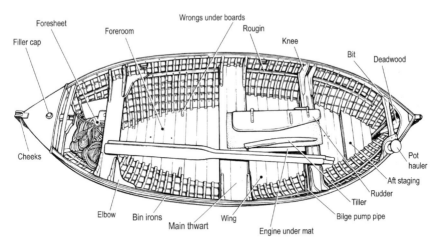

Foresheet

Wrongs under boards

Foreroom

Rougin

Filler cap

Knee

Bit

Deadwood

Cheeks

Pot hauler

Aft staging

Rudder

Tiller

Elbow

Bin irons

Wing

Bilge pump pipe

Main thwart

Engine under mat

building on average one crab boat a year. The firm was in the fortunate position of being the only one fishermen could go to at the time. Over the six years Alan worked there he built five crab boats, all for Cromer fishermen. They were built over the winter months, sometimes into the summer, two builders working at a time. As with the Sheringham boats, no two came out exactly the same. The shape best suited for fishing off Norfolk's beaches had been long established, but minor variations could be built in to take account of individual fishermen's views to make *his* new boat just that little bit better.

The boat length at this time was 21–22ft, catching up the size of the hovellers. The largest crab boat was Richard Davies's, built in 1970. Richard Davies:

> I was going to sea with my father in the *Autumn Rose*, and we had a row. I said, 'I'm not going with you next year, I'm going on my own!' I rang Billy May up and ordered a boat. For years people wanted boats an inch longer, and an inch longer – Billy May said, 'I suppose you want it an inch longer?' I said, 'No, a foot!' My father came to look at it; some of them said it would be too big. The *JJ and F* was 23ft, long for the time, usually it was 22ft, 22ft 6in. I asked the old man what he think of it. He said he'd give me £1 to name it – I was hard up – so he named it *JJ and F* after Julie, John and Fiona.

As noted above, crab boats had become quite beamy, 8ft being typical at Maycraft. Alan explained the length was always going to be restricted by what was possible to get up and down the beach – a fitted-out motor crabber weighed 2.5–3 tons – but there could be minor variations in width, or the bows or stern could be made fuller or sharper. Dennis Gaff: 'People always said for the first four planks you want as sharp as you can.' This was to make the boat more stable, but cutting deeper in the water it could be more difficult to bring ashore. John Lee told me this had been the case with *Our Provider* which was built sharper than her predecessor *Provider*.

As at Sheringham, Maycraft's crab boats were built without plans or drawings, but the shape of the hull was obtained by building up around moulds. Templates were first made from the interior of a boat with a successful design. This was usually from a boat already built by the firm[2]. Before starting the first crab boat, Dennis Gaff remembers Billy May coming to Cromer to take templates off 'Shrimp' Davies's *KP and K*. Dennis, who had first gone fishing in the *KP and K*, admired her sea-going qualities and wanted a copy. When completed, the proud owner, with accompanying proud builder, took the *William Robert* on the scenic route home. This was by way of the river to Yarmouth and thence by sea to Cromer. Later boats were to go by road. Within a few years Dennis told me there were a dozen new Maycraft boats on the beach.

The main sequence was: construct keel, hog (the plank over it), stern and stem posts, put in moulds and plank up; construct floor-bearers, timbers, gunwales, 'rougins' and thwarts. The keel, which established the length of the boat, was made from a single piece of wood. It was supported on stocks. The stem and stern posts, cut according to hardboard patterns, were assembled onto this. They were fixed with copper bolts. Internally there was an inner stern post, or 'deadwood', through which the propeller shaft went, while at the stem, there was an 'apron' and stem knee.

The planking was larch; the keel, garboard, stem and stern posts, and the top plank (sheer strake) were all oak. Alan emphasised all the wood used in construction had to be carefully chosen by the boat-builder: 'The larch is from logs with a slight bend. The grain follows the shape of the tree, and planks are cut which follow this natural grain. This eliminates short grain, producing a stronger hull.'

Details on how the shape was obtained are given in the Appendix at the end of the chapter.

Like the Sheringham boats, slow-grown English oak, straight-grained and free of knots, was used for the timbers. They were steamed in a steam-chest to make them pliable, the rule of thumb being one hour for every inch of thickness. The timbers, 1½in by ⅞–1in thick, were put in warm, and the builder got inside the boat and pushed or walked them into place with his foot. Some were in continuous lengths to provide strength to the hull. These were supported on small, curved oak 'floor timbers' in the 'V' of the boat so that the timbers ran 'sheer to sheer in a fair curve' and did not break. Other timbers were in two pieces, as in the sharper angle towards the stem and stern. About thirty-eight timbers were put in altogether, placed every 6in along the length of the boat, and fixed with nails where two planks overlapped. Alan explained:

> Where the acute turn in the bilge required the timber to twist, the trick was to place them amidships of their intended position and clamp the top at sheer level, then knock them into position on the turn of the bilge, thus twisting the timber into shape, making it a tighter fit onto the planks.

Alan pointed out that, unique to crab boats, there is a timber for every other nail in the planking; on standard clinker boats this is every third nail. To fit the timbers against the planks, the triangular gaps between them were filled with wedges. Hundreds had to be made, first cut out by electric saw, then every one hand-finished to fit. Handfuls were thrown into the boat and the builder sat inside, and with the wedge secured to a piece of wood, he cut the curved side of each one with a spokeshave, judging every fit by eye. This careful work took about two weeks. Reg Emery notched his timbers to make them fit, as found on Yorkshire cobles.

The three thwarts which held the boat crossways were pine. They were supported by curved brackets, 'knees' and 'elbows'. Alan emphasised that any structure built into a crab boat is rounded off to avoid it catching on the fishing gear. The stern post came down straight to house the propeller according to Emery's design. This was mortised onto the aft end of the keel. A hole was bored through the shaft log at base of the deadwood and through the stern post to take the engine shaft leading to the propeller. The engine was mounted on beds dovetailed into two oak transverse supports, 'cross-floors', at the bottom of the boat. At this time the firm fitted Perkins and Thornycroft engines, which were diesel, and Stuart Turners which were petrol.

The boats were fitted with hydraulic pot-haulers. made by P. & P. Duerr of Essex, and VHF radios. Pot-haulers came in in the 1960s, ending the era of hand-hauling. Fishermen had had them in Yorkshire since the First World War, and as Richard Davies of Cromer recalled, 'We were well behind times! When I went up there and spoke to an old Yorkshireman and said we were going to have a pot-hauler next year, he laughed!' He told me that when pot-haulers were first introduced to Cromer, the doughty fishermen had a go at beating them. But within a year or so everyone had one.

Maycraft's crab boats, like the later Sheringham ones, were built with 'lockers'. One was under the fore thwart to stow bits of equipment. Another under the main thwart is remembered by older fishermen as where they packed the crabs as the pots were emptied. It had a 9in gap at the top. The surplus went into the wings of the boat, but in time the thwart got bigger to accommodate larger lockers. Lockers were abandoned when plastic fish boxes became available. Easily stacked on the boat, these can carry either bait or catch. Washboards had been a feature of some of the earlier boats, before Alan worked for Maycraft. An example is a boat built by the firm in 1960, the 19ft *Pandora*, retired at East Runton. Boats then carried a 'slender sheer', so were not high in the water; the washboards helped stop water getting in the boat when launched from the beach. In later years, the bows were built higher at Maycraft to save the use of washboards.

To protect the keel, a steel band, or 'clamp', was attached with countersunk welded lugs. Bin irons capped the gunwales. When haulers were introduced, wear strakes were fixed to protect the planks where the pots came up. Later, this became a sheet of glass-fibre. Boards were fitted at the bottom of the boat for fishermen to stand on. In the 1980s Maycraft installed masts made of spruce. These were a legal requirement to take red and white lights for night-time fishing.

Red lead paint was used in some of the joints and between the planks. Cuprinol, a preservative, was applied to the finished boat, although Billy May regarded a boat soon to be pickled in seawater was well protected against rot anyway. In Alan's day, the boat was then painted with special marine paint. He was not in favour of household paint sometimes used by fishermen to paint their boats, or tar, which had traditionally coated the bottom of the boat to prevent it leaking. One retired fisherman told me he had taken the engine out of his boat, upturned the boat and spread tar on it with a blow torch. When Donny Lawrence was asked about leaking, he said:

> Oh no, the boats never rifted, only person I know had a rifted boat occasionally was old boy Charlie Brackenbury, and Cutler Balls – lovely old boys. But they never went out far to sea, just to outside the pier to get a few crabs. If they rifted, all they did was get a piece of twine and tin of tar, and they poked tow all in, and they'd tar it. Next morning it was waterproof again.

Alan reckoned it took about 2,500–3,000 hours to build a crab boat. In the years he worked for Maycraft he did not know how much a boat cost, but guessed somewhere in the region of £12,000–16,000. Today's wages of £30 an hour (in 2008) would make a crab boat worth over £75,000, too expensive to produce. In the boom boat-building years of the 1970s, grants had helped fishermen with the costs.

Another important boat-building firm in the story of the traditional crab boats was Hewitt Bros of Stiffkey. A gradual changeover to glass-fibre (GRP) started in the 1970s, and the days of the wooden crab boat were beginning to be numbered. This was largely due to the closure of the boatyards at Sheringham and King's Lynn.

David Hewitt sitting on restored wooden crabber *Welcome Messenger*, talking to fisherman Billy Gaff. *Aurora*, the GRP boat with cuddy on the right, was built by David in 2003. Stiffkey, 2005.

From 1976, David Hewitt provided an almost unique service for fishermen from Wells to Trimingham, restoring and extending the lives of their wooden crab boats and whelkers In addition, David gave a new lease of life to boats which had come to the end of their 'professional' lives. Spruced up as pleasure craft, they now bask in the creeks around the East Anglian coast.

David's father had been a marine engineer working for a firm in Blakeney, so David learnt 'the engineering side' from him. He works with his brother in a series of hangar-like sheds which lie in a swathe of agricultural land at Stiffkey. Brother George works in GRP, but David likes wood, so he is to be found making and repairing a variety of wooden boats. It was with some difficulty I tracked him down, but he kindly gave his time to talk about crab boats. Settling down at a workbench in his boatshed, he talked to me about building the last traditional wooden crab boat in Norfolk. This was the *Valerie Teresa* for John Balls in 1989. She was to become John's work-horse for the next fourteen years, until David made another boat for him of quite a different type.

David explained his method was much the same as at Maycraft, using moulds and without drawings or plans. The *Valerie Teresa* was 22ft by 9ft, the actual shape being based on Dennis Gaff's *Amanda Lynn*, which many regarded as having the best shape at the time. Measurements and cardboard templates were taken off the *Amanda Lynn* in Cromer, and at his premises wooden moulds were made from these. Only three were used to plank up and produce the shape of the *Valerie Teresa*:

> The overlap's the same all the way along. You cut all the individual strokes[3] to shape, the bottom of one from top of the previous. You mark out on the stem and moulds roughly where you want the planks to be, and adjust a bit. If you were to have, say, a 6ft high boat in twelve planks, then you'd have about 6in planks – as a guideline.

To my question about whether they were in continuous lengths, David replied, 'Yes, down below, then three planks up they go to two planks. All Sheringham boats were two planks all the way up, except the sand stroke (garboard) which was one.'

The larch for the planks, which came from the forests of Northumberland, had been seasoned six months for every 1in thickness. The oak for the timbers had been seasoned one year for every 1in thickness, but the clear long lengths of oak are now difficult to obtain. He pointed to a long plastic tube attached to the ceiling which had been swung down and used as a steamer for the timbers; a heat source was set up in the middle. Small wedges were made to go in the gaps between the planks and timbers. David counted 1,200 of these, each individually made for the *Valerie Teresa*. She was fitted with a Perkins 4108 50hp engine. Like Maycraft's finished boats, the *Valerie Teresa* was coated with Cuprinol.

For David, the building of such a boat had been a labour of love. He could still make a crab boat, but due to the prohibitive cost and the fact that fishermen now fish single-handed, at the beginning of the twenty-first century no fisherman would even want a wooden crab boat built.

Boat-builder David Hewitt inside the *Valerie Teresa*, in the latter stages of construction. This was the last wooden crabber to be built in Norfolk. Stiffkey, 1989. (Via D. Hewitt)

Many of the tools David used were the same as in Emery's day: augers to bore the shaft for the propeller, bradawl brace, rasps, marking gauge, planes and paring chisels. But not 'caulking irons', to knock in caulking. David said caulking was done between planks on carvel-built boats, but not on clinker-built boats as the planks swell and tighten when in the water. He knew that Emery and Johnson had used pitch and horsehair. I was slightly puzzled by this, but it has been suggested by more than one source that caulking might have been used on plank 'lands' (angled edges) near the stem and stern post, and for the garboard. Discussing the curved objects pinned on his wall and which I had seen in a reconstruction of Emery's workshop in Sheringham Museum, David explained these were patterns used by Robert Emery to make the transverse 'frames' which went in the bottom of boats. The patterns had notches showing the edges of the lower planks. In the museum, frames can be seen in the *Enterprise*, built in 1946.

Referring to his repair work for fishermen, David's boom years were the late 1970s to mid-'90s. So many boats had come through his doors, yet he could reel off information about any one of them. He told me that wooden beach-boats last fifteen or at most twenty years without a great deal needing doing to them, but they needed a proper refit after thirty to forty years. He did or made everything for them. This included converting the engines from petrol to diesel. Some Sheringham boats tended to come apart at stem and stern, a particular fault of the iron fastenings. A system of jigs and ingenuity was used to get them back into shape. Timbers became worn, broke, and lost rigidity, and wedges had to be replaced. Fisherman John Jonas reckoned the *Mary Ann* and *Duncan* had had all their timbers replaced over the years. Some boats had to have their gunwales removed and virtually be taken to pieces, a time-consuming and expensive job – and so much replaced they had become almost new boats. All suffered from abrasion along the keel. Rubbing boards to protect the bottom planks had to be replaced and patches applied. He could sometimes detect a slight asymmetry in Sheringham boats which had been built without moulds.

I was shown round large sheds containing crab boats in storage and in stages of repair. One superb little crab boat was being given a new stern post to take a propeller for an inboard engine. This 16-footer with six oar holes had been built for sailing, but used with an outboard engine until ten years ago from Cart Gap by Michael and Andy Williamson. She was one of just two boats built at Happisburgh, copied from one of Johnson's boats built in 1945. The standing boards had been removed and one could see the lovely shape of the bottom of the boat. David pointed out the sturdy curved 'wrongs' he had put in the bottom of a couple of larger crab boats to strengthen them. This had included the lightly built *Mary Ann* and *Billy Witch*, where there were fewer, more widely spaced timbers.

Besides the boatyards which did repairs, small repair set-ups existed along the coast saving the boat going out of the village. Mr Barker of Mundesley did boat repairs in his back garden during the 1950s. His steam-box for softening the timbers was a pipe made from welded sheet steel. This was propped up, and with a fire under one end, a gallon of water was poured down the other and plugged with a piece of sacking. With six timbers inside, it was left to steam for two hours. When they were placed in the boat, his young son would help as the planks were nailed. One customer was 'Old George' Cox, who paid Mr Barker in crabs or herrings depending on the season.

The first GRP crab boat built along the Norfolk coast was the *Paternoster* for Richard Davies in 1974. The firm Stratton Long Marine of Blakeney made a mould from 'Yacker' Harrison's old boat, the *Charles Perkins*. This came out rather heavy for its size, but the second boat the *Sarah Jane* was more successful and became a GRP milestone. When Richard's son John had his first boat *Gladiator* at the age of eighteen, she was built lighter too. The shape of the later GRP boats, such as made at Hewitts' boatyard, became dependent on what moulds were available. They were made in one piece, using a two-piece mould. A usual type was 22ft with 8ft 6in beam. Maycraft did not make GRP crab boats, but Alan Goodchild built one in 1979 when he moved to premises in Yarmouth. This was for Cromer fisherman 'Little' Billy Davies, the *Joanne Elizabeth*. She was built with a large head, a style thought safer for launching in a heavy swell. But time moved on for traditionally shaped crab boats even in GRP, and the *Joanne Elizabeth*, the last on the beach at Cromer, finally retired in 2006. The very last GRP boat still ploughing the waves is the *Anna Gail*, a 'descendant' of the *Charles Perkins*. She is worked from the difficult beach at Weybourne by Richard Matthews and Gary Mears.

# Appendix

At Maycraft, to make a wooden crab boat the moulds were normally 4ft apart. The same set of moulds was used for most new crabbers, modified according to what the fisherman wanted. Measurements were recorded in Billy May's notebook. To make a larger boat, splines would be bent around the moulds and the extra length of the boat calculated proportionately. Moulds could also be moved 1 or 2in for'ard or aft or they could be tipped to change the boat's shape. A mould moved for'ard with a spline round it would make the bow fuller; if tipped, this would lower the gunwales.

Moulds marked with plank widths (ticks) on their outer edge were placed along the keel. The moulds were kept in place by struts attached to a beam near the ceiling. One of these moulds can be seen on a photograph of the last boat built by Billy May. This was in 1985, after Alan's time at the firm. John'o Lee and his son John gave some assistance to Billy May and his son in its construction, and we are fortunate that John took some photographs.

There were twelve or thirteen planks each side, thickness ⅝in. Alan told me they were individually shaped, tapering to stern and stem and 'closer knit' at the turn of the bilge than on the sheer to avoid splitting. The lowest plank, or garboard, was put

Rare photographs taken by fisherman John Lee of a crab boat under construction. *Our Provider* was the last wooden crabber to be built by Maycraft in 1985. *Top left:* Wooden pegs clamping the strakes in place. The top of a wooden mould can be seen inside the boat. *Top right:* Planking-up stage finished. *Bottom left:* 'Apron' (vertical structure) with five 'floor timbers' and one 'cross-floor' in the bow. *Bottom right:* Stern, with deadwood (vertical structure), with a 'floor timber' and 'cross-floor'. Timbers, thwarts and gunwales yet to be fitted.

in first, then the other planks moving upwards one by one. Supports were added to the sides of the boat as it was planked up.

The shapes of the planks were obtained by means of a 'spoil board'. This was because there was no naval architect's table of 'offsets' (measurements) to refer to. The spoil board was a bendy piece of plank which was laid against the last attached plank on the boat. It was adjusted up or down until it abutted, or 'kissed', the moulds then fixed in position with large wooden pegs. Several pegs were used to hold it in place. A pencil line was then drawn along the spoil board where it met the lower plank on the boat. The spoil board was removed and this wavy line transferred on to the new piece of planking, to become the outline of its lower edge. The top outline of the new plank was obtained by marking on the required plank widths (referring to ticks on the moulds), laying a flexi-spline along them and drawing a pencil line. The plank was then cut out by band saw and pegged in place. Alan told me it was necessary to steam the last few feet of the planks near stem and stern. This was to help them curve and tuck neatly into the forefoot and stern of the boat.

Emery's pegs had been in two halves, with a wedge at the top which could be hammered down to bring the sides together; Alan's were in one piece, reinforced with a nail to prevent splitting.

The lands of the planks were planed to a width of ¾in, so that the planks overlapped snugly as they made up the hull. The angle of the landing was greater where the planks made the turn of the bilge. The planing, using a special coffin-shaped landing plane, was done by eye. The world of boat-building is sprinkled with special terminology for some of the tools and aspects of the work. For instance, Alan remarked, 'If it's fair it will be right on the boat,' and to check the fit, 'You'd wink along it by eye.' Getting the planks to fit together perfectly involved a special knack, which was not easily taught. 'The amount of planks you muck up and have to bin – and the old boy opposite is doing it not even concentrating but getting it to fit!' At the stem and stern of the boat, 'Here you've got to make the planks run into one. As you plane you twist, and the next plank you twist the other way. If you're good at it they fit perfectly when you put them together – if not, the boat will leak! You do struggle with that bit when you're learning.' About the fourth plank out at the turn of the bilge, oak bilge runners were attached for protection.

The planks were fixed every 3in with copper square-sectioned nails through the lands and the timbers. This was done by a rove-dolly, a bronze tool specially cast for the firm. Its end had a hole drilled down it, which was countersunk. Holes would first be drilled into the plank and the nails hammered from the outside. A small, domed copper 'rove', or washer, was put on the nail end, the dolly held over it, and the nail hammered again. Most of the end of the nail pointing through the rove was snipped off, and the point burred by hitting it with a hammer. The hammer used in these operations was a clink or pein hammer, a special round-ended hammer unobtainable in the shops and so made by the firm. Countersunk copper bolts and brass nuts were used to fix other areas of the boat.

Non-continuous planks were scarfed, staggered about 3ft, and were all the way down the boat except that the garboard was sometimes in one piece. When the boat was finally planked up, the builder would check its shape by bending over and looking back through his legs. His customer would do the same. This might seem somewhat strange, but the upside-down image gave a fresh eye on the shape of the boat in much the same way as an artist might look at his painting in a mirror.

End notes:
1. John Rogers of Church Street; Robert Allen of Tucker Street; John Mack of Brook Street.
2. The traditional way to copy a boat's shape was to obtain internal profiles using a 'cheating stick', a flexible rod with inter-linked sections, but the original builder did not always take kindly to this.
3. David in North Norfolk used some different terms from Alan Goodchild in South Norfolk. For instance, he talked of strokes – Alan's planks, or other people's strakes.

# CHAPTER 4

# POT LUCK

Towards the end of March, a frisson of excitement marks the beginning of the crab-bing season at Cromer. This is the centre for potting from beaches along the North Norfolk coast. After talking to each other for a few days, and wondering if the time is right, one day in the early hours of the morning, the fishermen bring their boats back to the seafront. Some had been taken away for winter repairs. Tractors with boats on trailers process down the Melbourne slope and onto the promenade, to slide back into their old positions at the top of the beach. Amidst quiet banter, the crews quickly start to load the gear onto the boats and 'bend' tows (attach ropes) onto pots, anchors and dan buoys. Over the next few days or weeks hundreds of pots will be set at sea.

The crabbing season was once from March/early April until July, when the crabs moult, or 'shoot their shells' to grow new ones. The season gradually extended to September, until finally to the end of December. It has become virtually all the year round at Wells, the boats potting on alternate days in winter. According to one of the older fishermen, Donny Lawrence, the crabbing season started when the temperature of the water was about 39°F, fishermen would then catch a few crabs that had not lain dormant in the sand all winter. When the water started to heat up to about 44°F, crabs could be caught which had come out looking for food. With the decline of whelking, netting and lining, potting for crabs and lobsters has become the mainstay for fisher-men in towns and villages along the coast, although options are kept open if other forms of fishing were again to become viable.

## Where to catch crabs

For best crabbing conditions, Richard Davies told me: 'For crabbing, you don't want the water too clear, you want a bit of colour, a little bit of movement. They're feed-ing better then, and they'll move too. If you go when it's fine, clock calm, crabbing's a waste of time.' Billy Gaff added, 'We know we'll catch more crabs if the water's "thick" rather than when it turns clear, "sheer as piss". The sea thickens up because of the gales during winter stirs up the seabed and gets all the sediment moving through the water.'

Potting grounds between Sheringham
and Trimingham, from fisherman Billy
Gaff's sketch. Some names refer to
features on land as seen from the boat.
*Inset:* Arrows show route to land boats
at Cromer avoiding rocks.

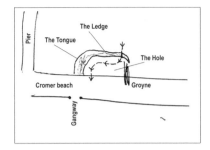

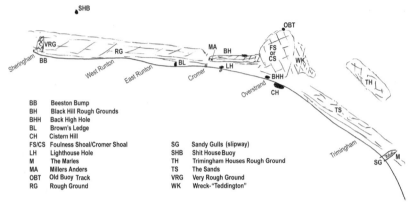

| | | | |
|---|---|---|---|
| BB | Beeston Bump | | |
| BH | Black Hill Rough Grounds | | |
| BHH | Back High Hole | | |
| BL | Brown's Ledge | | |
| CH | Cistern Hill | | |
| FS/CS | Foulness Shoal/Cromer Shoal | SG | Sandy Gulls (slipway) |
| LH | Lighthouse Hole | SHB | Shit House Buoy |
| M | The Marles | TH | Trimingham Houses Rough Ground |
| MA | Millers Anders | TS | The Sands |
| OBT | Old Buoy Track | VRG | Very Rough Ground |
| RG | Rough Ground | WK | Wreck-"Teddington" |

Crabs and lobsters like to live on the rocky ground off the Norfolk coast. Choosing
where to go crabbing is based on experience – and luck. There are no particular
'territories' owned by certain villages. Some grounds are reckoned to be consistently
productive, but good patches are found by the individual who is not likely to let on to
the others. Helping one another at sea and beaching the boats is one thing, but fishermen are fairly competitive in the matter of harvesting the sea and selling their catch.
A young or inexperienced fisherman will watch where the best fishermen go, and try
the same areas himself.

Norfolk's inshore fishermen often work a set route north-west to south-east, usually less than 3 or 4 miles out. Since the latter twentieth century, an area between
Blakeney and Mundesley extending to 3 miles out is a protected crabbing 'nursery'
area where trawling is not permitted. When the crabbing season starts, crabs can be
found closer to shore 'just off the beaches'. Retired Donny Lawrence, who worked
with Tony Payne:

When I first started, I'd never go more than 150 yards out to sea. We could find
enough crabs for his customers, especially off Overstrand, great big crabs, females.
Fabulous. But it's really a pot luck job where they are. If you hauled a shank of pots,
and done well out of them, you'd lay them near enough back again – if you don't
do well, you'd go out to sea a little further, maybe only a length of a buoy tow and
shoot them there. It's luck, same with lobster catching. You just hope you're laying
them on a little rough ground. If you don't, you shift it.

John Balls considered:

> For part of the year you can put pots anywhere and catch crabs, but you want quality
> as well as quantity. I personally start up¹ just above Overstrand, on the sand – I make
> a start up that end, and gradually work 'off', and back down towards the town when
> the lobsters start (July, August). You call the crabs then 'August jacks'. They come to
> the grounds to breed with the females which are shedding their shells. Anywhere on
> the hard ground you'll pick up jack crabs. The further you come in, in summertime
> and August, you pick up little jack crabs. The 'broadsters', the females, will shed
> their shells anyway, but you'll catch them more inshore than offshore – by offshore
> I mean about 3 miles. But at *this* time of the year, December, they're making their
> homes for the wintertime, digging into the sand.

Some fishermen like Richard Davies preferred to work the Sheringham grounds
where it was less 'crowded' with other fishermen. Willy Cox:

> You have your favourite little spots. Usually a shallow bit of ground is good, but it
> doesn't always work. We'd move our shanks about in different times of the year. I usu-
> ally first work south of Cromer, then draw down even to Sheringham in the summer.
> I work this way (Cromer) when the crab quality and quantity is not so good; also
> when the lobsters are coming on. So there is more than one reason to move.

Others keep working the same bit of ground, or fish to the south-east. Some fishermen become known for being good at catching lobsters, such as Dennis Gaff who
learnt from Tony Payne and Jack Davies, and Lenny West who taught John Davies.
However, the finer details of lobster lore are kept to themselves. Lobsters were caught
mainly 'inside', between Cromer and Sheringham; set 'just where you think you are
going to get something', was one enigmatic remark!

# Fishing trip

The weather forecast on TV and the radio shipping forecast are checked out the night
before. Billy Gaff: 'If it's blowing hard off the land we will still go. But if it's from
the sea from the northwest round to the easterly, we don't like those winds.' If the
sea looked rough, there were 'some large lumps of water going about' or it could be
'blowing up a hooligan'.

Fishermen usually leave early in the morning, something they have done since
having to deliver their own catch. Billy Gaff:

> It all depends on where the wind is blowing from, and what time high water is.
> Usually during summer when it's fairly fine all the time, we'll go away at daylight,

whatever time that is 3.30, 4.30, 5.30a.m. and work the tides to suit ourselves. But if there's a lot of wind blowing and a heavy swell we'll wait 'til after high water to launch, 'til we know the water's going back and safer to land the boats on an ebb than on high water. The swell 'makes' on the flood and drops away on the ebb on the beaches in North Norfolk.

Willy Cox:

You usually go away with the water going out, after high water, with the latter flood, and come home again with water down on the beach on the ebb tide. Depends on what tide is running – if you're hauling on the flood tide you go to the north end and work down, if on the ebb you go to the south end (and work the other way).

## Locating the pots

Fishermen describe how before the days of GPS, they located their gear with landmarks. After placing a buoy to mark the gear, distinctive features on land which lined up with one another were remembered so that finding it the next day would be easy. Some landmarks which located good crabbing grounds were secret, known only to the crew working a particular boat. John Davies:

How far you see the landmarks depends on visibility and weather. When you're working within 2 to 3 miles off, landmarks can be quite prominent, quite sharp. With a landmark you can line up a church with a hill or house or something, but once you get 5 to 6 miles off you lose all that.

Willy Cox explained the system: 'You use two marks if you can, a "long mark" for how far off you are, and a "short mark" for how far along the coast you are.' For a long mark, he had noted how patches of woodland move in relation to Beeston church as he steamed out to sea. Fishermen call one of them the 'Black Hill'. For the short mark, if he was, say, 2 miles off Overstrand:

Then you take a short mark, say the radar pylon at Overstrand, with a bit of property. You *could* locate all your shanks with marks, but you work all your gear from one end, one shank run on from another, parallel with the coast. So, you took a good mark where you set your pots and where you finished your gear, so when you come along the next day, on the flood you go to the north end, and you look for your upper mark.

The long mark for Willy's brother Bob, who fished from Mundesley, was taken when Happisburgh lighthouse disappeared behind Happisburgh church:

We call that 'blind light' because you couldn't see the lighthouse. We'd use these marks from both ends, so we might use Cromer pier as well, with the land you could see further on from the pier, whether the pier was on the pavilion, or if you was right out, on the Bath House (a building on the promenade). Then you'd also have your distance along (the short mark). Paston church or the windmill perhaps that would be over the Ship Hotel or the water tower on Mundesley seafront. You'd take these marks in case the steam boats cut your buoys off, or if you went in the dark and couldn't see your buoys, then you'd know where your gear was.

A frequent complaint among fishermen is that dan buoys locating the pots become separated from the underlying gear by large vessels ploughing through the fishing areas. Donny Lawrence described using landmarks to come ashore, at Cromer:

When we'd come into the beach at low water, we used the flagpole outside the old council offices – it had to be level with a chimney stack. If you got them lined up, you could come straight in, in the 'Hole'. It was quite safe then – so you didn't run aground at the bank or anything.

Older fishermen remember using a watch and compass to help locate their pots. Bob Cox:

We took a compass, though sometimes we forgot! It was only used when it was 'thick', foggy. When you shot away your last pots, you'd go straight in to the beach – or as near as you could with the tide pushing you one way or the other on a course southerly, southwestward or whatever, and you'd time yourself. Then the next day, you go along the beach to that point where you ran in, and if it's misty or foggy you ran off for that time.

Richard Davies:

My old man always got his watch out! We'd be washing down, stowing up, getting the crabs ready, he'd know his compass bearings, and know how long it was coming home. I used a compass all the time, couldn't go without it – fishermen still do, even with GPS. Especially when there's fog, and there's no GPS.

A compass could be placed on the floor or on an upturned box for the man steering to refer to; other times it was stored in a locker near the foresheet.

Using a watch and compass was once normal for fishermen from Wells who had to reach more distant fishing grounds. John Davies recalled, 'When we were first going out of Wells, Tony Jordan would be going out two to three hours at sea with a watch and compass. It's impressive to steam that distance and hit your gear! You don't do this every time mind, but there's not many times you're far out of the way.' John, who now works the large catamaran at Cromer, described how most fishermen find their gear today:

> We have GPS navigation and things like that, like what most modern boats have now. Hardly anyone uses landmarks now, they use GPS. It makes life so much easier. You can work that much more gear and go further off and not worry so much about it. Sometimes I shoot gear now without any markers on it at all, because I know I'm going to lose it where the ships are, but I just use GPS and go out there.

# Working the pots

Norfolk 'creel' pots are rectangular with a barrel-shaped top. These are placed in the sea for a season and worked in shanks. This is a row of pots, connected by pot tows. At each end are an anchor and a dan buoy. On the old double-ended crab boats two or three men worked about twenty-five pots per shank, and about eight to ten shanks, sometimes more in the main part of the season when parlour pots were added to catch lobsters. Sometimes a crewman would have a couple of shanks, and the skipper the rest. In the recent past fishermen hauled their pots every day, but now some work two or even three fleets of pots, hauling one fleet one day, another fleet the next day, so pots lie undisturbed for two to three days. Nowadays, for single-handed boats, there are fewer shanks, and fewer pots per shank. Willy Cox works a hundred pots in ten shanks. The parlour pots used now are bigger and take up more space in the boat.

In the days before the pots were set in shanks, they were fished singly, attached to a rope with several corks spaced along it. These pots, called 'swimmers', 'swummers' or 'swum pots', were bigger than today's crab pots. A pot was pulled up, then 'you steam a little way' and pull up another one, so it was a less energy-efficient way of fishing than working shanks. Retired fisherman Ivan Large of Salthouse remembers using swummers early in his career:

> A lot of people did then. Only trouble was if you got a blow (storm), you got a job to find them, because they'd go down to Sheringham or somewhere. They weren't anchored; it was just their own weight keeping them where they were. We'd have twelve to sixteen of them between here and Cley, big heavy pots. They seem to fish better on their own. It's like with a shank, the end pot always has more in, because it's not got to share with the next pot. We'd work about fifteen of these pots, the rest in shanks. About 120 pots altogether. Some would work just a few swimmers, especially if not full-time fishermen. But shanks were always there in my day. You didn't lose them so easy. If you had a blow, you'd find them, because they're anchored.

Retired fisherman Bob Cox had worked single pots as well as shanks earlier in his career:

We always had a few swum pots, though they could be a nuisance in the dark. You'd get them in the propeller. We'd work three or four big pots as swummers when we moved to Mundesley. In those days although you caught lobsters in ordinary pots, you also had a larger version for lobsters. We had a spot at Trimingham where we left our swum pots. Once when we had a north-east gale we expected our pots to wash ashore where we'd left them, but an old fisherman Charlie Rudram told us exactly where to find them, and we found them off Mundesley church – that was his experience! Of course, in his day there were just individual pots, no shanks then – they came in when the boats had engines. You could work more pots with shanks. In those days you had corks on the buoy tows, spaced all the way along. They were corks from the herring nets. 'Course, if you put a dan on one little pot, the tide itself would shift it. So you had individual pots with enough ropes and corks to reach the bottom.

There did not seem a particular problem locating the pots. John Jonas told me, simply, 'You knew your own pots, you can see the corks floating about on the water.' In his younger days he had had a few swummers spaced out between the Cromer pier and the lighthouse. These were 'right inside', or 100 yards off the beach.

Another device fishermen had used was the hoop net. This was a metal ring with a three-pronged strop on the top, a bait bar across the middle holding the bait, and a bag-shaped net. It sank to the bottom of the sea, weighted by three lead weights on the hoop. Retired fisherman Lenny West told me in his father's and grandfather's time hoop nets were used for lobsters and dabs. A pig's bladder float marked where the hoop net was. The bladder, obtained from the butcher, had a cotton reel in the opening fitted with a wooden bung. Bob Cox, who worked only four or five hoop nets at a time for flat-fish at slack water, used a thin rope with corks attached which rose to the surface. The hoop-net method involved setting them in a line, and after setting the last one, the boat steamed off to the top end of the line to start hauling them one by one. According to John Davies:

> Fishermen used quite a lot of them. They were left in a line in different places. You don't leave them in for long. When you pulled it up, the crab, lobster or fish would sink down into the net, and you'd haul up as quickly as possible. The skill was in bringing it up so as not to tip it, quick and efficiently, with the boat over the top of it so as not to drag it towards the boat.

Unlike pots, the hoops were brought back after the trip. Fishermen from Mundesley and Bacton told me of a type where the hoop consisted of two hinged half-moon rims. When pulled up the two halves would close. Another version was like a small bicycle wheel. Ivan Large from Salthouse:

> We used that for 'lobster snatching', in the wintertime when there were no crabs about. They'd be dotted about, singly. You'd be rowing round all day long, and

snatch them up. If there was a lobster in it you'd take it out, and put the wheel down again. Some were hinged. Fishermen made them; some might have been made by a blacksmith. It was an iron hoop with net hanging down and strop. You'd bend it round and tie it with string. It was used more Sheringham way, and off Weybourne.

# Hauling the pots

Before the days of mechanical haulers on the boat, pots had to be hauled by hand. This was done by some fishermen up to the 1970s, although pot-haulers had been introduced a few years earlier. It was hard work, and all of the older fishermen had experienced it. 'We didn't know no different! You just got used to it!' The last hand-hauling boat was 'Yacker' Harrison's *Charles Perkins* according to John Balls, who as a youngster had helped his uncle on it.

I talked about hand-hauling pots to the Cox brothers, some of the elder statesmen of the fishing fraternity. Willy Cox went to sea with his father and two older brothers, who taught him. Like the other fishermen I spoke to there had been no doubt about what he would do as a career, although after school he had a short spell trawling from Lowestoft. This was in the days of hand-hauling, and he was doing this when he had his own boat:

> You'd wear an old pair of socks, 'dannocks', with the toes cut out, or a piece of car inner tube with a slot for your thumb to go through. Otherwise the tows would cut your hands and blister them badly. But you can't prevent water running up your arms, and you got sea boils from chafing oilies (waterproofs) on your wrists and arms. You stood right aft, in the same position as you do now. You kept in the same positions, usually. The skipper baited up in the middle of the boat; there were usually three of you. You still hauled lots of pots, but not quite as many as now. The shanks were just as long as now, twenty-five, twenty or twenty-two pots. It was time-consuming, and you were probably out a little longer. There was relief all round when the winch came in! The first one was John'o Lee to have a hauler.

Brother Bob added:

> When it was me, my father and George, I'd be hauling all the while, and George would be pulling behind me, and I'd pass him the pot. If my father hadn't finished baiting, George would start to clear the pot. It was up to individuals how they hauled, some took long strokes, or they went quicker. It was worse when I first started – all the ropes were tarred in those days. Your hands would be covered with tar, like webbed feet! The dannocks only lasted a day or two.

Another fisherman commented that sometimes tows were so rough they were like grabbing hold of a hedgehog.

Hand-hauling placed some limits on the fishing trip. Richard Davies reckoned 1½ miles out was far enough out for hand-hauling, and not many worked outside the Cromer Buoy, 2¼–2½ miles out. He also reckoned that in his father's generation, they had landed a better quality of crab. Mechanical haulers have made crabbing more efficient, and some like John Jonas believe there are fewer crabs now than in their early fishing days. When hand-hauling, two men would work about six shanks or three men would work eight shanks; compare this with the ten shanks worked today. John added that mechanical haulers have meant fishermen are able to catch more lobsters now, because in hand-hauling days the pots did not come up so quickly and lobsters had more chance to escape.

Older fishermen have told me they 'stemmed the tide' when hand-hauling into a big tide. This made pulling up the pots easier. The boat was held into the tide, moving slowly forward and as they pulled the pots up, the tide caught underneath the pot,

Willy Cox and Brian Lee crab fishing in the 1960s. 'Setting in': a shank of emptied pots stacked in the foreroom will be shot in a different area from where hauled. (Via W. Cox)

giving it a slight lift. As noted above, the flood tide runs north-west to south-east, the ebb vice versa, so if working on the flood tide fishermen would go to the north end of the shank of pots. John Balls pointed out that on the ebb tide there was maybe 10ft less depth of water to haul through. The pots were all pulled onto the boat, stacked in the foreroom then shot back in the same bit of ground, starting where they had first hauled. If that area was not doing very well they would move the pots to a different area. This is called 'setting in'.

A different method, 'underrunning', used when a good fishing spot was found, is described by Donny Lawrence:

> You go to the north end of your shank, when the flood tide is running, pull the buoy in, then the man in the middle, or in the wing, like Willy – he'd take that buoy from me, or he sometimes pick it up. As I pulled the buoy tow in he'd coil it all up and lay it on top of the engine case, then I'd hand him the anchor which he'd hang that over side of the boat. Then the first tow from the anchor to pot, Willy would coil as well. Next thing is the pot would come on board. So I'd give the pot to Willy. He'd take all the good crabs out, throw away the small ones, and bait up. By then I would come nearly to the second pot. Now, Willy would get the buoy, throw it over the side, all the tows and the anchor – then when the second pot come up, he'd push the first one over the side – then when the third come up, he'd push the second one over side. That's what we call 'underrunning' – there's always two pots in the boat, and always one going over the side as one comes in. Pots stay in exactly same place as where you picked them up, in the same line. The boat is moving, the tide is taking us up – plus with us hauling that helps as well. Your hauler is running off the engine, but the engine is out of gear. And then you come to your final pot, then the anchor. When I come to the anchor I pull the little buoy tow in, and I say to Willy, 'Are you ready?', he says 'Yes,' and we put the boat into gear, and turn out, and Willy gets rid of that pot, and I'd throw the anchor over when the time is come, and the tow – and that shank is finished. That's how it's worked between you. If you're in a hurry and want to get back to shore for a delivery, or whatever, we'd underrun. It would only take about twenty minutes to do about twenty-five pots.

One man stood on the starboard side 'cleaning' out and baiting the pots, and packed the good ones into the lockers. These were compartments on either side of the engine under the main thwart. When the lockers were full the crabs were chucked into the wings between main and aft thwarts on the boards. Nowadays, stacks of plastic fish boxes are filled and 'trimmed' according to where weight is needed in the boat.

Hand-hauling could not be done against the tide, but with winches this became possible. Pots are shot 'with the tide', that is, with the tide coming towards the boat. The tows between pots end up fairly tight along the seabed.

Since the introduction of one-man skiffs, underrunning, which normally involved two men working together, is hardly done even when two men work on a skiff, such

John Balls midships unloads and sorts crabs into fish boxes. His son Michael pulls pots up with the hauler (obscured, in front of him). Pots are hauled and shot one at a time, termed 'underrunning'. 2003.

as Billy Gaff and Shaun Brown. Another difference is pots are now hauled at the head of the boat, rather than at the stern as on the old crab boats.

## The catch

Minimum landing sizes for crabs and lobsters were imposed in Norfolk following a report on the fishing industry by F. Buckland in 1875. He noted that the large numbers of small crabs, or 'togs', landed for eating or for bait, had the effect of seriously depressing the industry. Rules were also put in place which outlawed landing 'berried' (egg-carrying) crabs and lobsters. Willy Cox:

> Our crabs here are smaller than those in Cornwall, and possibly a bit smaller than the Yorkshire crabs where they work deeper water. Ours are like in Northumberland, further north. The regulation size is 4½in, this is fixed. There has always been a measure on crabs. It's not been recently altered, but lobsters, yes. But the crab has a bigger measure offshore than inshore, so the big boats at Wells have a bigger measure (5 in).

The minimum landing size for lobsters has increased in some fishermen's lifetimes, and recently with worries about lobster stocks DEFRA is investigating whether to raise it again. This would not be welcomed, as more will have to be thrown back to sea. Also, when over a certain size they become bigger than one person can eat, so they become less marketable.

In the past Norfolk's beach fishermen sometimes bought a boat and gear between them or worked as partners 'sharing everything down the line'. Crew working this way ran the risk of ending up with no money at the end of a week. Fortunately for them, weekly or daily wages became the norm after the war, but paying the crew is now less of an issue as skippers work mainly single-handed.

Catches vary year by year, from bumper harvest to dismal (see below). A run of bad weather can prevent fishermen even getting to sea. But I am told a beach fisherman expects to bring back six to seven boxes of crabs, and 20–70kg (less than a box to two boxes) of lobsters in the lobster season. If one refers to official landings records, over the years April, May and June are the best crabbing months for inshore fishermen. It is slightly later for those going on bigger boats from Morston and Wells, who go up to 30–40 miles offshore. Crabs can be fished all year, though fewer are found in winter when most go to ground. In the August holiday season when there are more visitors about wanting crabs there is a dip in the catches. This is because crabs are moulting their shells. But in July to September when lobsters are being caught these compensate for fewer crabs. However, too many lobsters about can bring prices down. Sold by weight, in July 2010 prices had varied from between £8.50–13 a kilogram at first sale.

Retired fisherman Donny Lawrence: 'I remember when I was with Richard Davies's father – and one day we'd brought 1,300 crabs ashore. Yes, the lockers were full, the wings were full – we had to stuff an oily in the orrock (oar) holes to stop them crawling out!' Donny's cousin Ralph Kirk reckoned one should get a hundred crabs in a shank for May/June. John Davies told me that when fishing was good, his father Richard and cousin Dick would land 20–30 peds, and at eighty crabs in a ped that was a lot of crabs. When Ralph was fishing with Richard he remembered one day they had done so well he and 'Speedy' Muirhead had cooked 2,500 crabs. Sheringham fisherman Richard Little recalled his best years were in the 1960s and '70s, especially when parlour pots first became available and he caught lots more lobsters than he had previously. He would bring back three full boxes of lobsters, as well as fifteen of crabs.

John Davies held the record for crab-catching for many years when he went from Wells. He managed eighty-one fish boxes from hauling 220 pots, and at about sixty-five to ninety crabs per box, this was a lot of crabs! His record has since been beaten, but by bigger boats going from Wells with a lot more gear. On the catamaran from Cromer John told me he could land thirty to forty boxes, if doing well. He has had 340 crabs out of one shank of pots. But this is exceptional, and every fisherman has experienced pots coming up virtually empty. In the disastrous year of 2006 some boats were only bringing back twenty crabs per trip.

# The catch once ashore

Older fishermen relate how their lives have got harder since having to process their own catch. Before this, they had sold their crabs live to fish merchants, each having their own marketing arrangements. Willy Cox related:

> In those days, when fishermen came ashore, they got the boat up the beach, they left the crabs in the boat, laid an oily or sack across the lockers and went home for breakfast. They came down an hour later, and packed the crabs into baskets or boxes. They would take them to the railway station, or the back of a lorry to wherever they went off to. Most boats had six or seven 'peds' of crabs in the lockers – in the days of hand-hauling there weren't so many crabs.

Some fishermen remembered the fisheries officer standing over them packing the crabs watching that no undersized or moulting crabs were put in. Packing was tight to restrict the crabs from nipping one another with their claws. The peds referred to were wicker baskets with hinged lids. They were made inland, such as at Hickling Broad. Being wicker they allowed the crabs to breathe and so last two or three days. In the 1970s ped-making died out and wooden boxes were used for a while.

Customers did not want damaged crabs with only one claw. Richard Davies:

> We used to give nearly all the one-footers away. After you gone home to have your breakfast, the people who'd look after your boat for you, keep everyone out, you'd give them all the one-footers. Old Wally Horness would go home with a sackful. With four or five kids helping, all wanting ten or twelve crabs, that's a basket of crabs gone every day!

Local youngsters enjoyed helping the fishermen hold the crabs down while they were counted into the baskets. Some bright sparks did quite well by selling their crabs on the way home to earn pocket money.

Ralph Kirk:

> Ted Cook would run the peds up to the top of Gangway for us. We'd put a label on, then there'd be a lorry come and take them to the station, to go on the freight van. He was a bit simple, but strong. We'd say, 'Come on Ted, the lorry'll be here shortly, you'll have to move quicker than this,' so he used to *run* up the Gangway with a ped on his back! He used to 'work' nearly all the boats.

Crabs and lobsters put on the train at Cromer were picked up by the fish-merchant at the other end. These were the days when a lot of freight went by rail. The fisherman's initials or mark were painted or branded on the ped so that when they came back on the returning fish van they could be identified and reclaimed. (Dennis Gaff told me everything then was branded: peds, crab pots, buoys and whelk pots.) The destinations were Norwich, Peterborough, Cambridge, Ipswich and other large towns. Set prices had been agreed with the merchant beforehand. Crabs were sold this way by number, not by weight as in other parts of Britain. Richard Davies:

> They still are! Unless they go to the Crab Factory where they buy weight. We'd carry them out in baskets, in peds, holding eighty crabs, mixed sizes as they come. Someone might want forty crabs, that's a half ped, someone would want three to four peds. We had one good merchant in Norwich who had eight peds a day, that's 640 crabs a day. They had their own boilers then.

Bob Cox:

> We took the crabs to the station, even if they were going just to North Walsham. *Some* you'd deliver. You paid at the station, they'd put them on the scales, but they'd only vary a few pence. The peds would go in the guard's van with a label, say, to North Walsham, and the guards would put them off there. When you sent the bill in (to the customer) then you'd charge them carriage. You counted eighty crabs into a ped; you mixed the sizes so they all got the same. There used to be a man at Cromer, Tom, with a horse and cart, he'd take them up the station and they'd pay him. We eventually got vans, first one or two, then all.

Bob suggested the number of crabs in a ped seemed to be related to counting crabs in 'long hundreds' which is 240 crabs, (or 120 'casts', a cast being two crabs), which is the traditional way of counting crabs. Three peds would be the same as two long hundreds, 240. He added that the long hundred was once easy for fishermen to deal in as there had been 240 old pennies in a pound, so if a crab was say 10d, a long hundred of them was £10.

Donny Lawrence:

> For lobsters, we'd box them up in newspaper or sawdust. We'd go to Travis and Arnold (timber merchants) and buy a big box of sawdust. You'd have layers of sawdust this high, then layers of lobsters like how you'd sleep as kids, feet and heads reversed. You'd cover them with sawdust and put another row in, you maybe had two or three rows, and put a thick layer on top. Then you'd put on the slats of wood and nail them down. That's how they'd go to London, to the Garden (Billingsgate).

Lobsters have to have their claws tied if they are to be sold live. 'Oh yes, but in those days you used to tie them with string. You had one between your knees, clamp it in, and tie the claws. Sometimes you got a nip!'

Live transport of lobsters. Billy Gaff (right) with crewman Shaun Brown tie up lobster claws with elastic bands to stop them fighting. Cromer, 2009.

He told me that lobsters which did not go on the train were sold to local restaurants and hotels, where the chefs wanted lobsters live. One hotel at Wroxham would take a dozen or more for parties; they had to be no more than 1lb in weight, each enough for an individual meal.

At Sheringham and adjacent villages, fishermen also sent their crabs by rail in peds. Richard Little recalled crabs had been taken in barrows to Sheringham station. One could tell how well-off the fisherman was by his barrow – poor fishermen had iron wheels on theirs which they had 'acquired' from farms, well-off fishermen had good rubber ones! Barrow-loads were also taken to a business in Cooperative Street run by fishmonger Henry 'Downtide' West. This was round the back of his fish shop in High Street. As Henry hired out boats to fishermen, he was able to sell their catch in his shop as well as send it away by rail – and even turn it into potted fish! He had a small factory after the war behind his shop, where women prepared the crab meat and potted it into jars. There was even a machine for extracting crab meat from the shells.

Bob Cox thought it may have been a rail strike which finished the practice of transporting crabs and lobsters by train, which had been going since before the war. Others blamed a hike in freight costs. Fishing families reacted by buying their own delivery vehicles. According to Richard Davies, Kelly Harrison was the first to buy a van in Cromer and deliver crabs, but it was mainly the womenfolk, including his mother, who taught themselves to drive and took over deliveries. The crabs all went live to shops and merchants, to Norwich and around the region. Richard added: 'We used to sell to a fella in Norwich, in Ketts Hill who cooked the crabs. My mother would take them there to boil – he told her he had a job to get up one day because his "trinket box" got caught in the bedsprings!' Bennett Middleton told me there could be fierce competition among fishermen. He had one secure buyer who paid £12 for a hundred, but with undercutting this went down to £10, and finally £6, at which point he called it a day.

In addition to delivering the catch, fishermen sent it to fish merchant Van Smirren of Boston by regular pick-up lorry. Richard Davies:

> We had one or two 'keep pots' at the end of the pier, for when Van Smirren come. So you could keep your crabs a weekend if you went Saturday – we didn't go Sunday unless we had gale of wind during the week. Cromer and Sheringham didn't go Sundays. Then the Cox family moved back, they were going Sundays, so then we all did! Sheringham had to row off and leave theirs at sea, we were lucky at Cromer as we could leave them on the end of the pier. On Monday we would haul them and pack them for when the lorry come.

The 'keep' pots referred to were crab pots, sometimes extra-big, without entrances. Donny Lawrence, who had worked with Richard's father, added:

> Van Smirren were for crab paste and that. A lorry come down from Lincolnshire down the coast, as far as Mundesley to where the Coxes were, and picked the crabs all up and take them back. We picked out the best for our customers, and they got the 'rubbish', the one-footers and big old jacks which we knew had nothing in them. Yes, Van Smirren was very handy! They'd give us 2½d each for them. They were put in wooden orange boxes we'd scrounged from vegetable shops in town.

## Present day: Processing, boiling and selling

The working day has got longer for today's fishermen, with more 'shorework'. First the option of sending shellfish by train finished and fishermen had to do most of the deliveries themselves, then crabs had to be boiled before they could be delivered. All this is after five to seven hours of hard work fishing. Once most of the merchants who bought the crabs cooked them; this meant that if a fisherman was back from his fishing trip by about 9 o'clock he could have them delivered to Norwich, Yarmouth or Lowestoft and other towns by dinnertime. But from the 1960s fish merchants weren't prepared to cook them, and fishermen began boiling in a small way themselves. By the 1970s, it was the norm. Later, merchants wanted them dressed too, as customers couldn't cope with doing it themselves. Only occasionally fish shops or stalls prefer live crabs to boil themselves or to sell live. Although most of the

Richard and John Davies sorting crabs at their former premises in Garden Street, Cromer, 2001.

live trade has died out, some will go to a wholesaler in East Runton or to Cromer Crab Factory. The latter, which sprawls on the outskirts of Cromer, takes shellfish, especially prawns, from around the world while buying in local crabs on a quota system, which it processes and sells to the major supermarkets. Local fishermen can get more money from processing and selling crabs themselves, but the factory is a useful place to take surplus. Lobsters are also taken there when there are no private trade outlets.

To keep surplus crabs a few days, today's fishermen have chillers on their premises. Live lobsters are kept in tanks by some. David Bywater, who once fished on a crab boat from East Runton, now goes potting on a bigger vessel with two crew from Morston. He explained that up to a ton of lobsters can be kept in filtered seawater, their claws tied to prevent them fighting. They can be kept until a good price is obtained: 'That's a lot easier than running around the countryside selling twenty here, thirty there, if I can get rid of them in one hit.' This might be to a wholesaler supplying big city hotels, or sent in vivier lorries to Spain or Portugal, where there is a big demand for shellfish. In the recent past lobsters were stored at sea, and references for this go back to the eighteenth century.

But to return to the cooking. Amidst thick swirling steam and a fresh smell of shellfish, these still operate cottage-industry style in lean-tos behind fishermen's houses or fish shops. A few fishermen have gone large-scale and have had special buildings built. The boiling is often done by a crewman, if not by the fisherman himself.

John Balls of Cromer started boiling crabs when he was eight or nine years old, something unimaginable today. This was for John'o Lee, who he later accompanied crabbing. Richard Davies told me when he started boiling it was just a few in a

*Above:* Richard Davies (front) with 'Speedy' Muirhead, Ralph Kirk and Mick Watts cleaning crabs before they are boiled. Cromer, 1990. (EDP)

*Right:* Billy Davies boiling crabs near the family crab stall, Cromer, 2006.

Burco boiler for one or two customers. His wife Julie would dress them after tea on the kitchen table. Meanwhile, he was delivering most live to Yarmouth, Wymondham and Norwich. Richard expanded the boiling operation using the sheds where his grandfather had boiled whelks. The boilers were originally old coppers with a fire underneath, changing to old school-dinner boilers heated using gas canisters.

'Blond' Billy Davies has his boilery close to where he sells his crabs and within sight of the sea. This is in a walled-in yard, which had been used by his father before him. Billy has had a long fishing career, and is a former cox'n of the Cromer lifeboat. No longer going to sea, he now buys crabs from other fishermen to process. These arrive by pick-up vehicles straight from the boats.

The copper is boiled up, and some water taken out and put with some cold water in an old tin or enamel bath. Crabs are shot into the lukewarm water to kill them, then scrubbed 'as clean as a sweep's arse' to get the scum off them. The coppers are topped up, reheated, and two loads of crabs from metal baskets added. Billy Davies told me the crabs go in loose to cook them evenly. Other fishermen boil the crabs in net bags once used for whelking. Lobsters go in at the bottom or the top of the boiler. When the water is boiling, they are cooked for fifteen to twenty minutes. Billy then hauls them out with a big mesh scoop at the end of a pole, which had been his father's. Others haul their bags of crabs out by a pole with a hook. The boiled crabs are cooled with a pressurised hose. At the end of the operation there is a fish box or metal basket full of nice pink crabs with a couple of bright red lobsters on top. More batches go into the boiler. Finally, the whole boilery is hosed down, walls, floor and all, so that it is hygienic and spotless before it is used again the next day.

After boiling the crabs, they have to be dressed (see below) and sold. They are sold to hotels, restaurants and shops in the towns and villages all over Norfolk. I am told one fisherman has lobsters taken to London where they are sold on the internet, probably a way of selling which will get bigger. Some like Billy Gaff will drive a batch of cooked crabs down to the fish quay at Lowestoft, where they are sold by numbers to a fish-merchant, unsorted, at a fixed price. They eventually reach outlets in the East Anglian region. Unlike some areas of Britain where distribution and bait-buying are centralised, Norfolk fishermen still prefer to be in control of their product from start to finish. Are Norfolk fishermen too individualistic? 'No, pig-headed!' says John Balls.

## Fish stalls and shops

Some fishing families sell direct to the public through their own fish shops and stalls in Wells, Sheringham and Cromer. There is also a tradition of Norfolk fishermen selling their catch from their own houses – even from the front window, as 'Buster' Grout did in Brook Street, Cromer, until recent years. Direct contact between fisherman and customer all adds to the appeal of Norfolk to the holiday-maker.

In Cromer, two cottages a stone's throw away from the sea have crab stalls outside. Health and safety rules mean that crabs are no longer laid out on marble slabs but displayed in chilled units, and one can no longer go inside where they are prepared. One is the crab stall at the top of the Gangway established by William and Faith Davies, now run by their grandson Billy, his mother Gladys – who has been dressing crabs for more years than she cares to remember – and wife Sylvia. The other crab stall was established by John'o and Kitty Lee outside their cottage in New Street. It is still run by Kitty who sells crabs caught by her son John. Similar delightful stalls are in Sheringham and Wells.

Although there are fewer fish shops than there were a generation ago, the survivors have direct links to fishing families. In Cromer there are two. These are owned by Richard and Julie Davies, and John and Frances Jonas. Typically, they had started small, Richard's father with a crab stall, John Jonas's father with a fish round. John, who had accompanied his father Reggie, told me:

> It would be cooked crabs and lobster mainly at weekends, fish in the week. He went round the country in his van to houses and that, and rang his bell. Same time every week so people knew he was coming. All round North Norfolk, he went as far as Aylsham. He did it for years.

Reggie's fish used to come in by train from Lowestoft, some of it from Scotland, in a special fish wagon.

> We had to go up to the station to get the fish. Just phone and order your fish, and it'd come by train. He'd keep the fish up at Chapel Street as a store, then when he

was ill in the late '70s he never went back to the fish round and started selling it there (in the present shop). When he started the fish round he packed up going to sea, apart from working a few pots in the early '60s from the skiff. He'd catch a few of his own, but he used to buy them in.

John later supplied the shop when he was fishing, and eventually took it over with his wife Frances. Fishermen also marketed their catch by fish round, first by cart then by motor vehicle, in Sheringham and nearby villages.

Retired fisherman Ivan Large described how he had marketed his crabs from the village of Salthouse:

> I boiled them up at home, in a shed. Then took crabs and lobsters to pubs at night-time, and a shop in Holt we'd supply. I had a vehicle then, an Austin 12. There were twelve or fourteen pubs in Wells then, and at that time there was no-one crabbing out of Wells. So I used to take crabs from Salthouse to Wells on a Saturday night around the pubs.

It is surprising considering the high price lobsters now fetch, that Ivan found that no one wanted lobsters then and they were difficult to get rid of. To my question whether there was competition between fishermen to find outlets, he laughed, 'There always was! Cut each other's throats. The price would go down to a penny a crab to sell them – that's when crabs were only 6d each. Yes, I was selling them at 6d each to the shop.'

He never took them down to the market at Lowestoft to sell, unlike some fishermen east of Salthouse:

> That's because Overstrand and Cromer used to start crabbing before we did. The crabs would start that way and come here, then by the time they got here they flooded the market, so it wasn't worth taking them to Lowestoft. When we lived down Beach Road, near the present fish and chip shop, we used to sell them from the window. My brother-in-law and wife June would help out. Crabs, lobsters, shrimps, cockles, whelks. Everything. It was a cottage industry!

## Bait

Holiday-makers taking an evening stroll along the beach might see fishermen getting their bait ready for the next day. In earlier years bait had arrived by train, half a mile from the beach. Dennis Gaff recalls collecting it by horse and cart. Others like Ralph Kirk and Bob Cox would take it by barrow the half mile to the Gangway. Ralph remembered going too fast, breaking the legs off the barrow and dropping his load down the Gangway. Some sent Ted Cook with the barrow up to the station to get their bait. John Jonas: 'We reckon he never could stop – so you had to get out of his way when you saw him coming!'

Bait includes 'scads' (horse mackerel), plaice, cod 'frames' and skate. Gurnard is almost off the list, having become expensive. After the fish van on the train was withdrawn, cardboard packs of bait are now delivered by lorry direct to the beach. Fishermen can pick it up from the fish dock at Lowestoft if delivering crabs there, or obtain it from a local wholesale agent or the Cromer Crab Factory. Some fishermen have facilities to deep freeze the bait in bulk.

For attracting lobsters the bait should be stinking. Horse mackerel, which has sharp barbs on its back, is recommended. In earlier years, some fishermen will tell you, a tasty bit of crab was put in the pot as bait. The problem was keeping the lobsters in the pot; if left too long they had enough cunning to escape. Bob Cox explained how fishermen tried to overcome this:

> We used to break up crab which was no good to sell, illegal now. We used to haul twice a day. When we did, we went in the morning to haul, and we'd bait up for lobsters to haul in the afternoon. But when we baited in the afternoon we put whitebait in so we got crabs the next morning. But it didn't always work like that. I remember when me and brother George were working for lobsters, and father and William were working for crabs, and they got more lobsters than us! But that's probably father's experience as against ours.

# Interview with John Davies

I talked about potting to John Davies, one of the present generation of fishermen fishing from Cromer. He works the largest beach boat in the region, going offshore as well as inshore. His main fishing season is March to October, but, like some of the other fishermen, he keeps some pots out all the year round. Steeped in fishing and seamanship, John comes from seven or eight generations of fishermen, and like his father Richard and his forebears did before him, serves the community as cox'n of the lifeboat. John enjoys his work, pointing out that every day is different.

John had been to sea with his father 'virtually as a babe in arms'. Fishing was the only job he wanted to do. He had gained some fishing experience as a schoolboy, especially in the summer holidays:

> As soon as school finished I went to the school of life! I was fishing with my father, aged fifteen through to nearly eighteen. At sea we got on well, but I had my ideas and he had his. He thought I was good enough to go on my own, and I did. But still being an eighteen-year-old, he thought it would be a good idea if I went with some-one quiet, but who wouldn't hold me back, but who'd look on things different from me and give me a bit of experience. So father fixed up Lenny (West, of Sheringham) to come with me. He was a great character at sea – not talk a lot. We got on very, very well. I bought a boat, the *Gladiator*, and Lenny came with me from Cromer.

And 'Speedy' Muirhead used to come with us – we left school together. I still did as I like crabbing, but as soon as we were lobster-catching Lenny came into his own. If Lenny could catch lobsters all year round, he was happy doing that. He taught me a lot on lobsters, I admit. When you caught lobsters in a four-bowed traditional crab pot there was a lot more art and skill, probably why not many people made a living out of lobsters then. The parlour pot has made fishing easy, especially lobster fishing.

John Davies discussed fishing for lobster:

Yes, they once used crab and that for bait. But the pots were slightly different, you could look at the pots and think no difference in the two, but they could be netted slightly different. The pots were a little bit taller, the crinnies a little bit finer, a finer neck. Just subtle differences. Lenny's pots always fished better for lobsters than mine, because mine were more crab-orientated and his were 'lobsters'. And you had to haul your gear different – you couldn't pull your pots about, because a lobster could get out of a wooden pot very quickly. You had to haul completely different, had to be on top of your gear all the time. And you got to know your ground better than you do with a parlour pot. You'd haul your pots every day, because a lobster can get out easily. But now, with a parlour pot the longer you leave them the better they fish. I wouldn't use wooden pots now to catch lobsters.

While at sea on the catamaran, I noticed John Davies wrapping the bait in little cloth 'pasties'. He explained it was a method copied from a successful lobster fisherman from Wells. Wrapping up the bait meant it was not eaten so fast by crabs and its smell had a chance to draw in the lobsters, though it attracted crabs too. 'Soft' bait, such as horse mackerel, could be made to last longer this way – it was not necessary to wrap hard bait such as skate and gurnard:

You had different places you liked to go, and different times of the year. Lenny fished from East Runton right through to Weybourne; he knew that inshore bit like the back of his hand. He taught me a lot regarding marks, different places he would go and different times in there. Now I work further off (up to 20 miles), in places Lenny would never dream of going. Although they did work little rough bits of ground further off, say a couple of miles, but not like I do now. And a lot of years we fished the bigger wooden pots, and they fished better with being bigger and more room in them. At the beginning of the season crab pots will out-fish parlour pots for crabs. But as crabs get quicker (later in the season), they will get out of crab pots, but not out of parlour pots. You could leave a parlour pot for a week or a month and there would be stuff in them, but not in a crab pot. The crabs might fight each other, but will live quite happily for a week or even a month, because they filter feed – they're not relying on the bait in there.

This is why some fishermen work two or more fleets of pots, hauling them only on alternate days. John Davies works three fleets, two inshore and one offshore, and can visit each fleet every three days if he wishes. They can be set in different areas unless crabs are 'thick' in one area. At the time of writing, one fleet is on an area of wrecks. John is now phasing out the traditional crab pot, because working three fleets, by the time he comes to hauling every three days the crabs which have become active have been in and gone from a wooden pot.

I asked John about crabbing offshore, and he had the following to say:

The North Sea isn't that deep, it averages 25–30m. The deepest we're working is 40m of water. I cut my (pot) tows about 17 fathoms, so sometimes have more than one pot off the bottom at once. They're the same crabs but bigger further 'off'. I'm convinced of that. Because when they moult here (inshore), what we call a 'shot crab', the female is feeding up, the pots will be full of them, great big crabs. But as soon as they're hard, they're gone! Then we start to catch them further out. They just walk 'off'. And they walk north. When I was fishing at Wells and catching a lot of crabs, the crabs were moving north all the time, and I had a job to keep up with them. The north end of my fleet of pots would do better every day, so I'd keep more pots that way, more pots that way every day. Once they've started marching, they're away!

Tagging experiments have in fact shown female crabs move incredible distances up to the Yorkshire coast. Here they release their spawn, which as newly hatched youngsters make their way on the currents back down to Norfolk. The males in contrast have no such wanderlust and stay put.

Fishermen sort their catch at almost unbelievable speed, crabs being flung back to sea or into a fish box below. John shakes his pots upside down onto a metal table midships, but on crab boats with less space sorting takes place inside the pot. I asked John about this rapid sorting, as so many crabs were thrown back into the sea. On a trip in July I noted only seven or eight crabs per pot were flung into the fish box. Some

Crab fishing on the catamaran *Laura Ann*, 2007. John Davies empties the pots, Steve Barrett does the hauling with slave-hauler, far left, while David Heir baits up the pots.

of them were quickly measured with a metal guage to make sure they were the legal size. The stipulation that the minimum landing size must be at least 115mm across the widest part of the shell means they are a few years old. John showed me a crab with a bulging abdomen which he quickly dispatched to the deep:

> Those with eggs you chuck away. It's like when on a typewriter every day, you get ever so quick at it – if on it once a month you're not so quick! If you see the big ones we chuck away, they're soft or no good. They're the 'shot' ones which have moulted and they're feeding up and there's nothing in them at all.

Crabs normally 'shoot their shells' in the latter part of summer. John explained their shells then harden up and when the crabs hibernate in winter they filter feed, so that by April/May when fishermen have started crabbing they have come out of hibernation, fed, and are fairly full of meat.

> You get crabs that moult later on in the year, so they're not completely filled up over wintertime, and they're not hardened up and so not good quality. You can look at a crab, if it's dark and brown and its legs are all brown and claws are jet black, that's going to be a good crab. If you turn some of them up and the legs are a bit gingery and quite clean and light, there's nothing in them – they're not fattened up over winter and they won't be any good until the end of June, July time. These we call the 'whitefoot' crab.

By law they cannot be landed until 30 June, so have to be thrown back to sea:

> The small ones will moult, but the big ones don't, the older ones. But the majority will moult every year, the males and females, but at different times. If the water's warmer and the females are moulting later, the males will moult even later still, because they mate when the female moults and the male is still in his old shell. When we catch the males, the jack crab, just before they start to mate they're better quality then, because they're all fit and up for breeding!

John told me about his spell at fishing in his younger days from Wells. This was on a square-sterned boat with a wheel house, previously used for whelking:

> At that time you had a job getting into Wells harbour, you couldn't just take a boat in there – you wanted a berth and a mooring. But previous to that, crabs were coming on quite big at Wells, and Tony Jordan – he had experience of working out of Wells for years – he wanted to know about crabbing, and I wanted to know about Wells harbour. You know I'm used to working a beach, not a harbour – and not a strange one like Wells! So one autumn we put the pots into Tony's boat – we supplied all the gear, and he supplied the boat.

You could be out for twelve hours, because it's a tidal harbour. He had a hoveller, built in Sheringham, a double-ender, one of the last double-enders to work out of Wells – a beautiful old boat, the *William Edward*. So that was like second nature to me because it was like a crab boat, but bigger. I was on this for four to five months, and we done really well, crabbing, We took some crab pots to sea and steamed off another 1½ miles and picked his whelk pots up and brought them home – that's how we started there. The boats were bigger at Wells because they had to go much further at sea, and they didn't have to get them up and down the beach. Yes, it was a harbour boat. You know when Tony finished he was perhaps working 40 miles out to sea, in basically an open boat!

This was a time when crabbing was taking off at Wells, before becoming the mainstay:

We were only going to the Race, perhaps 10–12 miles was as far as we were going, and not working nearly as many pots as they work now. We did really well, but there were lots of crabs there then. When we first started, we were hauling only 160 pots a day from Wells, which is nothing to what they work now – some of them haul 400 a day, and got 1,200–1,600 pots in the water, maybe even 2,000! That catamaran, the *Pathfinder*, she's the most modern one in the fleet now – that's working 2,000 pots!

But I suppose my heart was always in Cromer working from the beach, because that's what I'd been brought up to do and I enjoyed doing it. But working out of Wells, that was lovely, in the summer months, and when there's plenty of crabs it was very enjoyable. In wintertime when it's damp, cold and miserable, it's not the best place in world! It was a long way to drive, and long at sea, day after day – yes, that can take a bit of sticking, I admit. But when you're younger you can do it more.

Nowadays fishermen all along the North Norfolk coast fish almost exclusively for crab and lobster. John told me:

We shot a few lines this year but that was a waste of time! We specialise in crabs and lobsters and that is what we target. We work as much gear as we can, and have to stick to that. If something else turned up, such as a market for herring, we'd perhaps do some of that. But there's no market for them, so you can't catch them.

# Crab dressing with Billy Davies

Many people can dress crabs but not with the skill and speed to be found among fishing families. Dressing is done by men, such as retired fishermen, as well as by women, and particular ways of doing it are passed down each family business.

Billy Davies's father Bob dressing crabs to sell on the family crab stall. Cromer, 1990s. (EDP)

'Blond' Billy Davies's stall is at the top of the Gangway. Every morning in the crabbing season he carries baskets of freshly cooked crabs from his boilery to the shop to be dressed and sold. Before the days of strict hygiene rules, when one could freely enter the premises, I went in to talk to him. Sitting with several cooked crabs on a formica table, a kitchen knife, and a basket of discarded crab bits at his feet, he showed me how a crab is dressed – the proper way, Billy says!

> They are mostly males at this time of the year, June, because the females are getting ready to shoot the shell for mating. They'll be red roe then. When crabs first come out of hibernation, they're not quite full then. They are best when they've been out for about a month, so that's the end of March or April. You can tell if it's a good crab, if it will split round the front (underside), or at the back, it will split out of the shell.
>
> You'll find in July the females will spawn and there will not be anything in them at all – there will be nothing but water and fat in the 'cart' (shell). No brown meat in them at all. You can bring back males in the summer, but you're not allowed to bring back berried females.

Most breed in summer immediately after the moult, but when this is over crabs are good quality from September to November. They will have eaten well all summer for the coming winter, and those that moulted will have hardened.

First the crab is 'opened': a central lump from the underside, the 'shekel', with legs attached is pulled out. The stomach of the crab, in the middle of the shekel, is pushed with the thumb and pulled away. This comes out as a gelatinous whitish piece and is discarded. The gills, or dead men's fingers, from around the outside of the shekel are also discarded. The big claws and small legs are pulled off from the shekel, and the legs thrown away. The joints where the legs had joined the shekel are trimmed.

Returning to the cart, Billy pulls away segments of shell from its underside so that there is a wider opening in the middle. Brown meat in the cart is picked up with the knife, turned over and pushed to one side. He adds a little more brown meat from the outside of the shekel. The shekel is then cut through twice and small bits of white meat are scooped out from the pockets where the legs and claws were attached and put into the cart. This white meat is pushed into half of the cart, so that one half ends up as brown meat, the other as white meat. The claws are broken with a whack from the knife, the white meat cleaned out of them and put in the centre of the cart. The crab is put into a poly bag, and into the cool cabinet. Job done. It has taken just two to three minutes to prepare: 'Males and females are the same to dress, but the female's cart is deeper than the male's, so you can get more brown meat in a female.' These are the 'broadsters' with a broad apron on their underside:

> People do it different ways. Some people don't fold the brown meat back, some leave it and fill the hole in the middle with the claw meat. Some do not bother to pick the shekel out. But there's only one correct way – the way we do it! The way we do it, the meat from each crab is not mixed up like some people do – each crab has its own meat.

Blond Billy only dresses crabs with both front claws; others mix and match if one is missing. In the past one-footers were given away, as fishmongers wanted crabs with both legs to put on their slab.

To my question of how many are dressed per day, the answer was simple: 'As many as possible! But it depends on sales – what we've got on – hotels, pubs and that.' The final touch on some Cromer crabs is now a date stamp.

# The future of potting

What of the future of potting in Norfolk? Fishermen have an eye on changes in the marine environment, especially when there is a bad crabbing year. They are not sure about global warming, but agree that the seasons have been all over the place in recent years and fewer crabs go dormant. John Davies, with a deep knowledge of the industry, discussed the fluctuations:

> Years ago, they'd sometimes get bumper harvests, especially in what they call the 'bay' up at Weybourne – it's deeper water in there. And so they did here, Cromer, too. Five or six years back we had some good years, quite a lot of crabs. But then there was no one catching crabs further 'off' like there is now, and the effort now

on crabs. The increases, I put a lot of that down to depletion of the whitefish stock. Because in the summer months when there'd be dogfish and skate, and crabs in the late autumn – they'll all eat the crabs, suck them up like a hoover. If you catch any codling in summertime and gut them, they're completely full of crabs. Every fish will eat crabs. When we got depletion in whitefish stocks, I think the crabs have benefited from it. But why they've gone slow *now* God above knows.

But the seasonal weather patterns have changed so vastly I think that's really messed them up. Crabs haven't run to a pattern for a lot of years now like they used to. At certain times you could go to certain places you'd always catch crabs there, and if you went too far off you wouldn't get any. But that's all gone by the wayside. The crab can only go by the seasonal weather patterns, and they live their life by a season.

It's not just global warming. There's just no proper seasons any more. We don't get a winter at all, if you think about it[2]. Before, you come to December and the crabs begin to go to ground hibernating, and it's the middle of March before you saw any crabs again. Now, I keep pots out all year and we get a few crabs – not that many. But years ago you'd not get *any*, they'd be hibernating. But you see, (now) they keep feeding a little bit and a little bit so they're not coming out in spring starving hungry – they're not starving because there's good meat in them. They should be hungry, wanting to eat. (Before) you'd always get females, soon as we started. They'd sit like little balls in the pots, and you'd not get any 'rubbish', that's the small crabs with them. But, today I've been in February and the pots were half full of small crabs. We wouldn't see any of them until April/May time. Now they're already there, male crabs with them too. That's completely out of character, and it's in *my* lifetime!

I asked one of the older fishermen, Ivan Large, who had fished from Salthouse and Wells, if crabbing was the same years ago:

The catches kept the same as they are now. There were more fish about then, but there were no more crabs than there is now. Matter of fact, some seasons were worse, the odd season. I had a season and not get a crab all the year through! We put it down to the weather. If you got a cold winter and everything go to ground and hibernate, then it seemed you'd get a better year then. But the weather is more open now. The temperature doesn't go that cold. The crabs don't hibernate so much now, so they go crabbing all the year round now, don't they?

Other older fishermen confirm that catches had been up and down over their whole fishing life. According to retired Donny Lawrence, small decreases in the past were put down to crabs not being interested in the bait because there was enough food on the sea bed; in a week or so they would be caught again. Fishermen and scientists are now puzzled about the arrival of velvet crabs and their effects on brown crab populations. In 2006–7 they were appearing in the pots, when a few years earlier they were almost non-existent. Fishermen along the coast took to putting them in keep pots at sea and sending them off on weekly vivier lorries from Scotland to Spain or Portugal. Abroad they are relished as a delicacy, but they are not yet to the English taste, although some have appeared in supermarkets. Recently, they have declined. They had initially been more of a going concern at Wells, prompting construction of a new building with storage tanks. John Davies discussed the threats to the industry:

> It's not an easy way to earn a living, far from it. The biggest threat is going single-handed, because how is the youngster going to learn the skill? I can remember when there was always crew about, swapping and changing, and youngsters came in to work with an experienced bloke. He'd take him with him, and he'd work his way up. And training isn't something you can learn overnight! That's not there anymore.

This is a sentiment shared by fishermen generally. Few of today's youngsters can stick the hours, beginning at dawn. John on the catamaran has two crew members; one is an experienced fisherman who had formerly gone lining from Lowestoft, the other was, for a time, a rare school-leaver.

Since the days of mechanised hauling, the increased efficiency of parlour pots, plus more fishermen potting as other forms of fishing have declined or been restricted by quotas, more pressure has been put on crab stocks in the North Sea. Some Norfolk fishermen point out that offshore 'supercrabbers' working thousands of pots all-year from ports to the north must have an effect as they remove migrating females. Others say the interaction of offshore and inshore crabs is as yet unclear. Some fishermen I have talked to, like Ivan, believe there will always be upturns and downturns of the industry in Norfolk, but others are gloomy about the future.

In recent years fewer fishermen work full-time. For those coming up to retirement many say they have made a good living from fishing – the mantra being, 'What you put in, you get out!' But they did not see this for a youngster just starting. One of the older fishermen told me when he began fishing he had started with nothing, having come from a poor family, but with hard work he had done well in his career, even being able to buy two houses. He believed it would be impossible to pull oneself up in an equivalent way now. A lot more money was needed to offset the risks and the initial investments – 'One would now need to be born with a silver spoon in your mouth!' In addition, Norfolk's fishermen had once felt that they had had Government support, an example being the availability of grants which had once helped them buy new boats. This has not only gone but fishing has become beset by rules and regulations from DEFRA and other bodies. Some of these come like shots across the bows which make earning a living more difficult for the small-scale fisherman.

End notes:
1. Norfolk fishermen reverse 'up' and 'down' at sea.
2. Interview conducted before the harsh winter of 2010–11.

# CHAPTER 5

# SHEDWORK

In the past Norfolk's beach fishermen have made and repaired their fishing gear throughout the year, particularly when the weather was bad and they could not get to sea. Picturesque old photographs show them mending pots in their communal backyards. Nowadays, since the demise of herring-catching, long-lining and whelking, fishermen can devote more time after the crabbing season has finished to what they call 'shedwork'.

Tucked away in sheds or lean-tos at the backs of their houses, fishermen either do this work themselves, or employ crew-men or retired fishermen who like to keep their hand in. Until they moved to larger premises outside Cromer, the Davieses used former storage buildings within the town for fishing-related activities, which included boiling crabs and mending gear. Much colour and life was given to the heart of the town as their vehicles loaded with pots or boxes of crabs swung in and out, and if one could sneak a look at work in progress so much the better. Several fishermen now have facilities away from where they live, such as old farm buildings.

## Making and 'overlooking' crab pots

Fishermen have to make their pots and dan buoys ready for the next crabbing season, and also repair, or 'overlook' their old ones. Working together in the shed was often the time to share a few laughs and chat about fishing, and more than one working fisherman has told me how, when they were schoolboys, they had hung around and enjoyed the conversation of the older men, besides picking up useful information. The sheds did not have electricity at first. Ralph Kirk described how he would go to Jack Davies's shed, and see Jack's son Richard and cousin 'Little Billy', and 'Stymie' Blythe working by gas-light. They had a pot-bellied stove in the corner to keep warm, which would burn up bits of wood and 'cut-offs'.

Some of the work has now changed. Parlour pots, which have been widely used since the 1970s–80s, have to be netted and roped. These are worked later in the fishing season and are especially good for catching lobsters. Traditional crab pots in Norfolk are no longer made from scratch; Dennis Gaff may be among the last to have done so. Fishermen still like these pots as they are good for catching crabs at the beginning of

*Above:* Future fisherman Billy (W.H.) Davies (left) and friend observing Dick Davies making a crab pot. George Lusher repairing a cork buoy (right). Cromer, 1954. (EDP)

*Right:*Retired fisherman Dennis Gaff preparing pots for the coming season for his son Billy. Here roping up a parlour pot. Cromer, 2009.

the season, but many believe that in less than twenty years they will have completely converted to parlour pots and the traditional crab pots will be a thing of the past, as will the skill to make them. They aim to get a good few years of wear out of them, and repair them until it is no longer worthwhile, so several shanks of them are still to be seen stacked in their sheds.

Overlooking the gear is time-consuming but the situation has been greatly improved since the introduction of synthetic materials. The older type of pot had to be continuously made and a vast number overlooked each year. I will look at the preparation of parlour pots and dan buoys later in this chapter, but my first call is to visit Dennis Gaff, master of crab-pot making.

Dennis has his workshop in a back street of neat terraced houses in Cromer. It is an interesting emporium of ropes, pots, fish boxes and dan buoys. Dennis is a retired fisherman, who assists his son Billy in making and overlooking crab pots. The old stable building where he works has partly been converted to an area where crabs are dressed, which meets health and hygiene standards. The upper room, where once stable boys had slept, stored crab pots until recently, which would be lowered to the outside by a rope through the window.

Although related to fishing families, Dennis's father was not a fisherman and he was put into the painting and decorating business when he left school. Dennis had been to sea since a schoolboy, and soon gave up decorating in favour of what he really liked, which was fishing. His father asked 'Shrimp' Davies, a well-known fisherman in the town and lifeboat cox'n, to take him on. By the age of sixteen Dennis was fishing full-time. He has had a long fishing career in Cromer, and unusually for a beach fisherman had a spell on a steam-drifter from Yarmouth, a type of fishing long since gone.

Stacked at the main entrance of the workshop is a supply of newly delivered oak frames, which will be used as crab pot bases. Dennis is in the process of making a traditional, or conventional, crab pot. Several finished articles are stacked nearby. His worktable is an old herring-stool, which had belonged to his cousin Kelly Harrison, with whom Dennis had fished for many years. I settled down to watch Dennis at his work, while he talked all the while about what he was doing and his days at sea.

The method of making the traditional crab pot is very precise. They have to be very robust to withstand storms at sea and being knocked about during hauling. Fishermen take pride in their craftsmanship, and it is fair to say that the Norfolk pots are particularly neat. A fisherman initially learns his craft from a more experienced fisherman. Dennis was taught by 'Shrimp' Davies. Small adaptations become incorporated according to availability of materials and personal preference, so it is not surprising that fishermen can identify their own pots and can spot them when washed up on the beach. They can often identify pots belonging to another individual or another village 'where they make them different there'.

The basic creel shape has hardly changed since introduced in the middle of the nineteenth century. There is an interesting debate as to where the design came from. Local fishermen believe they originated in Yorkshire, the know-how probably coming down to the area with visiting coal ships in the second half of the nineteenth century. There is an official fisheries report by Frank Buckland from 1875, which suggests pots were introduced 1861–63. However, an article published in the *Whitby Gazette* in 1876 suggests it was the other way round. A fish merchant is quoted as saying that 'two old Sheringham fishermen' took the design up to Yorkshire *c*.1856. The Norfolk crab pot is generally similar to Yorkshire pots, but there are differences in weighting the pot, the method of netting and making entrances, and the number of bows. Inkwell-shaped pots had previously been used in Norfolk, according to old prints up to at least the 1860s. In more recent times this type of pot, which is now associated with the South Coast, has been tried here but found not suited to the ground. Similarly, a Canadian design, a round plastic pot in use at Whitby, was tried by an Overstrand fisherman, but found wanting.

At the bottom of the Norfolk crab pot is a wooden frame with an iron base which helps sink the pot in the water. The frame is well-seasoned oak, about 2ft 6in by 1ft 6in. The Gaffs have had these made in bulk by Donny Lawrence, another retired fisherman. Within the frame, the older type of iron base is called a 'music', because its parallel bars have a vague similarity to a music score. Musics are now hard to come by, as the local blacksmiths who once made them are no more. Dennis told me that in Cromer, Burgess of Corner Street had once supplied them. They were also cast by a foundry at Walsingham, if a pattern was taken there for a mould to be made. It is now unusual to find crab pots still worked with their original musics in. A derelict one might be 'cut down' to supply a metal base for a pot being restored, otherwise bars of iron or plate steel have to be obtained from a dealer.

The pot has four hoops, or 'bows', to which the netting is attached. There are two entrances, funnel-shaped 'crinnies', through which the crab pushes its way seeking the bait. Fishermen do not know the origin of the word 'crinny', but I like to think many years ago a vicar, well-versed in his Latin, had murmured the lily-shaped entrance looked crinoid and the word stuck.

The bows were traditionally hazel, superseded by cane in the 1960s, and later by polythene tubing. The piping lasts well, but 'nutsticks' are sometimes thought better, and cheaper. Dennis has obtained long lengths of them from a local gamekeeper; other fishermen have their own contacts. Dennis, like some of the older fishermen, remembers making unauthorised sorties into woods several miles away – and wobbling home with the bundles of nutsticks on his trade bike.

Some terms for parts of crab pots and parlour pots refer to parts of houses. The front and back of the pot between the bows are called windows, and the ends are called gables. Five 'sticks', are attached to the top.

For the pot I am watching Dennis make, no old-style music is available, so he uses two bars of iron (also becoming difficult to get hold of), with a wooden bar partly filling the space between them to stop crabs escaping. These are bolted to the frame. Dennis then wrestles with the plastic bows of the superstructure, forcing the ends into drilled holes in the frame, and knocking nails in from the base and sides to secure them. (Another fisherman told me he put small wedges in the holes which swelled in the sea and held the bows in place.) An electric drill is used nowadays, but not so long ago a large corkscrew-like device was all there was, as demonstrated to me by Sheringham fisherman Lenny West. His shed still contains one which his father and grandfather had used, their initials marked on the handle.

Dennis explained the bows of the pot were once forced into shape by bending them over the fishermen's knees – giving them sore knees. He now uses a 'bow-bender'. This is a thick D-shaped block of wood, with metal brackets around the edge, into which the wood lengths or plastic tubing are pushed. Dennis has several pieces of bent tubing ready. They had been softened by being dipped in the nearby crab-boiling vat before the crabs went in, then put into cold water before 'shoving' round the bow-bender.

The twine now used for 'braiding', or knitting, the crinnies and the rest of the netting for the pot, is synthetic 'corlene'. Before this, less durable manila, or 'pot stuff', had been used. Dennis remembers sisal which was worse still, which fishermen had to use during the last war when manila was scarce. At one time there had been rope-walks in Cromer and Sheringham, where fibres were twisted into rope and twine. Lenny West recalled his father had helped at a ropewalk behind his house and was repaid in twine to do his pots. But mostly, pot stuff, like other fishing equipment, had come from 'Fiddy' West's chandlery in Sheringham, now gone. Dennis, like the other fishermen, had soaked it in Cuprinol or bought it with preservative in it when that became available. He told me others had immersed the whole pot in Cuprinol, had soaked a ball of twine in tar before braiding with it or painted tar on the netted pot. He remembered Jimmy Davies blackened with tar and having to be cleaned with grease before setting out for the Red Lion.

In the days of manila, this only lasted one season, so the netting had to be stripped off the pot, and new netting braided onto it. This obviously presented a lot of work, with perhaps a hundred pots to do per season. In Lenny West's experience the netting sometimes only lasted four weeks, especially when the sea warmed up, 'It turned black and fell off! You were braiding all the time, bringing pots ashore and taking them back repaired the next morning.' Bob Cox:

> If we put new sisal or manila pots at sea at the start of the season we'd let them get a bit of wear, then change them over. We'd take them ashore and tan them with 'cutch' as used for herring nets, then tar them. When they dried we'd take them back to sea. To tan them, we'd put them in the copper, the whole pot. The coppers were like for doing washing years ago – larger. The whole pot went in the tar tub – a big galvanised tub; the wood came to no harm. Yes, it was a messy job!

The net-braiding needle used for pots is the same type as once used to repair herring nets up and down the East Coast, but bigger. Dennis prefers wooden to plastic needles, adding that women in days gone by had used larger versions to braid trawl nets in Lowestoft. He winds twine onto the needle, backwards and forwards around the spine. This comes in several colours, including 'unlucky' green.

The traditional way to make the netting for the crinny, as for the rest of the pot, is by hand. Dennis set about making a couple of crinnies, braiding onto a length of twine attached to two nails 3ft apart on the stable door. He explained that in the days when fishermen sometimes repaired or made fishing gear in their houses, he had made crinnies in his living room using a window frame as a support. A piece of electrical wire for the mouth of the crinny is bent round and secured into a ring then threaded onto the twine. Formerly, the ring had been a piece of hazel or split cane, but this was not long-lasting; better was a piece of elm, which hardened in seawater. Dennis showed me an old pot still in use, and identified it as made by 'Old Jack' Davies because he had always used cane for the ring.

Fourteen stitches are cast onto the ring. At the end of the first row, the second row is braided going backwards, the hand turned over with fingers pointing upwards instead of downwards. There are seven rows altogether, but for the last four rows only seven of the stitches reach the bottom, so forming a sort of flap, or top end of a lily-shape. Using his fingers and the needle Dennis works rhythmically, causing the stable door to rattle and thump. To make the stitches, the needle is threaded into a loop (stitch) of the row above, and secured with a knot. It is impressive that fishermen who do such hard work at sea are such deft craftsmen. Their fingers, which are quite large after years of hand-hauling pots at sea, are the ideal size, two for the width of each mesh. Dennis told me braiding had occasionally been done by women during the last war when there was less manpower about. There had of course been a tradition of women mending herring nets along the East Coast, especially at Lowestoft.

Dennis stretches the netting he has braided around the ring and laces the top half up, leaving the flap to hang down. The flap is necessary for fitting the crinny into the space between the bows of the pot. The rest of the pot has two rectangular sections of hand-braided netting (each 'twenty-three meshes, come down seven'), which Dennis wraps around each end of the pot. Each one is attached to two windows and a gable. Billy has farmed out the manufacture of these to another retired fisherman. I was told Cromer fishermen had in earlier days knitted up sections on the beach while waiting to hire out beach huts. Nowadays hand-braiding is rare, as most fishermen cut up factory-made sheet netting instead.

As he attached the netting to the pot with nylon cord, and incorporated the two crinnies, Dennis recalled the storm of 1953, which devastated the Norfolk coast and created havoc in many people's lives. His wife was pregnant with Billy at the time. In the night before the worst day, Dennis and other fishermen had rushed to pull their boats up to the top of the Gangway, almost up to street level. The boats were saved, but fishermen who were whelking at the time lost all their pots, which had been a terrible loss of working capital. Fortunately, a national fund was set up to help pay fishermen compensation. Dennis was later employed in the repair of the Promenade.

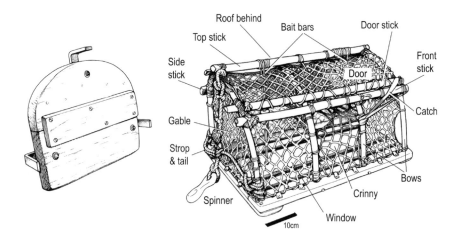

Traditional Norfolk crab pot. Dennis Gaff was among the last to make them, in 2005. Iron bars instead of 'musics' weight the base. *Left:* Bow bender. The bows are forced under the brackets.

Stacked in the shed was a bunch of straight hazel sticks about 9ft tall, destined to be roof sticks. They had become hard after seasoning so would last about four years on a pot – if put on fresh they would only last a couple. Dennis cuts four pieces the same length as the pot, and makes small notches in them. First the front-stick is tied on, the notches keeping the string in place. The netting and crinny at the front of the pot are pulled upright and threaded onto a line of twine which is tied to the front-stick. After a short break for a cup of tea, the side-stick is tied on and the netting and crinny at the back of the pot are similarly secured. To make the roof, a sheet of roof-netting is laid over the top of the pot and the back half laced onto the back wall of the pot and side-stick. The front half left loose is to become the 'door'.

Dennis now makes the bridge between the rings of the two crinnies by lacing twine backwards and forwards ('reins'). A space is left at the bottom for crabs to fall through and be trapped in the pot. The reins are reinforced with lacing across them, so that crabs cannot force their way out.

To secure the walls of netting onto the wooden base frame, Dennis folds small loops of oilskin around the bottom of the netting at intervals, and bangs nails in. The tops of the gables are then braided and sewn onto the end-bows.

The door-stick then has to be attached. Dennis first makes a loop 'catch' for it on the pot corner. This is a piece of twisted twine, bent over and tied on. He attaches a loop of tyre inner-tube to the other corner so that the door-stick will be kept in place when the 'door' is closed. This is a King's Lynn idea, replacing string ties. On the boat, the fisherman will be able to open the door in a flash and empty the crabs out. The door-stick is threaded through the edge of the door netting and secured. Sticks then tied at the apex of the pot and behind the apex, become the top-stick and back-stick, keeping the roof netting in place.

The next stage is to make two 'bait bars', which will have the bait rammed into them during the fishing trip. Dennis attaches a double nylon cord to the top-stick and through a hole in the base of the pot, which is secured with a 'peg' made of a small piece of hosepipe. A 'button' to hold the bait tightly is threaded onto the cords. This is a small piece of thick-walled piping, but Dennis had once used small circles of leather cut from old shoes. He gives the bait bars a couple of satisfying twangs to see if they are nice and tight, and closes the 'door' with the catch.

The final stage is to make the 'strop and tail' which will join the tows (ropes) when fishing. Dennis told me the incorporated spinner stopped pots getting 'spun up'. Previously, fishermen had periodically to unbend (detach) the pots at sea to take the turns out of the tow ropes; with spinners pots could roll about in the sea and turn independently of each other. Before the fishing season begins tows between the pots will be tied to the spinners.

At the end of this complex series of operations Dennis surveys his work. He says that it would be better to put the finished pot in the sitting room than at the bottom of the sea. It will last a couple of years before overlooking 'unless it gets a breeze on it', and these days there are less breezes than years ago, so it should last quite well. He reckons well maintained crab pots will outlast the modern parlour pots by several years, which succumb to rust after about six years. He recalled in previous times, a sisal or manila pot took about 1½ hours to make, 'But with synthetic, it's slippery and they take a lot longer. But they last a lot longer, so you can't have everything, I suppose.'

Later Dennis will next start overlooking a stack of old pots. Some have damaged bases, the superstructure, or 'shekels', being fine, or vice versa. Warped and worn hazel sticks will need to be replaced. Plastic bows which had gone 'cathedral-shaped' after 'taking a breeze of wind', will need to be reshaped in the bow-bender. Holes in netting have to be rebraided, bait bars and door fastenings renewed. I am told Cromer pots have an advantage over Sheringham pots in that when a section of netting is damaged it can more easily be cut out and replaced. Sheringham pots are braided in one piece directly onto the pot from a cord along the base.

In another part of Cromer Ralph Kirk works for Billy Gaff, netting up parlour pots for the next season's fishing. As a retired fisherman he has worked for other fishermen too, including making conventional crab pots for 'Little' Billy Davies. Ralph has a small shed at the back of his terraced house. Everything is shipshape and Bristol-fashion, perhaps because Ralph once did a spell in the navy, although most fishermen are by nature very tidy. Tools and materials are organised in neat rows around his workbench or within reach of his chair. Symbolically, his long fishing boots are hanging up, but visitors are told 'I'm still open to offers!'

As he winds on a piece of corlene twine onto his braiding needle, Ralph muses on the dying art of making and braiding up traditional crab pots. Although most of the fishermen on the beach can still do it he says, in a few years the skill will be gone in Norfolk. Ralph is a wonderful communicator, and enjoys talking to me about his shedwork and his fishing career.

The parlour pots he is to prepare are used in the summer months particularly to catch lobsters, but also for catching crabs. Lobsters were previously caught in conventional crab pots, made up bigger, but limited by what was manageable to lift, which was significant in the days before pot-haulers. Most fishermen had owned about twenty I was told, whereas now they own several shanks of parlour pots. Ralph considered that parlour pots had been invented by a fisherman rather than by a scientist or engineer and thought they originated in Yorkshire. Up and down the country fishermen have adapted traps to local circumstances and available materials, so it seemed reasonable that their experience of lobster behaviour would lead them to the parlour pot. I was told by John Balls that some Cromer fishermen had had a go at making them themselves, but gave up because the cost of buying them was less than the aggravation of making them.

The frames of the parlour pot are obtained from firms in East Anglia. The simple thin steel frame is plastic-coated (Ralph was contemptuous: 'Waste of time, it soon peels off'), or galvanised. They are bigger and heavier than a conventional crab pot, but dimensions vary, for instance Ralph has braided pots for John Davies which are longer than most, with thicker steel frames. Willy Cox has large parlour pots but also likes to have some shanks of smaller ones which are more convenient to handle now that he fishes solo.

The pots are bought as a grid-like base, with three thin bows, and thin struts on the top. Most parlour pots are top-opening, although a few fishermen use 'D doors', where the pot is opened at the gable end. The crinnies incorporate 'hard eyes', or rigid rings, as for crab pots. A large part of the pot is a compartment called the 'parlour'. Lobsters find their way into this via a funnel-shaped piece of netting with a 'soft eye' opening made from twine. Because they cannot easily get out again, the great advantage of the parlour pot for catching lobsters is that they can be left in the sea longer without having to be hauled up every day. After a while lobsters make a getaway from a crab pot.

Ralph is almost unique in the region in hand-braiding the netting for parlour pots. Most fishermen cut up pieces of sheet netting bought from a wholesaler. John Davies had shown me pots with netting wrapped around the four sides or over the whole pot and gathered at both ends. Ralph admits that economics might force Billy Gaff to go this way eventually. Pots with hand-made netting are slower to make, but better fitted. In the meantime Ralph continues to braid them up by hand, having adapted the method for making traditional crab pots learnt many years ago from his mentor, 'Tuna' Harrison. Like Dennis, Ralph uses traditional wooden needles. His favourite one has become worn over time and the central spine distorted. He has had it for over thirty years, and it wasn't new then. Ralph sometimes uses a modern plastic 'Norwegian' needle. This is easier to load, the twine being passed through a gap at the top so the needle need not be turned round continuously.

As Ralph finishes loading up three needles, we talk about the fact that while boats are insured, fishing gear is not. He explained that it would be too easy to put in a false

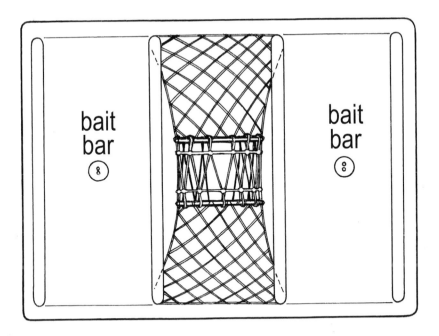

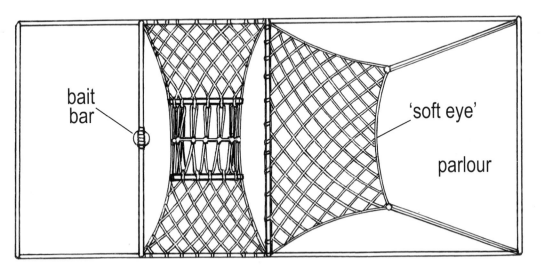

Diagrams of traps of crab pot (top) and parlour pot (bottom), looking down. On each pot, two opposing crinnies are joined by 'reins'. Positions of vertical bait bars indicated.

claim that pots had been destroyed in a storm, when really they are still at sea. He recalled a time when he was fishing with Richard Davies and a storm blew up:

> We didn't go to sea for ten days. We lost three shanks: two were washed up off Overstrand; they were rolled up and taken by the tide. We got divers to help – there were fifty pots in a heap, we used a grapnel to pull them up on deck, but they were damaged beyond repair. Another time, nine shanks were lying in a heap off Cromer. We used the lifeboat's winch to try to get them up, no good, so we got the *Strandline*, which was a stern trawler from King's Lynn, I think, to drag them up on his deck. Oh yes, you can lose thousands of pounds worth of equipment, but I wouldn't like to say how much a shank is worth. You see, it's not just the cost of the pot, but what it can earn you when at sea.

As with making a conventional crab pot, the order of the stages and details of technique are particular to the fisherman. For Ralph's parlour pot, the gables with adjoining windows are made first, then the roof, the tops of the gables and the crinnies. He has worked out through trial and error the number of stitches for each section.

He first casts stitches onto a loose piece of twine secured by two nails a couple of feet apart on the workbench, and proceeds to go back and forth forming rows of a sheet of netting. Ralph told me the technique was called 'backward braiding'; Dennis had done the same when making crinnies. Ralph's tutor 'Tuna' Harrison always went one way, left to right, called 'braiding on a single string'. (Here, a loop of twine knotted onto a nail is turned round each time the end of a row is reached.) But Ralph reckoned the method shown to him by 'Shrimp' was better as it resulted in a neater net. When he emptied a needle-full of twine he sealed the end with a flame to prevent it fraying, and with another needle-full tied on the new twine, having first sealed its end. Ralph is very particular about sealing the ends of any piece of twine: 'I don't like my ends to get all fluffy!'

When he has braided two sheets of netting they are tied around the bottom of the pot with nylon cord. Wearing a rubber glove with the fingers cut out, Ralph makes several small knots to secure the cord to the pot, tugging hard at every knot. Next, he braids the top of the gables, stitching them on to the end bows. Fishermen who attach sheet netting to their pots still have to braid in this part in by hand.

The ring of the crinny is plastic, bought ready-made from Mr Williment's chandlery in Gorleston. Ralph often uses old rings, first scraping off the barnacles. The ring is wider than for a conventional pot, and completely circular, not slightly oval. Ralph makes crinnies slightly differently than Dennis does for a conventional pot. After attaching them to the pot, a bridge is laced between them, leaving a hole for the lobsters to go through. Ralph told me some fishermen offset the crinnies from one another, lacing each one to the opposite wall.

Ralph next makes a sheet of netting (thirty stitches wide, ten rows down) into a funnel-shaped bag and ties it inside the pot. Its narrow end will form into a slit (the

Retired fisherman Ralph Kirk 'netting' a parlour pot. Here stitching the gable. Cromer, 2006.

'soft eye') when in the water. Having entered the pot through a crinny and dropped through the hole at the bottom of the bridge, the lobster will wander over to the bag and push its way through the slit and into the 'parlour'. It will find it can't just wander out again because it is difficult from this side to prize the slit open.

Ralph attaches inside the pot a bait bar of nylon cord, with a plastic-disc button. A sheet of roof netting is sewn partly on to the bows, and as for a conventional pot, half of it is left loose to become the 'door', which is reinforced with twine along its edges. To form the front for the door, Ralph uses a broom handle, but hazel sticks are preferred. The broom handle is notched at each end so that it will 'sit' easily on the pot, then threaded through the loose edge of the netting and stitched in place. A small door 'catch' is made with twine twisted into a loop and reinforced with blanket stitch.

Some fishermen make a small hole in the pot to allow small crabs to escape, but many will escape anyway through the grille at the bottom. This is unlike a conventional crab pot, where smaller crabs cannot easily get out.

After a cup of coffee, a roll-up, and a noisy visit from Ralph's Alsatian, he starts on the next stage. This is 'roping up' to protect chafing of the struts and the netting. Ralph admits this is the boring part. Using old tow rope, a five fathom length is cut, and one end secured to the bottom corner. It is bound round and round the bottom bar, the four sides, the bows at both ends, across two roof bars, down two central bows, to end up along the top bar. The pot has then to be 'stropped and tailed', as on conventional crab pots. The only thing Billy Gaff has to do is attach a piece of inner tube, as a door-opener.

Ralph surveys his handiwork then adds the finished pot to a stack of others outside the shed, 'They're too good to go in the sea! As my mother used to say, if a job's worth doing, it's worth doing well. These will last several years if they don't take too much rough weather.' To my question as to how long the operation took him:

> Well with making the net, it takes longer than with sheet netting which you cut out. It takes maybe three hours to braid the net. Then an hour and a half to net the pot. Then to rope it, it'd take an hour and a half to two hours, if I got stuck in. I do one pot at a time – braid the net, put it on, rope it and finish. Then the next one. If I really got stuck in in the morning I could do one in a day. It's possible, but I like my coffee and having breaks! My cousin Donny, he can do two in a morning with sheet netting, but without roping. He doesn't like roping.

Ralph enjoys his work, which is satisfying and helps maintain contact with his former colleagues on the beach. He will continue working until, as he says, 'I can't get out of the shed!'

Other essential parts of a crab fisherman's gear are the markers, or dan buoys. I made my way down to John Davies's shed where he and his crew were getting their gear ready for the next season. They are helped by John's father Richard, who retired from fishing a few years ago.

The basic shape of the dan buoy is a pole with a marker flag at the top, a float of some kind, and a weight below sea level to keep the dan upright. Over the fishing season dans collect weed and debris, and become 'roughed up' during storms, so they have to be scrubbed and repaired, and new ones made. When I visited John's shed I was shown how they were made from scratch. All around are overlooked crab pots and parlour pots piled high. Workbenches and materials are arranged around the room, and everyone is busy. Crew member Steve Barrett is engaged in making dan buoys for the coming season. Already over a dozen are leaning against a wall.

Fishermen's dans, like the crab pots, can be recognised as belonging to a particular fisherman by slight variations in technique and materials. John told me he did not rely on them so much now, as he found his pots by GPS – dans were more to warn other boats where his pots were. Some fishermen have said that with more uptake of GPS, dans and the skill in making them will become a thing of the past; others say they will always be needed. John likes to have a good supply, as some of his fishing is several miles offshore where dans are vulnerable to damage by shipping. Numerous buoys get separated from the underlying tows, 'They're foreign and English, all sorts: cargo ships, ferries, tankers. When the weather's not fine they can't see the small buoys – and they go in closer in than they should do.' Some are container ships from Humberside which cut in close on their way down to Felixstowe. Inshore fisherman Billy Gaff makes twenty dans at the start of the season, more throughout and repairs others. They could last two seasons, or be lost the next day if a ship cuts them off.

Dan buoys have to be securely made, so ties and knots are extremely tight. The procedures worked out are very precise, but a series of rapid movements results in a dan being made in a matter of minutes. I counted just seventeen minutes from start to finish, with time included for chat. As he worked Steve told me he had gone lining for a few years from one of few remaining fishing vessels at Lowestoft, a 14m, sheltered-deck vessel. The catch was the same as once for beach fishermen: dogfish, cod and skate. He had been introduced to crabbing when working with John Jonas during weekends a few years ago.

The poles of the dans are 'nut sticks', about 9ft long. It is not worth the expense of buying cane, as used by some fishermen, because there is such a turnover of buoys offshore. First the bottom of the pole is to be attached to a strop with a spinner, which on the boat will be attached, or 'bent', onto the tow and anchor. To make the strop, Steve takes two fathoms of rope and burns the ends in the flame of the gas-heater to prevent them fraying. The rope is doubled up and the folded end pushed through one of the holes in the spinner; the other end is knotted. Some fishermen reinforce the strop rope with hosepipe tubing. Steve knots the strop rope on to the lower part of the pole and secures it with twine at intervals. Small notches have been made in the pole so that the twine does not slip.

He next ties on two small sash window weights; others might use one long weight. In the past the weight might have been a bar of iron or large bolt, but recently fisher-men have had a good supply of weights as old wooden windows have been replaced by UPVC, but the source will eventually dry up. About two-thirds of the way down the dan is the float. John Davies's floats are made from sheet polystyrene cut into 1ft squares. Some inshore fishermen like Willy Cox use moulded polystyrene floats bought for £2–3 from a chandler. Steve sandwiches three squares of polystyrene between two round plastic lids from jellied eel containers, pushing the pole through the centre of each. He measures three fathoms of rope and ties the float on all four sides to the pole so that it ends up looking like a bound parcel. The end of the rope is laid against the pole under the float, knotted on to it and secured tightly with twine.

Lastly, marker flags are attached to the top of the pole. These are cut from a sheet of brightly coloured plasticised cotton bought from a nearby tarpaulin factory. Fishermen working their shanks day in day out know their dans and don't normally confuse them with other people's even though no particular colour is 'owned' by a fisherman. John's are blue or black; black being good as it stands out well. As an added extra Steve attaches a 'butterfly' to the top, made from a folded sheet of plastic. Some fishermen use two flags or vary their shapes. One fisherman told me he had used old Walls ice-cream flags, another had cut up old deckchair covers.

The dan buoy is now finished, and looking very serviceable. Steve stacks it with the others, and gets on with the next. Richard Davies, John's father, came in to show me an old cork buoy, of the type fishermen of his generation had used It was about 7ft high, and had layers of 'Scotch' corks arranged in circles for the float. The corks had come from old herring nets, which were sold off as strawberry nets when the herring industry at Lowestoft and Yarmouth collapsed. They had been bought in sacks by the thousand. When polystyrene first became available in the 1960s it 'held the tide and tended to sink under', but when it improved, it was a godsend as it took longer to become waterlogged than cork and was more easily cleaned. A complete set of cork buoys once had to be made every season. They also took much longer to make. Their poles had been hazel or cane, or a broom handle, with another smaller pole attached bearing the flag. A heavy stone from the beach was tied on as a weight.

Elsewhere in the shed John was making strops for anchors and pots, to which tow ropes would be attached later. John explained that the strops had changed when bollard haulers were replaced by slave-haulers. As he worked, he told me about the Herculean task of moving tanks, fridges, and other equipment to the new premises. Here there was a lot more workspace and they had been able to arrange it how they wanted it. Easter was a time when demand for crabs is fairly high, but this year not much fishing could be done before Easter as the sea temperature was still low. He might go to sea the next week, the end of March, to 'turn over the gear and see what's in it'.

On another occasion I had seen the tows prepared. From huge reels of rope, these are measured by arms outstretched across the fisherman's chest, each span being about 6ft, or a fathom. Fifteen fathoms are standard for tows pot to pot, and anchor to pot, but this varies depending where fishing. The lengths were coiled and thrown into a heap, to be taken to the boat and bent on to the pots. The tow leading to the anchor will be forty fathoms, or shorter where boats work on shallower ground.

Before the days of polypropylene, fishermen had the trouble of treating ropes with preservative. Lenny West from Sheringham described how tan was boiled up in a copper, and poured over tows stacked in old beer barrels. The tows were jammed down tight and left all winter covered with sacks. Rope bought ready-tarred had to be tanned, if after a season the tar had come out and the rope had softened up, but fishermen also tarred it themselves. Donny Lawrence recalled, 'We used to tar the ropes. We had an old 6ft bath, and they'd go to Norwich, buy some tar, pour it out of the cans into the bath. Had a line stretched across; and they'd dunk the tows into the bath, hang them up and just let them drain. When you first started crabbing you were black from blooming tar!'

Steve Barrett making dan buoys. Securing the polystyrene float with rope. East Runton, 2006.

Steve ties twine to secure a rope below the float. The weight is already tied on.

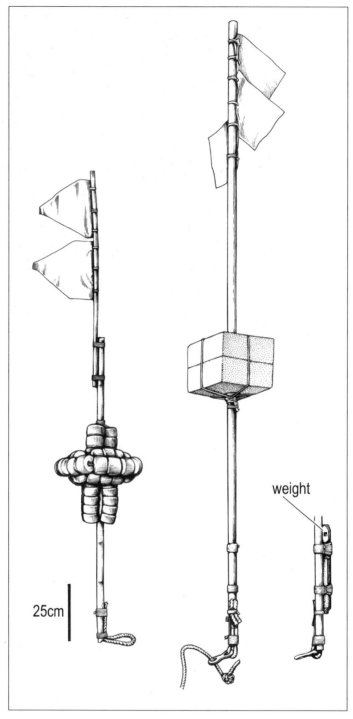

weight

25cm

Old type of dan buoy with cork float made by Richard Davies (its weight removed). Modern version made by Billy Gaff, slightly differently from Steve's.

*Above:* 'Laying away the anchor.' (John Balls on *Aurora*, Fran J. Weatherhead 2004)

*Right:* 'Awaiting the tractor.' (Andy Pardon and 'Tozzy' Osbourne, FJW 2004)

*Above:* 'Unloading the catch.' ('Tozzy' Osbourne, John Lee and John'o Lee, FJW 2002)

*Right:* 'Dan buoy aboard.' (John and Michael Balls, off Cromer, FJW 2003)

*Opposite above:* 'East Beach II.' (FJW 2002)

*Opposite below:* 'In the shallows.' (Keith Shaul and Steve Barrett with *Joanne Elizabeth*, FJW 2006)

*Above:* 'Carrying the catch.' (John Balls and son, John, FJW 2002)

*Below:* 'A calm day, Cromer beach.' (John Lee and Ralph Kirk on *Our Provider*, FJW 2003)

*Above:* 'Onto the skeet.' (Billy Gaff and 'Tozzy' Osbourne with *Joanne Elizabeth*, FJW 2005)

*Below:* 'Cleaning the pots.' (Mark Windows on *Aurora*, FJW 2006)

*Above:* 'Beginning of the season.' (*Mary Ann*, FJW 2004)

*Left:* 'Pot-hauling on the *Mary Ann*.' (Charlie Jonas, FJW 2004)

*Right:* 'Pulling up the pots.' (Michael Balls on *Our Provider*, FJW 2003)

*Below:* 'Preparing bait on *Laura Ann.*' (John Davies, Steve Barrett and David Heir, FJW 2006)

*Above:* 'Laying away pots.' (John Balls on *Aurora*, FJW 2006)

*Left:* 'East beach IV.' (FJW 2005)

# CHAPTER 6

# WHATEVER'S OUT THERE

Fishing for whitefish using the traditional method of lining has all but disappeared along the Norfolk coast. This is true for Norfolk's beach boats, but even the once healthy lining fleet at Lowestoft is much reduced, and the smaller one at Yarmouth is almost finished. The method involves laying a long line at sea with a number of hooks to catch low-feeding fish. The fish caught this way are regarded as of better quality than those pulled up in a trawl net.

Lining had once been a mainstay for North Norfolk's fishermen in the winter months when the crabbing and herring seasons had finished. They fished mostly for cod, but it depended on what fish were about. Sometimes they went after skate, dogfish, and flatfish, and sometimes the catch was mixed. Retired fisherman Richard Davies told me that lining had once been more important than crabbing in Cromer. Huge amounts of cod had been landed, 'and the further you go back the better the years seem to be'.

The heyday seems to have been during the First and Second World Wars. All the trawlers fishing the North Sea went on war work, so there were plenty of fish about for fishermen to catch who had not been called up. Retired fisherman Dennis Gaff recalled that fishing boats would often catch 100 stone a day, earning fishermen a lot of money. Some did so well they invested in property. When the trawlers started again after the second war, the catch was somewhat smaller but there were still plenty of fish in the sea to provide a good income for many years.

For fishermen who have retired or are coming up to retiring age, their lining years were in the 1970s–80s. John Jonas recalled the 1960s had been quite good, but the best years were the early 1970s when he started lining. Today's younger fishermen, like John Davies, experienced this boom when they were boys accompanying their fathers. This was mainly a time before quota restrictions, which apply even to small beach boats. Ivan Large, chairman of two local fishing societies, summed it up: 'You could catch what you like and do what you like – as long as they were sizeable.'

Lining could be done at any time of the year, and sometimes was, but it was usual in the winter months. Not all fishermen took part, especially if put off by having to bait the lines, which had to be done before each fishing trip. Some went whelking or did non-fishing work instead like sprout-picking or building work; others went whelking and lining later. When Richard Davies went lining there were only three other boats lining from Cromer.

Dennis Gaff, one of the older fishermen:

I'd go with Billy Davies; two or three of us would ship in together. It was from October right through 'til spring. Some of them were still lining when crabbing come through, then they'd pack up and go crabbing. You didn't go that much because the weather would stop you half the time in the wintertime, but you always found something to do. We'd go about 4 miles out I suppose, go up to Happisburgh and that, there's a good place round there.

When his son Billy went, this was after Christmas until February, sometimes into March. Cod had been the main fish lined in his day.

# The gear and baiting up

For lining there was less gear to be made and maintained than for crabbing and whelking, but there was a lot of preparation. Hundreds of hooks had to be attached, or 'whipped', to the lines with short lengths of twine, or 'snoods'. The snoods were 1½ fathoms (9ft) apart. An unpleasant task was baiting the lines. Nowadays, there are automatic baiters for larger boats which are still lining, but for Norfolk's beach boats this had to be done by hand.

Willy Cox of Cromer described how after a fishing trip, and after a short break for a meal, fishermen would have to get ready for the next day's trip. There was always the possibility that bad weather might prevent fishing, in which case the baiting work would be wasted. Fresh mussels or whelks were used as bait. Mussels were preferred if there were a lot of fish about, but if not, whelks had the advantage of being harder and kept on the hooks longer so could be left longer at sea. At the time the beach fishermen were lining there was a lot of whelking going on at Wells, so whelks could be obtained from fishermen there. Lugworms could also be used, such as were dug commercially in the region. Several fishermen went bait-digging along the coast to make money in wintertime, but as Bob Cox pointed out, doing both would mean a very long day, so they were usually bought. If fishermen knew someone who was going shrimping, they could ask that shrimps be kept back for bait.

In post-war Cromer, the job of baiting up was done in sheds or old wash-houses in fishermen's backyards. In former days, it was sometimes done on the beach, as shown on old photographs. Several people pitched in. It could be a cold, miserable experience. Dennis Gaff: 'There's a lot of preparation for lines, sometimes there were about ten of you would go in together, if only three go to sea!' These were often retired fishermen, with the incentive of a plump fish for supper, or sons of fishermen, who later became fishermen themselves. Some, like Bennett Middleton's son, managed to bait a pack of lines before going to school.

Jack Allen and Richard Davies baiting the lines with mussels. Cromer, late 1960s. (EDP)

John Jonas: 'You'd buy the lines, and have to rig them up with hooks on. Some packs had nearly 300 hooks on, some 200. If you were doing ten packs, that's 2000 hooks, so it'd take you a while to bait them all up!' He told me whelk shells were smashed with a hammer, the shell knocked off and the whelk extracted by knife. It was not a difficult job, but unpleasant and messy, and the creature inside had to be live. Care was taken not to get any shell on the bait, because the fish would reject it.

Before baiting the lines, they had to be 'tricked'. This was removing the weed and old bait from the previous fishing trip – a dirty, smelly job. For a busy fisherman, a young son would come in handy for this. Richard Davies who was lining with 'Tuna' Harrison and 'Stymie' Blythe, roped in his son John and friend 'Speedy' Muirhead.

In earlier times the baited lines had been coiled on 'rips' or 'rip boards'. Some fishermen in their sixties remember using them when they first started fishing, such as Richard Davies and Willy Cox of Cromer. Most rips have been thrown away, but Roger Seago of East Runton showed me one still in his shed. It consisted of a steel hoop, about 40cm in diameter, braided with netting. Over this was a circle of oilskin, tied at the edges. This formed a base onto which a mound of baited lines was coiled. They were tied down to keep them in place. Nylon twine was threaded through two rings and a small block of wood attached to the hoop. The block of wood had the fisherman's initials inscribed on it. Baited rips were carried to the boat for the fishing trip, and afterwards returned to the shed with the empty lines to be re-baited.

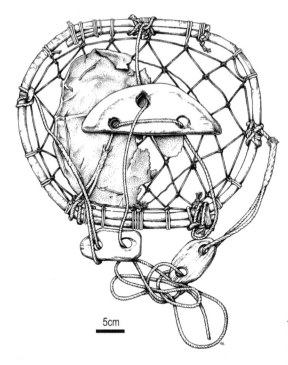

5cm

John Jonas's rip, formerly used
for long lining. Lines were
coiled on it and tied with the
cords.

John Jonas produced an earlier rip which had been his father's. This was about
the same diameter as the rip mentioned earlier, but made of cane bent into a circle.
Before cane became available, hazel stick would have been used. The base was made
of braided string supporting a round piece of leather. A length of thick string was
threaded through three small blocks of wood to keep the lines in place. Bob Cox
mentioned another version consisting of a square piece of board with rope attached
through holes at the edges. These rips, like so much of Norfolk fishermen's gear, were
entirely homemade, or like Roger Seago's, would only have required a blacksmith to
make the ring base.

When the rip had lines coiled on it, it was called a 'pack'. In later times, the lines
were coiled into metal baths of the type once used for bathing small children. Some
fishermen still have them stored away in sheds with coiled lines. Baths were used up
and down the Norfolk coast, thought by some fishermen to have been introduced
from Lowestoft or Yarmouth. A bath was easier to use than a rip as the lines had only
to be coiled inside, rather than coiled into a heap and tied up. Richard Davies: 'We
put the lines in right-handed. We were different from Sheringham; they were left-
handed, they still are at Lowestoft and Yarmouth.'

Bob Cox: 'The bait would be say 12–3 o'clock on one side of the rip, then perhaps
9–12 o'clock on the other side, so it's not all on top of one another and to avoid foul-
ing the hooks.' This method differed from in Yorkshire, where the bait was humped
up on one side. Billy Gaff, referring to the baths:

You try to keep the hooks to the outside of the bath – no, not over the side. Some people used to separate them with sheets of paper. It varied from place to place, but here the bait wasn't all humped up on one side. You tried to keep them fairly even. You could get in a muddle if you weren't careful.

Frequently, six or eight packs or baths of lines were used but ten or twelve were possible, which were stacked ready in the boat. A 'long pack' was eight lines joined together in a bath or pack; a 'short pack' was six lines joined together.

# Laying the lines and hauling

It was somewhat unpredictable where the fish were; one boat might do extremely well, but the next boat along might get almost nothing. Sometimes the fish were close to the beach, sometimes farther out than where the fishermen went crabbing. In the 1980s, Richard Little told me he went from Sheringham 5 miles to the back of Sheringham Shoal, which was much further out than his father and grandfather, who had to row their boats. Billy Gaff, at Cromer:

> You went as far as you felt like going! It all depended on the conditions of the day
> – if it's a nice fine day you might go 5 or 6 miles out. You just go on instinct , and if
> at the time there were several of you going after cod, one might get a lot more than
> you, so you tend to go to where he'd been that previous day!

Left to right: Paul, Peter and David Bywater long-lining off East Runton, April 1979. (Brian Hunt)

Richard Davies: 'If you came across fish – yes, it was luck – they'd all be in a "stream", and so the next day you would know to go a bit further out or in.' John Jonas recalled on one good day with a smooth sea, he got the compass out and took some marks – he referred to a chart when he got home and worked out he had been 13 miles out. 'That's a long way in a crab boat! But normally you'd go off not that far, for twenty or thirty minutes, then lay the lines, and tides would perhaps set you to either west or south a bit. A mile to 1½ miles out.'

At Cromer and Sheringham lines were 'laid' at sea, although some fishermen say 'shot' like at Lowestoft. A single line was forty fathoms (80 yards), so five 'long packs' would stretch nearly 2 miles. I asked if the lines ever got crossed. John Jonas:

> Sometimes, but usually there weren't so many lining at the same time. Say, Overstrand or East Runton, you'd get two or three boats from there, too. They'd all lay the same sort of way, on a full tide just as it was starting. Say if high water was 12 o'clock, you'd start laying your lines at about 9 o'clock. The lines were laid according to the direction of the flood tide. You chucked one hook at a time, if 200 hooks on a pack you did that 200 times. If you had 2000, you did it 2000 times! And the quicker the tide, the quicker you had to go!

Sometimes he laid twelve packs. There was a buoy and anchor at each end of the pack or bath of lines. The baited hooks would be fifteen or so fathoms down attracting the fish. Some fishermen laid the lines by hand, picking up the hooks which were arranged around the top of the bath; others like Richard Davies or the Bywaters at East Runton used a stick to flick them out. A third man would be steering the boat, which was going along slowly. Dennis Gaff, who shot the lines by hand from rips, told me:

> That's why the hooks are laid all one way. You got to keep them going, you can't stop. If you stop the whole lot would go over in a lump. Someone would join the lines while you were laying it. There were anchors in between the lines – that was a Yarmouth idea. They say the more anchors the more fish.

Small anchors every thirty or forty hooks helped keep the line at the bottom of the sea. The baths of lines were joined to each other with strops, two to three fathom lengths of thicker rope. Billy Gaff:

> You could have two lines running at different angles. If I had six baths of lines, I might shoot three baths of lines away together, all joined together in one long line, then perhaps go out away from that area say a quarter mile, and then shoot the other lines away. I don't think I actually shot more than six baths of lines while I was going, but there's fishermen up at Lowestoft now who will shoot more than that, a lot more – that's probably how they make their money.

John Balls: 'You lined with the tide. It depends on what bait you were using, and how far out. If using mussels, you'd shoot the gear just after slack water, leave it one tide. I used to shoot the gear in the flood tide, let it work that tide, then start hauling.' One could shoot and wait two or three hours, or go off and haul some crab pots and come back later to haul the lines. Lugworm need only be left about an hour, but whelks were left for longer.

If shot about 4p.m., the fishermen would go home leaving their lines overnight and come out the next morning to haul, although they might have to wait at sea if they thought the weather was going to be bad the next day or if there was fog about. To avoid the trouble of having to beach and relaunch their crab boats, Cromer fishermen had a system of tying their boats onto the pier, where they had left a small skiff. They used this to return to shore for a few hours. If the crab boat was left on the flood tide, they returned before the tide eased and the boat drifted up against the pier. The boat could also be moored at the pier buoy. Richard Davies:

We turned over one day! It was wintertime, snow on the beach, we'd been and shot in the dark. We were coming in, had tied the boat to the pier buoy and had got on this skiff and I was rowing ashore on the skiff, a square-sterned thing, with no rudder on it, just a pair of oars. Willy Cox was sitting aft, Clive (Rayment) was for'ard. And I see this big sea coming, and I thought this is too big for us! We pulled like hell, lovely and straight, then it started to broach. I knew it was going over! Clive dived away from the boat, and when it went over I swam out from under it, and when I came up I was out of my depth. Got my oilies and boots on, but the boots were tight against me so it was alright. I saw Clive, and he said 'Where's Willy?' I said 'I dunno – he can't swim!' We see the skiff further in, and got to it – it took some time – and we lifted the skiff up, and Willy came out like a rocket! It ripped his oily and slop it was so forceful. We had these balaclavas on Clive's mother had knitted, which hung down. I burst out laughing. Willy asked, 'What's bloody funny?' But we were so relieved to see him. It was so bloody cold!

Richard and Willy hurried home to revive themselves in warm baths, while other fishermen who had been anxiously waiting on the beach got the skiff up.

The hauling experience could be very rewarding when the hauls were good. The occasional fish weighed 20–25lb, the biggest at Cromer being a 56-pounder caught by 'Shrimp' Davies. But hauling could take a very long time. John Jonas:

Yes, especially with a lot of fish and the weather not too good. I remember one day we were hauling for ten hours! When you're hauling as the tide is easing, you haul with the tide. You'd start one end and the tide would be taking you that way – and sometimes you'd get halfway through and the tide would slack water and start going the other way, so you'd let go there and go to the other end, so you're hauling with the tide that way again.

Dennis Gaff with fish, long-lining with Billy Davies and others on the *Ellen*. Off Cromer, 1970s. (Roger Godfrey)

The fish were flicked off the hooks as the line came in, or for a big fish a gaff, or a hand-made pick, was used. John Jonas used a meat-hook attached to a stick handle, which he also used 'to work the engine' on his old boat the *Duncan*. While one man was hauling and another steering, the third man was coiling the lines up and putting them back in the baths or on the rips.

Billy Gaff: 'It's all by chance when to haul. But you wanted to get them hauled before dark. You usually put them into fish boxes and gutted them when going home. Fifty stone of cod was a good day's work, but you could get up to a hundred stone.' Several Cromer fishermen recalled colossal hauls from the 1960s onwards, sometimes using only four to six baths. If doing well, the hooks would be re-baited at sea and the lines shot away again. Richard Davies recalled that because there was so much cod about in the 1980s it wasn't always worth much. In February and March you could almost fill the boat up!

Most of the beach fishermen I spoke to liked long-lining. They recalled the sense of sport they got from it, especially when they anticipated a large fish about to be pulled up on the line. Richard Davies: 'I loved it, had some fun! With different people, though Clive Rayment was with us all the time. Willy Cox come in with us, and we had some laughs!' Donny Lawrence, who didn't like long-lining and only went twice, referred to the dangers as the line is going over the side non-stop:

I've known fishermen get the hooks in their hands, they could go right through. You had to come ashore and be taken to hospital. Or it would hang onto their clothes and nearly take them over the side. When you haul them it's not so dangerous; you put your hands between the hooks.

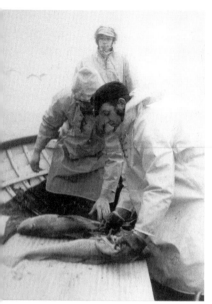

*Above left:* Willy Cox gutting cod on the *Mary Ann*. Off Cromer, December 1976. (B. Gedge)

*Above right:* Roger Seago and other East Runton fishermen unloading cod, January 1974. (EDP)

The cold could be another factor, for lining, as with whelking, took place in the wintertime. John Jonas: 'I've been lining when the water's been freezing on the outside of the boat! When you're at sea and moving about it weren't so bad, but sometimes when you've been tied up at the pier and go back, you'd have ½in of ice on the outside of the crab boat!'

Some fishermen like Richard and John Davies went after small cod, or codling. These kept close to the beach, and so as to cover the ground but keep in the area where the fish were thought to be, the fishermen would make a zigzag of lines parallel to the beach, shooting alternately a short pack and a long pack. Sometimes when skate, dogfish, whiting and dabs were about these were targeted. Mackerel or herring was used as bait for skate, and later squid which came in frozen packs from Lowestoft and had to be defrosted. Salted herring was used as bait for dogfish. Bob Cox who went lining with his father and brothers:

> We had good hauls for skate and cod. We went from Cromer and Mundesley. Once for cod we got 60 stone for two short packs. Skate, 30 or 40 stone would be good too. We went from Cromer for skate; we went as far as Weybourne and shot lines there. Skate was in the summer. Dad just liked doing everything. Every now and then we'd try for skate during the course of the season, but sometimes we'd get nothing. Father would say, 'We'll get a box of herring from Lowestoft market,' and we'd bait the lines. We'd shoot the line, then go and haul the crab pots, come back

and haul the lines. They were left as long as we were crabbing, on the same fishing trip. You had a rough idea where to go for them, where you had them before. Once when we were only laying two packs, as we hauled we got two or three turbot, which were worth having. So the next day we went further off to reach ground where there were more turbot, but we were still on the outside end. It happened again the next day; three days on the trot leading us further and further out.

Fishing for skate, or 'roker', seems to have been quite popular in North Norfolk. They came inshore to lay eggs. Donny Lawrence recalled them being caught on sands at Trimingham only a few hundred yards off the beach. His cousin Ralph, who fished off Mundesley for skate, thought they had not been around for years. John Jonas:

> One day, I was crabbing at the time, we went early in the morning and only laid two packs of lines at the back of the Buoy. We come in, hauled the crab pots, and went out and hauled the lines. We had ninety stone of dogfish! Nearly every hook had one on, and where there was space without one, the hooks had gone – they'd taken the hook! They went to Lowestoft, and made £1 a stone. Now they'd make a lot more than that!

Following the decline in cod stocks, dogfish or 'rock salmon' became increasingly marketable.

## Selling the catch

In earlier times all sorts of fish had been sold at beach auctions in Cromer and Sheringham, which lasted until the 1930s in Sheringham. The price was fixed by clapping two stones together. The practice of carrying the cod up the beach on the narrow part of an oar, or lum, from the early crab boats (which had to be unloaded before being carried up), is still remembered by older fishermen like Lenny West and Bob Cox. Two fishermen each bore the end of an oar on his shoulder, from which hung several stone of fish on large hooks. Some of the fishermen's catch was hawked round their villages by barrow. Richard Little of Sheringham recalled that in his grandfather's time the fish was picked up by horse and cart and taken to be sold to nearby towns, even reaching as far as Norwich. From Wells, fish was carted similar distances, and at one time the mode of transport had been by motorbike.

During the last war fish was needed to feed the nation. It was rationed, but cheap. Richard Davies of Cromer told me that local boats were required to supply regulated amounts of fish to particular fish shops. The Davies's fish went to one in Aylsham. Post-war, Richard Little from Sheringham remembers taking fish to the wholesale fish market in Mountergate, Norwich. Some of the Cromer fishermen's wives who delivered the catch for their husbands also drove it to the Norwich market. Julie

Jack Allen and Richard Davies's father Jack packing the catch after long-lining. Cromer. (Via R. Davies)

Davies took fish there for her husband Richard, sometimes with crabs if there was a glut. But the Norwich fish market was dwindling by the late 1960s, and finally closed when it was not updated to comply with hygiene regulations.

In spite of some fish going out of the vicinity, from talking to today's fishermen it seems that a lot had been sold through local fish shops. What could be better than fresh long-lined cod almost straight from the boat? This was a time when people ate a lot more fish than today and there were a lot more fish shops. Fish and chip shops also took a lot of local fish. Some fishermen, like Richard Davies and John Jonas in Cromer, could sell their catch through their own shops. Others, like Willy Cox, supplied two or three different shops. In the 1960–70s, when Bennett Middleton was lining from Sheringham he was able to take his cod into fish and chip shops in Wells: 'They knew nothing about lining at Wells then – they were too busy whelking!'

Billy Gaff told me that if there was an exceptional amount of fish, more than could be sold locally, it was boxed up and driven down to Lowestoft. Being winter, it kept cool so arrived in 'good nick'. Ralph Kirk lined with 'Little' Billy Davies and his father Dick Davies:

It was easy enough, took them straight down to Lowestoft. Coles it was mainly, down on the Fish Quay. Billy did all that. If we came home late, we'd load up, go to Lowestoft, dump the fish on the market, then go and buy the next lot of worms.

I imagine it'd go in the auction. We'd put paper tallies, proper printed ones, stick that on the tin or box that we had, so people knew whose fish it was.

The whitefish was sold by the stone, but prices depended on how many other fishermen had a big catch: one day it would be £5 a stone, the next day £10. Ralph was one of the Cromer fishermen who took off to Southwold in Suffolk for a season of lining.

'Little' Billy said, 'Fancy going down to Southwold? Me and 'Goose' (Chris Craske) will take the boat, you take the van and we'll meet you down there.' A chap in the pub, he had a caravan down near the harbour so we lived in that, then when the caravan site closed he moved his caravan alongside his pub, so we lived there. 'Little' Billy had only just got married so he went home every weekend. We got our meals in the pub, and were wired up to electrics, so it was ideal. He lent us a shed to keep the gear in, and bait up in. We used to go sea most days, from the harbour, weather permitting. You didn't want it too rough, not to haul on – the line was strong, but the snood between the hook and the line could snap if you got a decent size fish on. We had one really good day at Southwold, quite a few boxes of cod. But it was quite good all the time and we wished we'd gone down earlier.

# Other fishing

In less than a lifetime, several fishing methods used by Norfolk's beach fishermen have disappeared. One which was mentioned in a local newspaper as far back as 1894 lingered on into recent times. Bob Cox:

Seine-netting for us, that was a regular thing, but not for the others. Now it's rarely done. You'd go round (in the boat) in a semicircle. The net is left in a semicircle. There are three of you – one would stop on the beach and hold the end of the net. On the boat one would row, the other would shoot. You'd come round, you had to gauge it properly, but 10–12 yards away from completing the half-circle. You just had a rope on the end of your nets. Once you got ashore you started to pull the net in. The net would have like a pocket, like the end of a trawl, and perhaps a white-painted cork in middle of it so you could keep it level. You'd have trout, sole, dabs, anything in it.

When we were at Cromer we fished for trout from the beach, draw-netting for sea trout. Father would work where there was little tide, on the Runton side of the pier. See, at Cromer there's no tide like there is here at Mundesley. On top of them 'horseshoe rocks' between Cromer and Runton, we used to shoot a net straight along with an anchor on each end. Parallel to the coast, not have to be far out. Two people would be rowing on the inside between the beach and the net, and one would be banging down on the beach side of the boat – from the stern – with a big

George Cox (senior) mending a nylon draw net for sea trout on Cromer beach, late 1950s. This was a time when herring nets were still cotton. (Bob Cox)

stick. That'd drive the trout out towards the net. Then you'd go along to the net, and haul the nets, and they'd be there with their teeth stuck in the net and you'd pick them out. Now it's not commercially viable. Nowadays with monofilament nets, they get wound up in it. In those times when we were draw-netting for trout we also caught what we called 'bessies', proper name bass, and they'd be cut up for crab bait – now it's probably the most expensive fish in the sea!

Bob explained another method: 'Sometimes you'd see two people with a net on a couple of poles, walk into water up to the neck and pull it along, but it's rare.' His brother George added:

There was young Sargent from Cromer. One would have half the net on his shoulder, the other the same. They'd walk out, then walk away from each other, in an arc – they're not in deep water, they can't go out of their depth. They just walk and pull the net between them. It didn't take long.

Another method dating back to the late nineteenth century or earlier, and used up to twenty years ago was inshore trawling with a small beam trawl. This was dragged along the bottom of the sea from the stern of a crab boat to pick up low-feeding sole. It was done along the Norfolk coast where the sea bed was not rocky. This was off Mundesley and Bacton, east of the non-trawling zone. Andy Davies of Overstrand believes sole are probably still out there, but he, like others, is now exclusively crabbing. An 8½ft trawl from former days was hanging up in his shed, a metal beam with triangular end-pieces ('shoes') and a net to collect the fish.

# Fishing from Salthouse and Wells

For experience of Norfolk's coast to the west of Cromer and Sheringham, I talked to retired fisherman Ivan Large. Ivan had fished from his village at Salthouse, and later from the harbour at Wells. From the shelving pebbly beach at Salthouse, he told me fishing was much the same as for other beach fishermen. He went lining for cod, skate, dogfish or for whatever fish there were about. This was no further than a mile out. At night-time in June–July he went seine-netting for sole, sea trout and mackerel. Then in the early 1970s he decided to go fishing from Wells from larger boats, including a small trawler:

> The fishing wasn't going so well off the beach then. Had a chap at Wells, Paul Linehan, ask me to go out as crew, said I'd have a go. I was still self-employed, as I was taking a 'share'. Then I got the *Remus* in the '80s. The *Remus* was built down at Faversham, Kent. She was one of the ones brought up here in the '60s, when she was brand new. They used her here for ten to fifteen years, then old George Leggett died. Then someone else bought it and my brother-in-law bought it off him. She was just under 40ft. We used a trawl mostly when I was on the *Remus*. We used an otter trawl – yes, like the Grimsby ones, with two doors that open and you let the net out. We were fishing for skate mostly in summertime, sprats and whitebait in winter. There was no crabbing done at all at Wells when I first went there.

The *Remus* was part of a new generation of boats with wheelhouses to arrive at Wells. She had originally pair-trawled with her sister boat the *Romulus*, and was worked by the Leggett family. After their fishing trips, they would send a massive 16–18 tons of sprats at a time up to a canning factory in Scotland. These and other boats had come up from Whitstable to fish, and their owners settled in Wells. When Ivan bought the *Remus*, he continued pair-trawling, as well as working singly. I asked Ivan how he adapted to going from a harbour after going from Salthouse beach, 'It was easier, but there were longer hours because when you went to sea you had to go on the tide, see. We went every day if the weather was fine. It wasn't harder work, in fact we thought we were in heaven when we had a winch!' He pointed out that tidal streams coming from different directions meet out at sea from Wells, something not experienced by boats closer to shore. As was normal at the time, Ivan timed the journeys from the harbour with a watch to locate his gear:

When I first went to Wells we had a compass, and that was all, and an echo-sounder so we knew the depth of water. That was on the first boat, and on the *Remus* as well. Then we had radar. Then I worked on another boat called the *Strandline*, a big steel one in Wells; she had a Decca navigator, and we thought we were in heaven with that!

When the tide goes out, that dries out on the 'bar' and you can't get back in the harbour any more. Fishing trips were ten to twelve hours, you've got to go twelve hours because you've got to go with the tide, see. If you go at 7 o'clock in the morning you can't get home until 7 o'clock at night. And if the weather turn rough you've got to stick it out 'til the tide come in again. Yes, a very long day! But we always got back OK. Then you had to take the fish to market, or you had to ice it down and take it to market the next morning. Or get someone to take it to market for you. Yes, we used to get someone to take several loads. When skate fishing, there were four or five boats working together. We had big ice boxes on the quay, put skate in them today, and it'd go down to market tomorrow, someone would take it by lorry to Lowestoft or Grimsby.

The skate was trawled westwards inshore to the Wash, and eastwards to Happisburgh avoiding the protected crabbing area:

Whitebait, the tiny herrings, we used to catch them and if there was a large amount we'd send them to Coles of Lowestoft, or they would pick it up. Used to sell them at so much a stone. If there was a small amount we'd freeze it down ourselves in one-pound bags and send it out to restaurants and hotels. Trouble is if the weather is like this, hot like today, you can't do it, because by the time you get back from fishing they're all rotten, as fish don't keep in the sun. If there were any mackerel about off our beaches here, the whitebait'd wash up on the beach. The mackerel drive them, and they jump out of the water onto the beach. We went pair-trawling for white-bait, with another boat at Wells. Two boats tow a net between the two of them. It'd be fine mesh for whitebait. Two boats side by side, you come up together, and you let the net over the side, go apart and tow the net between the two of you.

Spratting at Wells went from outside the harbour to Blakeney, and from off Brancaster to Hunstanton:

In the wintertime we'd get sprats, and they'd go to Coles as well. That was in the '70s when I was working with Paul Letzer. It was mid-water pair-trawling, at night-time. You set the net to the depth where the fish are. You find out where they are with the echo-sounder. You shoot your nets say 10ft from the surface. You have attached a small buoy with a rope attached so they're shot 10ft down, a Heath Robinson method. The sprats also went to Grimsby to the fish-meal factory. We had a day's fishing in the Wash close up to Grimsby; we'd steam up and unload it at the factory at the fish dock. They had a lorry to pick it up, and they'd grab it out of the hold with big spoon-like things and put it on a conveyor belt. We had to join a queue with other big boats there – they had 150 tons of sprats and we had 6 or 7 tons! It was all for fish meal.

For cod we went up to the Wash, as far as Skegness and Mablethorpe off the Lincolnshire coast. There would be 20 or 30 other boats from Grimsby, Skegness up there too. And we used to come down to Cromer, and fish off there to the Happisburgh Sands, in wintertime. Yes, avoiding the non-trawl area. Used to get soles, all sorts of flatfish, dabs and all that as well. There weren't so many gas plat-forms off there then, but we were always in the shipping lanes, yes.

Wells was a busy place then, a lot of fishing, Wells had lots of whelk boats then. Used to be lots of shipping come in to Wells. Export corn, and import spuds, apples, artificial manure for farmers, in the '70s. We used to work on the ships as well when they come in on the tides – help unload the ships, as casual labour. Oh yes, a bustling place, more than it is now. But you still get visiting boats, now.

The occasional shrimper might come from King's Lynn or the south-east. While at Wells, trawling had been Ivan's main occupation. He had hauled a few whelk pots outside the harbour on his way back from trawling, and when whelking dropped off had tried crabbing, but this had never been full-time. On trawling trips, in the hour-and-a-half break between shooting and hauling Ivan would be busy making his crab pots. These were bigger than conventional pots, and the whole of the net was braided at sea. I was told the Frary family were first to go crabbing from Wells to just off

Roger Seago
'cleaning'
fish from
monofilament
nets. Cromer,
2008.

Weybourne, but crabbing only really took off from Wells in the late 1980s–90s when crabs were found further off in the Race channel. All trawling has now stopped.

Over the last twenty years in North Norfolk there has been a lull in lining, but some net fishing survives. Heaps of nylon nets with fine filamentous mesh are occasionally seen on old net stools by the boats at Sheringham, Mundesley and elsewhere. They are set on ground where fish are thought to occur, and hang in the water to trap them by the gills. Sea bass, which started to appear in numbers in the late 1990s, has been targeted, especially by part-time fishermen. As yet there are no quotas on bass, but minimum landing sizes must be observed. Local fisheries officer Ady Woods, who helps fishermen beach and unload their boats, keeps an eye on the sizes of fish landed. Some cod-fishing with trammel nets also occurs at Sheringham.

I talked to Roger Seago at Cromer who has for several years been catching bass, cod and anything else he can find, off-season from crabbing. With his son Jonathan he had gone netting from East Runton before the beach became too rocky and they moved their boats to Cromer. Roger was going after bass when I met him on the beach in October 2008. A Sheringham fisherman had earlier been spotted netting off Cromer, giving the signal that bass were about. If lucky, he could get twenty stone of fish and earn good money; if unlucky, he could get nothing. In December, he was getting a few cod and dogfish. A large ling in the catch was reckoned unusual. They were to be sorted into fish boxes then taken to Lowestoft market and outlets in Norwich.

Roger or his son sets the nets in the evening. These are 100–200 yards out, anchored at each end and marked with red buoys which are visible from the shore. He goes out at first light with his son to haul. 'Cleaning', or emptying, the nets takes place in the boat when he gets back. When I met Roger he had been at it for several hours, patiently picking out each fish. At the beginning of April 2009, unlike the other fishermen at Cromer, he had not started crabbing, but was about to do so. He was still doing well with 'nurse hounds', a type of dogfish, which can be sold as bait.

## Quotas and the uncertain future

Norfolk's beach fishermen are generally pessimistic about the prospects of reviving lining or other forms of fishing for whitefish. Many believe that there now are less fish about, and concentrating on potting in their area of the North Sea is best for a living. Billy Gaff last tried for cod in the mid-1980s. He put in six packs of lines at Sheringham Shoal, and got one cod! After this failure, he never tried again. Richard Davies reckoned if you shot in a 10-mile area, you might get only three or four cod: 'The boys at Lowestoft are finishing, and they lay a lot more lines than we do. Some are laying 15–16 miles of line! They come off here, lay lines for cod, and *they're* not getting a living, so we wouldn't!'

In 2007, the lining fleets had reduced to about six full-time boats at Lowestoft, and two at Yarmouth. Richard's son John mentioned that fishing from Lowestoft had improved around Christmas-time, 'The most cod they've seen, since the 80s. It looked quite good. But with restriction now on it, and the expenses, I don't think it will come back like it was.' He had recently tried lining from Cromer, 'For the hell of it, but we did no good at all, so I chucked the lines back in the shed, and they can stay there till whenever!'

Even with whitefish commanding high prices, beach fishermen are not tempted to go lining. Willy Cox, who last went about twenty years ago, thought £10–15 a stone was now the going price. When he last went and the price rose from £1 to £1.05, fishermen had thought *that* was good!

Fishermen are reluctant to blame other fishermen, but agree that years of factory trawling have had a lot to do with depletion of fish stocks in the North Sea. Billy Gaff:

> The rot set in the '60s, when these trawlers got very sophisticated, with fish-finders they could pick up fish, and clear the sea beds. There was a big British fleet then which has gone now, and obviously the Dutch had a lot to do with it as well. There was a lot of trawlers up Yorkshire way, and Grimsby and Hull. If it had just been down to long-lining, the way *we* were fishing, there'd still be plenty of cod.

Ralph Kirk:

> Years ago we used to see the trawlers mainly at night, because the crafty devils used to sneak 'inside'. There was the Foul Ness Buoy roughly 3 mile off, they were supposed to keep to the back of that. But you'd see their lights at night; you'd say, 'Hello, he's come inside to trawl!' It was the shipping lane just at the back of the Foul Ness, ships were supposed to keep to the back of it because of the working area, crab pots and that. Trawlers had to keep 3 mile off.

This is the crabbing area protected by byelaw between Blakeney and Mundesley. Foreign trawlers must stay over 12 miles offshore, but Belgium has special rights to fish between 6 and 12 miles.

Ralph blamed foreign trawlers for causing most damage, one country in particular for flouting net mesh-size restrictions. To help conserve diminishing fish stocks, the quota system, which varies depending on boat size, fish species and fishing area, came in with the EU's Common Fisheries Policy. This includes inshore boats operating on cottage-industry levels. Many fishermen consider the CFP flawed and those making decisions on fishing lacking in-depth knowledge. On large offshore boats, the system becomes senseless when fish (often dead) get thrown back overboard if it is bycatch, or if the quota allowance for a particular species has been used up.

Ivan Large explained how quotas worked:

> The quotas vary month by month. Thing is, there's fish about you're not allowed to catch, even here along the coast. You're not allowed to catch mackerel now. Say if there is 200 ton of mackerel in the southern North Sea for the year, and one 80ft

boat out of Grimsby catches 200 ton in a day, no one can then catch them for the rest of the time. We used to have our own quotas, 200 ton for the year for inshore vessels, and that helped us through the summertime. They're not doing it this year (2008).

They're stopping you from catching mackerel – anglers can catch them off the beach, but you can't catch them commercially! Herring are on quotas; you can catch a certain amount, but when the quota's caught you can't catch any more anyway. There are cod out there but you aren't allowed to catch them now. They (DEFRA) work on a rule: if you didn't catch any last year, you won't be able to this year. So if there's no cod about last year and you didn't catch any, and this year there *is* cod about you aren't allowed to catch any!

This applies to many beach fishermen, and is resented. They are forced to stick to potting. The bigger boats fishing out of Lowestoft can continue catching cod because they had been catching it a little bit all the while, but the Wells boats cannot do so because they had not caught it recently.

John Davies discussed restrictions on the region's bigger boats *vis-a-vis* inshore beach boats:

Dogfish is something the long-liners caught a hell of a lot, probably more than the fish could stand. But they're a slow-growing fish – you're allowed 5 per cent of your total now. Once you could catch as much skate as you wanted, but now this year its been brought in you can only have 25 per cent of your catch can be skate. I was talking to a fellow the other day, and he was talking about going out of Lowestoft, he's only allowed to catch 1½ ton of cod a month, and 25 per cent of that can be skate, and 5 per cent dogfish – that worked out about £4,000 worth of fish. He goes to sea on average thirteen times a month, and that cost him over £300 a time to go to sea, and if you work it out he's in debt from what he's allowed to catch! So how can he make a living?

And an *inshore* boat can't work on that sort of basis! It has to catch what comes in its inshore area, and what's only there at certain times. An inshore boat can't steam hundreds of miles to sea to target a species. You can go basically *where* you like, but you haven't the capability of doing that, have you? For mackerel – the majority is all caught up off Scotland, and they have quite a big quota down in Cornwall. But *here*, often before the mackerel get here, there'll be a ban on it because it has already caught the quota.

He told me a few years ago a glut of mackerel had appeared off the Norfolk coast, but a ban had just been imposed and, frustratingly, local fishermen had not been allowed to reap the rewards.

# CHAPTER 7

# A DOLLOP OF HERRING

Herrings were once plentiful and cheap in this country. Many people over a certain age remember their pungent smells wafting around the kitchens of Britain. The herring industry was then an important part of the national economy. Every year shoals of herring swam around the British coast, and as they moved from the Shetlands down the North Sea and round to the English Channel, fishing vessels emerged from their ports to go after them. As well as ending up on our breakfast and supper plates, vast quantities were processed and sent abroad.

There seems to have been a long history of herring-catching from North Norfolk's beaches, even going back to medieval times as at Great Yarmouth. A clue to this is a medieval will of a Mr Fawkener of Cromer which includes four twelve-score nets[1]. Catches of herring with other fish, crabs and lobsters, were noted in a Cromer guide of 1800 and there are other references and museum photographs for the nineteenth century. Herrings would have been a source of cheap food, as a novel set in 1823 Cromer illustrates: 'During the long and tedious months of winter dried fish and an inferior supply of herrings with a less proportion of other food had been the sustenance of numerous poor families.' (*The Cottage on the Cliff*, by Catherine Ward.)

At the beginning of the twentieth century, the Fisheries Annual Report for 1913 shows healthy catches of herring and less of mackerel at Cromer, Runton and Overstrand. Sheringham did less well with herring, but better with mackerel. Beach boats all along the coast were probably involved, as shown by a photograph taken at Bacton in 1926 with herring nets spread on the beach.

The major centres for fishing and processing herring in the region were at Yarmouth and Lowestoft. Yarmouth was the herring capital of the world. Huge quantities were landed there from November to February, when the shoals swam along the East Anglian coast. The Scots, who had brought their drifters down to join the local fishing fleets, introduced curing by gutting and brining in the nineteenth century. Up till living memory, cured herring were exported to the Baltic States, Russia and Southern Europe, overtaking export of the Yarmouth 'red herring'. But a slow decline set in after the First World War when demand slackened from abroad. Even the British Herring Industry Board, with its slogan urging people in this country to 'eat more herrings', could not halt the decline.

After the Second World War things improved slightly, although over-fishing in the North Sea, especially from trawlers which scooped up small herring as well as full-size fish, and the increasing popularity of whitefish, were both having an effect. This was a period when some of Norfolk's beach fishermen took up work on the steam drifters from Yarmouth and Lowestoft. After September, when the crabbing season finished, there was a need to earn an income. If herring-catching was good from a crab boat where they lived, they did this instead (discussed below). From Cromer and Overstrand the drifter fishermen included Dennis Gaff, the Cox family, Reggie Jonas, 'Buster' Grout and David Davies. Buster would walk the 8 miles from Cromer to Mundesley to get a lift to Yarmouth with the Coxes. The Coxes went drifting consistently for years, once having three members of the family on the same drifter. Dennis reckoned the Yarmouth fleet, though much reduced at the time, still had forty of its own drifters, and 300 others were 'Scotsmen', while Bob reckoned Lowestoft had just as many of its own boats, if not more. Most of these wonderful old fishing boats have now been scrapped, but one survives, the *Lydia Eva*, a boat 'Old George' Cox had worked on.

The drifters they worked on 'fished up the North Sea' – where 'up' geographically means down – landing herring at Shields, Hartlepool, Whitby and Grimsby. The fishermen were consequently several weeks at sea, coming in to port if they had big catches, otherwise it was boxed and iced until it was worth landing. Dennis had been a 'yunker', or junior deckhand, paid as a 'three-quarter half quarter', which related to a complicated system of being paid in shares from the catch. Galloper, Dudgeon and Dowsing, Smith's Knoll and Gabbards were some of the grounds fished as the shoals moved south. The drifters worked by the Coxes reached grounds off the Dutch and French coasts, and would go in to port at Calais and Boulogne.

Sadly, by the late 1960s to early 1970s the main herring industry centred at Yarmouth and Lowestoft had collapsed. The buildings and numerous businesses associated with the industry, including the factory smokehouses, disappeared, and the workforce was absorbed by the new oil and gas companies.

## 'Herringing'

From talking to some of today's fishermen, I gather that up to the 1960s–70s several had gone 'herringing' from Norfolk's beaches. All along the coast, lights on their crab boats had glistened like glow-worms on the night horizon as they fished. Most of these fishermen are now retired, and only vestiges of the industry hang on. A few part-timers go herring- and mackerel-catching from the beach at Caister, just north of Yarmouth, and in October 2008 one of the fishermen did a spot of herring-catching from Cromer. But many fishermen regard the era of herringing, like lining and whelking, as finished. Some still have nets piled away in their sheds from former glory days, but do not bother to go. Lenny West thinks herring are still out there:

But if you work your nets like we used to, and you got a lump of herring, you couldn't even *give* them away! The herring ban finished it. All the curing houses have gone. It'd be OK with a couple of nets, you could sell them around, but if you got eight or nine cran you'd not do anything with them. Just shoot (chuck) them on the beach!

# Conditions

Along North Norfolk, fishermen went herring-catching after the crabbing season was over. The pots had been brought ashore and pot-haulers removed. The season was mostly at the end of September, October (the best month), and November, and before whelking started. Some years were better than others; it was very variable, but the 1960s had generally been good years. When 'the herring were running', for three or four weeks on their way south, fishermen would go after them day after day, weather permitting. It is said one could tell if they had arrived by sticking a finger in water and giving it a lick. Billy Gaff:

> Yes, you could pick up an oily slick on top of the water, you could see this when you were out there still after crabs and could tell the herring were about, you'd see the gulls working at times, and the seals working as well, so you knew they were about – and that being the time of year for them anyway.

The basic technique was to have the nets hang like a wide curtain in the water and let them drift with the tide; one end was attached to the 'bit' in the stern of the boat. Billy Gaff: 'It all depends which way the tide was, well basically you used to follow the herring. They could be up off Mundesley, Bacton way, so you'd go up off that way to start with, and just follow the tide. Yes, you could do 10 miles along the coast, just drifting with the tide.' Some drifted just a few miles. From conversations with Cromer fishermen, it appears Happisburgh or Sea Palling was about as far down as the Cromer boats went; those to the west did not go so far.

Herring fishing was not done on a rough night: 'It had to be smooth.' Bob Cox described the best conditions for going out:

> Fine, or a gentle bit of wind is better than too much. None at all sometimes caused problems. We reckon we were better off fishing on the flood, or at a change of tide, the end of the ebb and lift of the flood, because sometimes herring would swim at that particular time. They might swim all the flood. But we rarely fished over the ebb here. You'd get Cromer boats up here (Mundesley), they'd stop off here over-night; they'd fish on the ebb as well, just have nets in the water, but they might not get so much. But we found we didn't want to, what we call, 'drive' on the hardest of the ebb.

Billy Gaff, who went with his father in the late 1960s on his part-namesake, the *William Robert*, was one of those who fished on either the ebb or the flood tide. Richard Davies:

> I'd go with the old man, or 'Tuna' and 'Yacker' Harrison, lovely old boys! We'd go day after day, about 4 o'clock as the sun was going down. You'd not go off in the dark with herring nets – that was dodgy. You'd really like to go on the 'shutting in', going dark, and if you can have a change of tide that would be ideal. You didn't get many on a hard flood.

The idea was to have the nets in the water at the time when the herring came up to the surface to feed on plankton, and in the dark they'd not see the net. Three men in the boat was usual. There could be long hours waiting unprotected in an open boat and hard work when the nets were full or a wind blowing. If lucky, they could be home by 9–10 o'clock at night, otherwise waiting for the shoals to get in the nets could go on all night, and they might not finish until the early hours of the morning. This was not to all fishermen's liking, and it was difficult to have a social life. At the time Richard Davies would rather have been courting his future wife Julie, but others liked it as a change from crabbing. But as Dennis Gaff summed up, 'You knew no better, anyway you *had* to do it, to get a living!'

# The gear

The nets now used by the few beach fishermen who go after herring are nylon. Only rarely will cotton nets, which had been used in the days when herringing was common, be sought out from the backs of sheds. These cotton nets were once bought from Yarmouth or Lowestoft. Second-hand factory-made nets from the drifters, called 'Scotch' nets, would be cut down to make them less deep. The depth was measured in 'scores', each twenty meshes. George Cox:

> Each net would be roughly the same length. But where there were thirty score meshes deep on the drifters, the deepest net you'd use out of a crab boat would be 14–15 score. You wouldn't have all your nets in the crab boat at that depth – you'd have some only eight, nine or ten score because of the way your beach shelved. So you have a deeper net for deep water, and when you're on top of the beach you just had a shallow net.

The nets were 35 yards wide; these became shorter once they were in the water. Anything between twelve to twenty were joined together and shot from the boat in one long 'stream'. Dennis Gaff told me that when he had worked on drifters they had worked an uneven number of nets, such as eighty-seven, because driftermen were

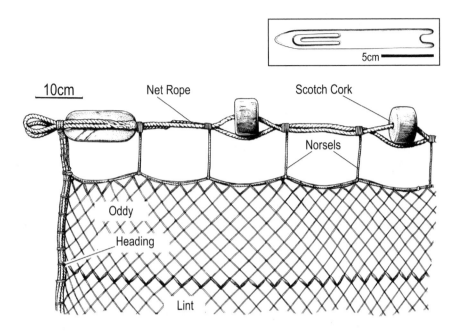

Net needle and herring net as used up to the early 1980s, Cromer. The two strands of the net rope wind in different directions to help stop it twisting.

superstitious about even numbers. They could stretch to almost 2 miles, but from a small crab boat a few hundred yards was long enough.

'Scotch' nets could be bought from the drifter-owner and net-maker Paul Williment, at Gorleston, south of Yarmouth. Unless the fisherman did it himself, Paul would cut them down and attach corks at intervals to a rope at the top. The net, which was called the 'lint', was hung from the head rope by short lengths of twine called 'norsels', but unlike on the drifters longshore boats did not have bottom ropes attached to their nets. The corks were round for herring-catching, rectangular for mackerel-catching. Mackerel nets were made not as deep as herring nets and had larger mesh.

Paul Williment, son of Paul (Senior), owns a chandlery supplying beach fisher-men along the coast in his father's old net chamber. It is also a pick-up point for bait. Paul told me net chambers on either side of his were not in use, and his was the only one which still has a connection with fishing in the area. Others[2] in Lowestoft, Caister and Sheringham have also been converted to new uses. Women 'beatsters' had once repaired nets in them. At Mr Williment's, one enters a very long first-floor room from the steps outside. It is an Aladdin's cave of fishing impedimenta, tools and workbenches, and has a wonderful whiff of history. Paul pointed out a long beam at the top of the room from which in earlier days had hung the herring nets . His father had been a 'ransacker', someone who checked the nets for holes. He also 'set them up' from the beam, that is, attached ropes, norsels and corks. Paul told me nets today were

Paul Williment in his net-chamber demonstrating one of the ties which had secured herring nets from a beam. Norfolk fishermen who came south to fish slept overnight on piles of nets in the compartments on the right. Gorleston, 2009.

imported from Japan and China, and were usually 'made up' along the South Coast. Until nylon nets came in the late 1960–70s, cotton nets had to be tanned to preserve them. Up until this period, every year or so at the end of the herring season, fishermen like Dennis Gaff brought their cotton nets to Paul Senior to be tanned. Paul remembers his father boiling up water with 'cutch' (gum catechu) for the nets, and tarring the ropes. The cutch, which had been extracted from a tree resin, arrived from the East in boxes lined with exotic-looking leaves. I was shown where there had been a tanning tank at the back of the building, which had a boiler next to it. The nets were pulled out onto a trough next to it and left to drain. They were then hung between posts set along a long stretch of ground at the back of the building.

Some fishermen had their own means of tanning the nets. Richard Davies mentioned tanning had once been done by Cromer fishermen in two big cast-iron 'coppers' in a hut in what was known as the 'fishermen's field' where their horses were kept, now the Runton Road car park. The Davies's coppers had originally been used for boiling towels and swimming costumes after they were hired out in the days of bathing machines. 'Old George' Cox had other sheds with a tanning copper in the Runton Road field.

After tanning or at the end of the season, the nets had to be dried, which could take several days. George Cox:

Herring nets drying on the promenade at Cromer, 1969. **(EDP)**

> If you were in Cromer October-time when they were longshoring, there was not
> one bit of railing round Cromer town which had not got a herring net on it! They
> were all down the Melbourne slope, past the Regency, Cliff Brow, even on the sea
> wall. We had to spread them on the prom at Mundesley. Now there are synthetic
> nets, so they don't have to be bone dry – cotton ones could combust!

Donny Lawrence added: 'When we finished with them we'd hang them out to dry.
When dry they were rolled up and tied and put them in a big old bag, so mice did not
get in – rats and mice could be a damned nuisance if they got in. Now I don't think
you can get a cotton net anywhere, no.'

Mending, or 'beating', nets is a dying art in this region. In North Norfolk there is
probably only a handful of the older fishermen who can still do it, including Lenny
'Teapot' West and Bob Cox. Even years ago, it was a specialist skill, done by fishermen
or their wives. Those who could braid nets for crab pots couldn't necessarily mend
nets as the technique was different. The needles were the same as for crab pots, but
smaller, and were once wood or bone, now plastic. Lenny West, who had once set up
herring nets, has a net shed at the back of his house. This had also been used by his
father and grandfather before him. Lenny told me his mother had mended nets in the
living room, and some of the needles were made out of a bone from the weekend
joint. Bob Cox:

Not many can mend herring nets. Half the job is cutting it out to start with and getting it ready. You don't just have a hole and fill it in, you have to cut the meshes so when you start to mend and braid you pick up the right meshes in the right places. I was taught the technique by my father; my mother did it as well. It was done in the sitting room.

He told me others who had mended nets were Richard Davies's grandfather 'Old Jack', and 'Shrimp' Davies. Some fishermen had had a go depending on how big the hole was, but most sent their nets to Paul Williment to mend once the season was over.

By the 1970s herring drifting from Yarmouth had collapsed and it became harder to get the traditional nets mended and tanned. Longshoremen in North Norfolk took to using nylon nets. These were good in that they were cheap and lasted longer, but they could be more damaging to the fish caught in the meshes, which took longer to pull out.

# The fishing trip

The traditional way to carry nets to the boat was to use a 'net stool'. This was like a small wooden table with four handles projecting outwards so two people could carry it. They go back to the 1890s, as shown by a photograph in Cromer museum, if not earlier. They were disappearing by the 1960s, but the odd one or two can be seen in Sheringham and other villages piled up with modern gill nets. Others have been used as work tables in fishermens' sheds. Bob:

> You had seven or eight nets on a stool, which is as much as you wanted to carry when they were wet. You 'ran' the nets off them into the stern of the boat .You'd join them from each stool as you ran them into the boat. So if you were standing where you steer, right aft, you ran the corks in there, and the other man would run the lint nearer to the engine house. They take up a lot of space in the boat.

Richard Davies recalled using three stools of nets, 'Might be two or three "sixes" and an "eight".' Nets were joined at the sides by short lengths of potstuff. The nets were shot at right angles to the tide; and a long line of nets snaked off into the distance, the corks bobbing about on the surface. A 'pole light' marked the end of the nets. This was a dan buoy cut down with a hurricane lamp or flashing tilley light on top. A series of nets connected together was known as a fleet.

John Balls described how the nets were shot:

> If you shot your gear at night, nine times out of ten it would be fine and you'd get a breeze off the land. So therefore you always start on the inside end and shot your

Austin 'Stymie' Blythe and Dick Davies 'running' herring nets from a net stool into the boat before a trip. Cromer, 1954. Boats at this time rested on skeets and stools, not on carriages as now. (Via Joyce Blythe)

nets to sea – and you drifted with the tide. You shot straight across the tide. If a light 'outly' wind was forecast – the forecast would have to be beautiful – you shoot your gear from seaward end in towards the land, because the weight of the boat would hold the net out outstretched.

If the wind changed, and you were lying on the outside end and there was a slight air or wind off the land, and then the wind come off the water, the boat would slacken away off the net, so the nets would lay loosely in the tide. Sometimes you'd get the pole-end blow out towards the other end of the nets, and that would 'cuddle' together, turn round together. There's nothing worse than that – you get the herring 'doubly swum'. That's when they go into both sides of the net. Normally herring go one way. If they're doubly swum, and the net's muddled up as well, it's a job to sort out! But not impossible.

Fishermen usually rowed as the nets were cast over the side. Donny Lawrence, who comes into Cromer twice a week to meet some of his old fishing friends for a drink, told me about herringing with Tony Payne:

It was lovely. My brother-in-law went with us, he was not a fisherman but he loved going to sea with us. We got him on an oar. When you used to shoot herring nets you shot to the horizon, put a pole buoy on one end, and you gradually chuck the net over, cast over and cast over, and if tide was taking her head round too far I or Tony would say to Gordon, 'Pull on that bloody oar, straighten her up again', he'd pull on the oar and straighten us away so we were straight out to the horizon.

Two people would shoot the nets. I'd cop over the corks, and Tony'd put over the lint. You had all the corks in the stern of the boat – you went backwards and forwards when you put the nets in, so when they go over the side they automatically come unfolded. I used to get hold of some corks, just cast it out into the water, and Tony would put the lint in, then I'd cast some more out and he'd put the lint, and I'd cast some more out. Then we'd tie one net to another net and we'd do the same thing again. It was OK (as they were going over), you could hang onto them. The engine's not on or you'd get the lint caught up in the screw (propeller) then you'd had it! The lint would be so many score deep – we had 'sixes' and 'eights' – you always had the six on the inside, so when you first chuck your pole over with the light to mark where you are, you always put the shallow ones, six score ones there, and you'd join the eight score ones onto it as you go further out into deep water.

On the boat, if they found one end of the nets in the water was producing a few herring, they would join on another 'stoolfull' of nets to this end. Each herring net had an 'eye' at one end in its rope, the other end had two tails called a 'fid'. The fid was 'bent' (tied) on to the eye. Sometimes, if lucky the nets were hardly shot, the corks on the nets would go down indicating fish in the net, and it was time to haul. Other times, wait. Donny continued:

And you'd just sit there – it used to be lovely. You'd wait maybe two to three hours. You'd just sit there rocking, and could fall asleep. You could stretch out on the boards and have a doze. We only had one little light on the mast, so other boats could see us. It was pitch black. You could have a brew up; some of the boys had a little kitchen thing. If they had what they call a 'look on', and if there's half a dozen they'd cook those herring and eat them at sea. You'd wait quite a while, and when the turn of the tide come, I'd haul at the rope in and have a 'look on' and see if the herring was swimming – you'd haul so much of the net in and if it was full of herring – Tony and I'd discuss if we should haul. If they were swimming, or had swum, we'd haul all the nets. I used to haul top rope, I'd have the corks, and all that. Tony would haul the lint, the fine cotton mesh where all the herring were, caught by the gills. He'd be shaking some of the herring into a tin or shoot them into a wing (between aft and midship thwarts); they went loose into the wings. Or if there were too many we'd leave them in the net, and come home and shake them out on the shore, and put them in tins and take them to market.

I had heard the expression 'herring running on the beach' for herring close in to shore. Bob and George Cox had regularly gone herring-catching from Cromer and Mundesley, with their father to start with. Bob described fishing close to shore:

Towards the end of herring-catching, I can't remember the years, we used to shoot much further off – we could go half a mile before we shot the nets. Whereas when we first went to sea, it was nothing unusual for us to back in to the beach, just round the first breakwater at Mundesley. You'd back the boat in to the beach, put a net on to the beach, jump back into your boat, and it gradually pulled off as we shot the rest of the nets up along the beach. Because it seemed as if the herring was coming out of the beach, out of the cliff! They always used to be on the south side of the net, the net is going parallel with the beach. But it's not possible to do this now as there are too many groynes.

The hauling was a slow business, sometimes taking hours. The nets were pulled in on the starboard side, because to quote John Balls Senior, 'Jesus pulled his nets in the starboard side. *Everything* goes in the starboard side.' Richard Davies:

> You didn't want too much wind, even off the land because you got to pull that net in and if it's blowing hard it is hard work. The man aft would be hauling the corks, he'd have all the weight. The man in the middle would have the lint with all the fish in. There'd be a man on the oars. You worked too many nets if there were no herring, or too few if there was a lot! It was a dodgy job, you could go out and get nothing; another night you'd fill her up. Clive Raiment and another, with me, were hauling for nothing, we had the nets in the boat and were going home, fed up. Spoke to Dennis who was hauling, he said, 'They're still swimming!', so I said, 'Thanks' and shot away. I got the most herring I ever got in my life. If it hadn't been in the boat I had I'd have lost a lot of nets. It was a fibreglass boat with no orrock holes in so it could hold more weight – twenty-odd nets! There's an old saying on drifters, if you're getting a few herring, they'd say 'spin up!', and you get a few more. We got a lot that night! I've not been herringing since.

Bob:

> You kept in time with one another. It was no good one trying to get the net back in boat before the other, you got to haul together, one on the lint, one on the corks. The boat's not stationary, you're pulling the boat to the nets, going backwards slightly if you were hauling them into the stern. You'd probably haul half into the stern, the other half into the head of the boat. If you think it's going to freshen up too much, you get your hauling cut back and come home. It can be smooth when you go, you'd not necessarily have wind but get a lot of swell. One night we were off Bacton. All of a sudden, you go up the swells and as the swells went past towards the beach, that cut out the land, you couldn't see the cliffs! So we came home.

Beach fishermen always point out that a crab boat was not built for herring-catching, as a lot of weight can be taken on board. Flatter bottomed boats are better. In the days of the smaller crab boats and hovellers an extra strake was put on the sides as they could end up well down in the water. When 'Old George' Cox was herringing in

*Left:* Willy Cox
hauling herring nets,
1977. (B. Gedge)

*Below:* Peter and
David Bywater
hauling herring
nets on the *Charles
Perkins*, 1981. (Martin
Warren/Cromer
Museum)

the 1930s his boat had an extra strake. These were slotted through rings onto the top strake, which did not at the time have gunwales.

Care had to be taken where the catch was put in the boat, and returning a fully laden boat to shore through a 'swelly' sea was particularly hazardous. The weight of the catch of herring was referred to in cran, as traditionally used at Lowestoft and Yarmouth. Each cran was about 28 stone, or a 'thousand' herrings – which was really 1320 herrings. Baskets which measured a quarter of a cran had been used for hoisting the catch ashore from the drifters. Dennis told me they had a crown on them indicating this was a legal measure, so presumably, the word cran had come from 'crown'. In terms of catch on a crab boat, five to six cran was a good night's work, ten cran from perhaps three good shots was exceptionally good[3]. But a boat just 300 yards away might miss the shoal and get virtually nothing. If they were getting a cran in a net, and had fourteen nets, that was reckoned too much for a crab boat, although John Lee and Richard Davies had both once brought home more than this. Donny mentioned one night when he'd foregone herringing with Tony Payne because it was darts night at the pub. He missed a bountiful ten-cran harvest; Tony's boat was so laden with herring, some were washed out as they came ashore in spite of oilies stuffed into the orrock holes. Two tractors were needed to drag the boat up the beach instead of one.

Bennett Middleton of Sheringham recalled the *Welcome Messenger* being so far down in the water only the top blue strake was visible: 'They was up over the top of the engine case, from one end to the other she was level full of herring!' John Jonas talked about going on a converted harbour boat which he had at Cromer at the time:

> It must have been about '79 or '80. I had a good catch on the *Reap*. Lot of swell when we come ashore that night. When we started running into the beach in the dark we couldn't see how much swell there was, I thought what am I doing here amongst this lot! Got to the beach alright, but it was a good job I was in the *Reap* 'cos if I was in a crab boat it'd sunk it. It'd have filled up – a wave coming in and hit the stern of it. But the *Reap* has a high stern.

Sometimes the boats could not carry the weight safely back to shore. George Cox:

> Where you'd joined the nets together you 'unbend' it, where you decide you've got enough. You go to the nearest boat and say, 'We've left three or six nets,' or whatever, 'You can pick them up'. They might even have returned to shore and got a call that nets could be picked up. That was the tradition – one had the herring, the other got the nets back.

## Scudding

Fishermen talk about cleaning, or 'scudding', their nets to empty them of the herring which were caught by the gills. Billy Gaff:

> Sometimes if you didn't have that many herring you'd clean them as you were hauling, but if you had a dollop of herring, probably you'd be pulling them all into the boat and get back onto the beach and clean the nets there. Sometimes you'd moor at the pier, at a flood tide, if you couldn't get ashore if there was a hard flood running and not much beach, and if there was a bit of swell running. You'd wait off

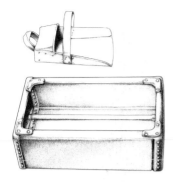

*Above:* Herring scoop and herring tin.

*Right:* David Leeder on *Carnival Queen* using a scoop to transfer herring from the wing and foreroom into tins. Nets were piled up aft. A battery lantern and reused car headlamp are attached to the boat. October 1967. (S. Harrison)

there for a while. Sometimes you had to clean the nets at the pier then go ashore after high water. You'd have some fish boxes with you, but more than likely you'd just clean them, scud the herring, into the wings of the crab boat.

Two men would clean the nets while one man steered. In the above image, David Leeder is shown using an aluminium 'scoop' to transfer herring, which had been scudded into the wings and foreroom, into tins. This scoop, a bit like a coal scuttle, was the same as was used on drifters at Lowestoft, where it was called a 'scutcher'.

The nets were sometimes scudded when the boat was ashore. Willy Cox:

> The nets were run from one end of the boat to the other was more usual – over an oar across the beam of the boat – we ran the nets from aft to for'ard, and shake them out, sometimes with help. The more the nets opened out, the more herring dropped out. You put them in 'tins' – you might get 30 tins, and you'd know you have five cran. Also we got mackerel, sometimes as many as herring in the same net – they were harder to get out, you can't shake them out – you take them out by hand. They'd make a hole, but you could do this yourself getting them out.

Youngsters who liked to watch the fishermen shake the nets out were allowed to have any that dropped onto the beach. Sometimes the catch was scudded onto a tarpaulin stretched out on the promenade. In the late 1990s some Cromer fishermen had decided to have a go at herring-catching, by then a very unusual event, and I was lucky enough to see a little group of them doing this. At Caister, where some her-

A group of fishermen scudding herring nets on Cromer promenade, late 1990s.

ring-catching still goes on, the nets are scudded in a car park near the boats. Weighing machines on-site are used to weigh the catch into fish boxes.

A good night's catch could mean several hours cleaning the nets, an endurance test which could last until the early hours, and the boat was messy afterwards. Dennis Gaff: 'Herring was a dirty job, your boat would be full of herring sometimes. It'd take hours to wash out the boat.' The 'tins' previously referred to were standardised metal boxes, which were used to sell the catch. They were introduced at Yarmouth when wicker baskets were replaced in 1960. Later, plastic boxes replaced tins, but a few fishermen still have piles of tins in storage.

Bob and George Cox had gone on herring drifters from Yarmouth, George on the *Wydale* which was the last steam drifter working from Yarmouth, so I asked, was going from a beach boat better? Bob:

> We were home everyday, that's the difference. If you wanted to sleep, a drifter was more comfortable even on a sack of straw than laying in the bottom of a crab boat! The drifters had one cabin for all to sleep in. On the crab boat all you had was an oar through the orrock holes, with a tarpaulin on it. When we'd go mackerel-fishing it was the same. We'd take an old crisp tin with a primus stove in it, and take ingredients to make coffee, also a flask of coffee – when that was drunk you'd boil up. But methylated spirits from the stove give a taste – it give us sore throats!

Fishing on a drifter was just as unpredictable in terms of the catch. George referred to the fact that fishermen had been paid on a share system when working on drifters, whereas they had received a weekly wage on trawlers: 'On drifters you could haul a hundred odd nets for nothing – get not even enough for breakfast! Half a share is just the same as no share when there's nothing!' A share system was also used by those fishing from crab boats, where pay depended on the amount of catch sold.

## Selling

In Cromer and Sheringham, and probably other villages too, herring and other fish had once been sold at beach auctions. There were then plenty of merchants who came to the beach or near it, to bid for the fish. This went on until the early twentieth century, as recorded by photographs of the time. One of these in Cromer museum, shows a sale of mackerel at the top of the Gangway in 1895. The small crab boats were unloaded of catch where they landed, recalled by Lenny West of Sheringham from his early days. The herrings were carried up the beach in wicker baskets as used at Yarmouth. The merchants would have clattered round to the surrounding villages and towns by horse and cart to sell the catch. Former cockle-picker Mrs Dowsing remembers them bringing herring from Wells to Stiffkey and villages along the coast. Fishermen also hawked the herring themselves, by cart and later by van. In the 1950s, two fishermen are remembered in Cromer pushing a barrow through the streets with a ped full of herring. They would ring a bell and shout 'Longshore herring!', which were sold at five for a shilling.

For transporting further afield, the herring had to get there as soon as possible – 'You didn't hang around!' In the mid-twentieth century, this was usually by the fishermen themselves, but in Cromer some of the wives who had learnt to drive before their husbands took over the deliveries. Herring was sold to the fish shops along the coast and inland. Some of the older fishermen who had 'a good few herring' recalled taking them through to the former fish market at Yarmouth, where the herring landed from drifters was auctioned. Bob described how he, his brother George and their father had got five cran one night, which their father drove down to Yarmouth. He and George carried on fishing to get another three cran and took the sea route to Yarmouth. Bennett Middleton told me the price was settled by a clap of the hands. The aim was to get to the market early before the drifters returned with their herring. He recalled one night's 'shot' raised £100, which was a small fortune at the time. The fish from the market was loaded onto rail lines which led to the main line station, from there to be distributed around the country. The Yarmouth market closed in the late 1960s, so after this, if a fisherman had an exceptional lot of the herring, it had to be driven the extra distance to Lowestoft fish market.

Only a few of the older fishermen can recall the Norfolk system of counting the herring, as had been used at Yarmouth and along the coast. This was how the Coxes had sold herring to shops early on:

When we started we always sold them in 'long hundreds', that was 33 warp and a warp was four herring, so there were 132 herrings to the 'hundred'. Eventually we got round to stonage. We'd measured them out where the boat was. They'd only be put in tins when they were going to market, to be sold by weight. By that time you'd sell to shops by weight as well – there were 4½ stone in a tin, 28 stone in cran.

During his fishing career Bennett Middleton had sold by weight but remembers his father selling by warp: 'My father did. He went up to Holt – yes, with motorbike and sidecar – and stood right outside the fish shop and said, "If you don't buy them, *we'll* stand here and sell them!"'

Donny Lawrence, who fished slightly later, recalled:

We'd not count them then, just shove 'em in. When we went to Lowestoft market, we'd fill the tins right up level. Then we'd keep say two tins apart, so by time we got to Lowestoft, they'd probably sunk down a bit, so we could top them up so they looked a good 6 stone. I don't *think* they were weighed. No we just put them on the market and sellers would sell them. There was one firm there called BFP, Better Fish Prices we called them, but that wasn't the name of them – we thought we got better money from him than from Cole's and people like that. We didn't wait around because we'd been up all night. We wanted to get back and have a couple hours sleep. Had to bend the nets back into the boats, and that, so had to be back on the beach by dinnertime. Then we'd go home have some dinner, then go back and go to sea! Take a flask of soup and a few sandwiches.

John Davies, like all the younger generation of fishermen in the region, now does just potting, but went herringing as a youngster. He told me the catch had to get to Lowestoft by 7a.m. in order to put it on the market. They did not go herring-catching on a Friday because there was no market on a Saturday, but they could go on Sunday as there was a Monday morning market. So while herring-catching, they always had Friday evening and Saturday off. Fishermen who did not wait around to see what prices their herring fetched, got their money in arrears at the end of the week, sometimes after two weeks. Dennis Gaff:

Sometimes we got a good price for them, if there were no herring at Yarmouth or anything. If you got five or six cran, that's a good night's work out of a crab boat. You want a lot of herring, but not for the others! But the more you got, the cheaper you got because they didn't look so good! The prices would go down.

This had happened to Richard Little who had 10,000 herring one night, and spent all night getting them up the gangway at Sheringham. That morning plenty of other fishermen had good catches to sell at Lowestoft, and the value plummeted. Donny Lawrence: 'I went with Tony Payne in the *Amanda Ann* in the 1970s. We couldn't sell them, we were going to Lowestoft sometimes and only got £5 for a six-stone tin. Waste of time. Then "Little" Billy and Gary Humphries went one day, they got about four cran, and got nothing for it!' One of the fishermen had a nice little earner selling his herring to local zoos, but Coles of Lowestoft got in on the act and finished it for him.

Others took to fishing out of Yarmouth or from towns and villages on the way to Yarmouth. Richard Little took his boat and worked off Hemsby beach for three or four years. He and other fishermen shared a bungalow, although Bennett Middleton recalled when he first went from Hemsby he had to share a bed with Richard in a garden shed. They had had a couple of hours sleep after returning from the pub, but were out on the beach by 2a.m. In the late 1960s, Cromer fisherman Billy Gaff fished out of Yarmouth harbour as a youngster with his father. There had not been so many herring around Cromer then. They tied up the *William Robert* at the Lifeboat House at Gorleston and dossed down on piles of old herring nets in Paul Williment's net chamber. Other fishermen from Cromer, Sheringham and Mundesley were there too. Bob recalled it had been colder than charity: 'No, there was no breakfast! But we could get bread rolls down the road. After fishing, Mabel Harrison, "Tuna"'s wife, would come through in her van and pick "Tuna" up and give others a lift home.' Paul Williment's net shed was also a convenient dropping off point for fishermen who did not want to drive on to Lowestoft to sell their herring. He took it to the market for them, charging so much a box.

# Smokehouses

Although there had once been several smokehouses in Yarmouth which took herring from the drifters, the main one mentioned by the North Norfolk fishermen I spoke to was Henry Sutton's. This factory took large volumes of longshore herring. I was told the herring was delivered 'tinned up' and sold at a fixed price which was paid at the end of the week. The herring which were steeped in brine pits as part of the process also provided fishermen with bait for whelking.

There had once been several smaller smokehouses in operation along the coast for the locally landed herring[4]. By preserving some of it, it would last longer for local consumption. The 'backyard' smokeries were small, two-storey brick buildings, some of which are still standing, at Cromer, Sheringham, Overstrand and East Runton. Some were used within living memory. One of the East Runton fishermen told me he had even helped to build one which was later demolished. Some of the fish shops had their own smokehouses out the back, such as behind the former Cox's and the Jonas's in Cromer; and behind former 'Downtide' West's and Scotter's in Sheringham.

One in Cromer is owned by fisherman John Jonas, and according to John the only authentic, working one in the region. This is a smokehouse with history; it is mentioned as working in 1877, in Savin's history of Cromer. The smoking chamber is a small, dark room a few feet across, its walls blackened from years of smoking fish. It is a smaller version of the former smokehouses in Yarmouth. Attached to the walls are row upon row of horizontal bars, rather like the bars in a gymnasium. On entering the chamber, one is surrounded by a lovely resinous, fishy smell.

Unlike the former 'factory' smokehouses of Yarmouth, John smokes his fish in modest quantities, cottage-industry style. At the back of the fish shop he prepares the fish to go in the smokery, using a method he and his father Reggie had worked out, but which is similar to other smokehouses. The herrings are first soaked in brine in a plastic box. Ones destined to be kippers are gutted and split open, then soaked an hour if large, three-quarters of an hour if small. Those destined to be bloaters, which are put in whole, are soaked for several hours or all day. Much depends on the size, as with the times of smoking. When ready, John attaches the kippers by their gills onto small spikes on wooden bars, or 'speets'. Several rows are laid across from the sink to a table, the goggle-eyed faces of the herrings staring upwards.

For the bloaters, which are whole fish, these are attached one by one onto a different sort of speet, a narrow rod which goes through the gills and mouths. John smokes his kippers and bloaters at the same time, but the kippers are smoked overnight, and the bloaters at least twelve hours, depending 'on the look of them, or if the fire goes out!' The speets are hung across the chamber resting on the horizontal bars attached to the walls. John straddles the bars lower down the chamber and moves up into the

John Jonas 'speeting' bloaters. Kippers already speeted, below. Cromer, 2008.

John Jonas holding up a speet of bloaters ready to go in the smokehouse. Cromer, 2008.

darkness placing the speets across the upper ones. When all the speets are in place, he spreads untreated oak shavings obtained from a carpenter in Sheringham on the floor. When lit this gently smoulders, giving off a cloud of smoke and enough heat to cure the herring. The smoke exits through windows at the top of the chamber. John also smokes mackerel and salmon at Christmas, and sends kippers by post on behalf of happy holiday-makers to the folks back home – special size to go through a letterbox!

John has also made the famous 'red herrings' which are dry and coloured. These are the traditionally cured Yarmouth herrings as made at Sutton's, which were exported to the Mediterranean region and predate kippers and bloaters. ('Bloatering' was also invented at Yarmouth.) John told me the 'reds' take a lot of time: two weeks being dry-salted, then six to eight weeks smoked in the smokehouse. The smoking is not continuous, as they are left in the smokehouse while other things are being smoked at the same time. Traditional smoked red herring should keep for years; I was shown one done a year ago, which was still in good, edible condition. However, John is not smoking reds at present, as it is not so easy to get the large herrings which are needed, as they will shrink to half the size in the salt. Another pickling method was mentioned by Richard Davies. The family, like other fishing families, once ate a lot of herring, and to help them keep, his mother used to steep them in brine in a stone jar in the pantry with lard poured over the top.

# Mackerel

Mackerel were caught in the summer months off North Norfolk. As they went off easily they had to be sold the day they were landed or be thrown away. Therefore commercial mackerel-fishing was not so popular from the beaches, especially as most fishermen were crabbing at that time. In addition, mackerel have barbs on their backs which meant the catch had to be tediously hand-picked out of the nets. At Cromer, Richard Davies thought mackerel-catching was done more in his father's or grandfather's day, but it had once been much more important in Sheringham. At Mundesley, Bob and George Cox recalled doing it in their earlier years. Bob:

> When we went mackerel-catching, we went twenty-six nights on the trot! Dad said no other crab boat ever did it before. That was a particular June. We used to go mackerel-catching in mid-April until the beginning of July, and crabbing as well! And lining as well, if Father had his way, and if we find a few more we'd put a trawl in as well. We did a lot of different fishing then, not just crabs. We'd be going off at night trawling, and April to July probably be mackerel-catching as well in drift nets. If you recall when the gas site was being constructed, about 1968, the latter part of the time, we'd go off there and shoot away from that for mackerel. Mackerel-catching was further out at sea than for herring. At that time, we didn't have crab pots so far out at sea, and we fished further off than where the pots were.

You couldn't now go mackerel-catching where *we* went because there's too many crab pots in the way. Because in those days, there were no hydraulic haulers (on the boats) and people didn't go so far to sea crabbing. We took good catches of mackerel to Lowestoft, if we got more than we could sell to shops.

George added:

When we were mackerel-catching, we'd go away from the beach maybe five in the evening, come back to the beach two to three in the morning. If there was any mackerel, someone had to drive them to market. Then you got to turn round and haul the crab pots, then when you come home again someone's got to deliver the crabs! You put in a long day if everything went right!

After fishing, Bennett Middleton of Sheringham recalled taking a shot of mackerel to a factory in Yarmouth where they were canned in tomato sauce. Lenny West told me in Sheringham mackerel had been caught in nets, but when he went he sometimes used revolving 'spinners', laid from the back of the boat. The shininess attracted mackerel which were caught by hooks on the spinner. This was also done at Cromer, mainly on the way back from crabbing, but seems not to have been done commercially in later years.

# Herring ban

As a response to over-fishing, a herring ban was imposed by the Government on the North Sea, 1977–80. Longshoring for herring from Norfolk had to stop. Fisheries inspectors kept a steely eye on what was brought ashore, on the lookout for 'black herring'. At the time mackerel-catching was permitted, but any by-catch herring had to be chucked overboard. Fishermen I have talked to consistently blame the herring ban for putting the kibosh on the herring industry. As with lining, another part of their livelihood went to the wall. When the ban was lifted, it was reckoned that, although only three years, consumers' tastes had changed and fishmongers had taken to filling their slabs with other fish. In addition, there were fewer older people about who ate herrings, and younger people, who grew up without eating them, did not want the pungent smells in their kitchens. For those who still want herring, most now in fish shops comes from Scotland or Norway.

The problem was due to the modernisation of fishing methods, particularly when British and foreign trawling was revived after the war in the North Sea. Super-trawlers with the latest fish-finding instruments, nylon nets and all-year-round fishing caught too many fish, far outstripping traditional lining and netting. Richard Davies summed it up: '*We* were taking bugger all out! And the drifters never did overfish!' Dennis Gaff:

What stopped it was foreign trawlers. First one here came from Holland and got stuck on Happisburgh Sands. We went on Cromer lifeboat – had to have fire-brigade pumps to pump the water out. She was *full* of herring! Everyone said this would have an effect. Like with everything the trawling done, there'd be plenty of fish now, but trawling took everything including the small stuff.

Bob Cox:

I think the trawlers who fished for herring used a mid-water trawl, as opposed to a bottom trawl. Foreign boats were very ahead in this form of fishing at this time. Nowadays, there are very big boats from Scottish ports who use purse-seines and are very efficient and successful. But *here* the home-fishing became uneconomical. The shoals would not shoal with consistency like years ago. If a pair-trawler had been through, that broke them up!

Brother George added:

On a drifter if you shot a hundred nets, you could haul thirty to forty and not see a fish, then in two or three nets you could get five or six cran per net. The pair-trawlers ploughed them up, took the lot – including small herring. The drift nets never killed the herring stock because they used a net size for the fish they were after – if it was too small it didn't get the big ones, if too big the herring went straight though. A foreign pair-trawler could steam towing a net faster than a Lowestoft or Yarmouth drifter – you never could catch them! You got East German, Polish and Russian boats. It was frightening too, you'd see them on deck, an armed guard to keep the crew in order!

Billy Gaff explained that in the period after the ban, if it 'was hard to sell the things', that was when he and other beach fishermen took them to Suttons. Most other smokehouses, and the businesses associated with them, closed because trade had dwindled away. The Baltic states changed to getting their herring from Norway. Today, there is only one firm which still does commercial curing. This is in part of the former Sutton's smokehouse. Its herring and mackerel are imported, and most of the product is exported to the Mediterranean, only a few going to London and local outlets. Another smokehouse has been converted into the Time and Tide Museum, a wonderful museum of Yarmouth's herring industry but a sure sign that the real thing is no longer extant. John Jonas:

There are quotas after the herring ban. Yes, on beach boats – it depends on the size of the boat a bit, but I don't know how these quotas work. They keep changing every five minutes – there're letters coming through all the time! They keep cutting them down all the time. If you get too many fish, you fill your quota up. Years ago it was a free-for-all, you get what you like. Boats didn't even have to have licences, just have to be registered. Then when they brought licences in, they gave you another number, to be carved on the boat. The quotas not come in till the '90s. Different sea areas have different quotas. They (DEFRA) think they know what's rare, but I'm sure they don't!

From talking to some fishermen, it seems quotas aren't really the issue; it is that herring-catching has been a waste of time, financially, for years. John Balls reckoned that about 1980 was the last time fishermen went commercially, and that even if one took a couple of hundred stone to Lowestoft market it might not sell and end up being condemned. The last time Willy Cox had sold herring on Lowestoft market was for £1 a stone, even though it was being sold for ten times this amount in the shops. Later he had not been able to sell it there at all, and had to pick it up and take it to Wells to sell as whelk bait. The amount he got did not even cover his expenses. At the end of the 1990s a few Cromer fishermen had tried a few trips, but didn't catch much, so didn't bother again. One fisherman who tried in 2008 using nylon set nets and cotton drift nets did a little better.

I asked fishermen if there were herring out there now. Billy Gaff summed it up:

> Yes, sure there is. Fact is, not many fishermen go after herring along this piece of coast any more, so there must be plenty of herring at certain times along this piece of coast because no-one's actually catching them! The Dutch go for them in a big way still, and they come within sight of the East Coast after them.

But as fishermen point out, even if they wanted to bring back herring-catching from Norfolk's beaches they couldn't because the market for them has gone and there are now too many pots in the way at sea. In the 1980s one or two fishermen had continued potting until Christmas, then more and more, until today when they only remove pots for two or three months at the beginning of the year.

End notes:
1. Norfolk Record Office, Norwich Consistory Court Will Register. 'Aleyn' Folio 34.
2. In Cromer, three women from fishing families are listed as net-makers in the 1841 census.
3. Bob Cox pointed out that a drifter would be catching in the region of 50–150 cran, but very big catches were not necessarily an advantage. It meant a lot of hard work, a long time hauling, and by the time one got to market the prices could have fallen, especially if a lot of fish were already landed.
4. Nineteenth-century trade directories list six 'curing houses' in Sheringham, four in Cromer and one in Weybourne.

# CHAPTER 8

# WHELKING

Whelks have for centuries been a convenience food in Britain. They became popular at seaside resorts when mass tourism took off in Victorian times. But in the modern era, with increased demand for foreign and fast foods, whelks have dipped in popularity perhaps more than other shellfish.

In Norfolk, great whelking centres rose and fell. First there was King's Lynn, with its early rail connections which helped establish the market in the late nineteenth century. Whelks were sent cooked to London (Billingsgate fish market) and other towns, and live to northern ports as bait for cod-lining. The nation's penchant for fish and chips had already begun, so bait was much in demand. Fishermen in towns and villages to the east of King's Lynn caught whelks for their own lining, also selling some to local resorts and to Norwich for human consumption. But when Sheringham became connected by rail, it soon outstripped King's Lynn in supplying whelks to London and the Midlands. Its whelk grounds were closer to the coast so there were shorter fishing trips, and the smaller beach boats could be worked by fewer men. Small boileries sprouted in the town. A Fisheries Inspector's report (cited in S. Worfolk, 1992) stated that there were forty whelk boats in 1889, although 100 cited one year later does seem difficult to believe, and perhaps includes smaller crab boats.

According to retired fisherman Lenny West, in his grandfather's time Sheringham fishermen fished westwards off Blakeney, a 20-mile round trip. This was in hovellers or small crab boats without engines. The latter worked the tides to make life easier, going on the ebb and returning on the flood. If there was a wind they sailed and 'went like hell', but otherwise they had to row. Some Sheringham fishermen moved to the busy port of Wells and to Brancaster, where they could work from harbours on bigger boats'. In 1899, nine whelk boats or 'whelkers' are known to have worked from Wells. Wells had a rail link since 1857, but with the impetus coming from the newcomers, by the early to mid-twentieth century it had supplanted Sheringham as the whelking hot spot, with Brancaster well behind. In the 1960s Wells was catching 6–800 tons of whelks a year. It became not only the major centre for whelking in Britain but for the whole of Europe.

Although the industry had declined in Sheringham, whelking still did well early to mid-twentieth century. Fisherman Henry 'Joyful' West in *Memoirs of a Shannock*, described whelking as an arduous, day-long activity. About twenty whelk boats were whelking then. The boats had engines, some installed by major fish-merchant Harry Johnson, who bought and marketed the fishermen's whelks, as well as their crabs, lobsters and fish. The whelks went by donkey and cart to Sheringham train station to be sent to London, Clacton, Southend and elsewhere. Johnson's boilery on the seafront, where men were employed to cook the whelks, is now the 'Whelk Coppers' café. Just before the Second World War, whelking took a serious dip and became a poor earner in Sheringham. Some fishermen switched to lining instead.

## Whelking from Wells

Alan Cooper still goes whelking from the harbour at Wells, one of a dwindling band to do so. This is now a mere whiff of the former whelking industry which had gone on there. Before and after the war there was much activity on the quay. As ships and barges offloaded fertiliser and coal and took on agricultural goods, the whelk boats would be unloading whelks. They were taken to the boileries in Wells, as most then were to be sold cooked for eating. Fishermen sent them out all over the country including to London and seaside resorts, with some going to the continent. Some were sold locally, including by barrow boys who took them round to the local pubs. Wells at one time supported a whelk factory which processed them. In his working life Alan reckoned Wells's heyday was in the late 1970s–80s, but fishermen had been making a good living from whelking one and two generations earlier. Crabbing took over when crabs were found on Race Bank in the early 1990s. Since then crabbing has been the main livelihood for Wells fishermen.

## Alan Cooper

Alan is a great source of knowledge about whelking from Wells. I managed to catch him off-season while his boat was being serviced, and he told me about his whelking career:

> Since 1959 when I started, there has been just one year I've not been whelking, that was the year before last (2007). But last year we worked just three months, and I think we cleaned them up, and we couldn't find nowhere else – just that one little patch. We used to haul crab pots as well closer in, to help out – on the way off or on the way back, whichever way the weather was going to be.

The Coopers were originally a Sheringham fishing family, and like the Coxes, helped Wells take off as a whelking centre. Alan's father Robert 'Diddy' Cooper (b. 1904), uncle David and grandfather William 'Demon' took up whelking from Wells. After being based at Wells for part of the week, 'Diddy' settled there when he married a Wells girl in 1928.

At sixty-four, Alan is still a full-time fisherman, crabbing as well as whelking from Wells. He has fished from Wells all his life. He took a week's holiday after leaving school, then went fishing in his father's whelk boat, the *Knot*. His father had not encouraged him to take up fishing as a career, wanting him to go to Lynn Tech., but Alan was not interested.

## Boats

Alan's grandfather and fishermen of his generation had gone oystering outside Wells harbour, which had been an important industry at the time. This was in rowing-sailing hovellers about the size of large crab boats. The whelkers which followed were bigger. Alan told me most of the hovellers and whelkers used at Wells, such as the *Knot*, had been built at Sheringham, although it is possible some might have been built at King's Lynn.

Alan Cooper pulling up whelk pots on the *Ann Isabel*, with a pile of whelks behind him. Fishing from Wells, 1970s–80s. (Via A. Cooper)

Whelk boats were built larger than hovellers to take the heavy gear and go further out to sea. One or two can still be seen at Morston, converted to pleasure boats. Fishing trips were long and arduous, and they had to go out and come back according to the tides:

> In the *Knot* we had a petrol engine in it, but we carried a sail with us, and would pull it up to help us along. My father always had a petrol engine – I can't say he ever rowed. When I went, my father was in partnership with a chap, Ernie Jarvis, so there were three of us. Most were three-handed, some were two.

When Alan's father 'Diddy' fell ill Alan continued fishing with Ernie Jarvis. At the time there were eight boats whelking. The *Knot*, built in the late 1930s, was typical, an open boat the same shape as a crab boat but bigger. She was 26ft long, 10½ft beam. The *William Edward* built for Cyril Grimes of Wells in 1949 was the longest whelker at 30ft, and weighed 6 tons.

The Wells whelk fishermen later used converted RNLI lifeboats, which at 35½ft were markedly bigger than the whelkers. The Coxes had three, one acting as a spare. Alan got hold of another, the *Ann Isabel,* and had it done up so that he could improve his working capacity. Around the 1970s, new styles of boats with wheelhouses were appearing in Wells harbour. This was after small trawlers with cabins had come up from Whitstable. As more modern fishing boats became available, Alan bought the 32ft *Ma Freen* in 1987, made by Alan Goodchild's firm in Burgh Castle, Yarmouth.

## Whelk grounds

> When my grandfather went, they used to go 5–6 miles off, no further. When *we* first went whelking we used to go just to the back of Blakeney Overfalls. Then we used to go 5, 6, 8 miles out, past the Race Buoy. That was 9 miles to Race Bank. It'd take us two and a half hours. We used to go just beyond the East Dudgeon Buoy – not as far as the Cromer Knoll. Then when we had the lifeboat we used to go past the Cromer Knoll nearly to the Haddock Bank; that used to take us four hours. We used to go to the back of Dudgeon Shoals, from Wells harbour that's about 24 miles.

When crabs proliferated on Race Bank, eating whelk spawn in the area, fishermen moved further offshore to find new whelk grounds:

> With the boat we've got now, the fibreglass one, we go right out. It was about 40 miles where we finished up whelking, it'd take four and a half to five hours to come home. But there are hardly any whelks there now. Last year (2008) we did three months between crabbing, and couldn't find hardly any – they had just gone!

Some blamed the Grimsby fishermen who had come down to work off the Norfolk coast, each boat working 3–4000 pots. Alan:

> It was in the '90s when they came here. This was when there was a big call for whelks. When the whelks come on and we used to be able to sell lots of whelks, they turned over from crabbing and went whelking in these big vivier crabbers, 50–60ft boats. They went to the Pickerill Field, between off here and the Humber, and they came here and in the Race Channel. Since all these big boats from Grimsby have been doing it, they've cleaned all the grounds! They've all gone silty.

# Fishing trip

Alan described the working conditions:

> We'd go out first of the tide, and be twelve to fourteen, sixteen hours at sea – now we go crabbing, it's not quite so many hours, but nearly. You'd pack sandwiches and a flask of coffee. On the whelkers, there was a little cuddy, and you could get in out of the weather. You couldn't sleep on them. The cold was the thing – you were better standing and stamp your feet than lying in the cold. We went all the year round. On the lifeboat there was no cover – no canopy to get under.
>
> We looked at the weather, heard the weather forecast. We've had the lifeboat come after us once or twice because it had come on rough. The off-land winds won't hurt you, that's the south, south-east, the east isn't too bad, the west – but anything outside of that, when it comes onto a gale of wind that's when you've got to get back to the harbour. When the sea starts building up, and you got to run into the harbour when the harbour's rough, that's the trouble. When the lifeboat came after us, we'd got caught there. But in the open sea, you don't take any harm, if you keep watching yourselves. With the boat we've got now, when you see a big sea you either ease her down or put her head to it, or run with it. You don't catch it on board so long as they're not breaking. The open boats, they would fill up, but on a big boat like ours now, it would just come on board and run out again. On the *Knot* we had a hand pump, and we had a motor pump run off the engine, that would pump her out.
>
> When I first started whelking with my father, we worked 216 pots, six shanks of thirty-six pots. We now have forty pots in a shank. We work six 'forties' this year. When there were lots of whelks about years ago we worked ten shanks.

The method is the same as used for crabbing, moving from shank to shank, but the pots are shot against the tide to make sure they sit upright on the bottom. Hauling is usually with the tide, as for crabbing. Each time the whole shank is hauled on board, and the boat held above the pots so that as they come up the whelks do not spill out.

Salt-herring loaded as bait for whelks on the *Alison Christine* by the Frary family. Wells quay, 1985. Small trawlers *Romulus* and *Remus* are behind, the latter owned by Ivan Large. (EDP)

They are emptied and rebaited, then shot against the tide in a continuous operation, timing it so that a line of pots linked by tows will be spaced evenly along the sea bed. At each end of the shank there is an anchor and tow leading up to a marker buoy. The length of tow between the pots is reckoned by the depth of water so as to prevent two pots being lifted off the bottom at once. They are hauled on the following day's trip.

'We used to use herring as bait. A lorry came up from Yarmouth with seven or eight tons at a time. Now we can't get it, we use scad and cod pieces same as for crabbing.' He told me the herring was once stored in a partitioned-off part of a whelk house on the Quay, and the fishermen bought their own, not as a co-operative. The herring was salted, broken in pieces; not fit for human consumption:

'If the whelks were small we put them through a riddle, a round thing with bars in it. Buyers do not want the small stuff, so the small ones were thrown back over to leave them to grow – but they never did!' Nowadays boats have riddle machines which sort out undersized whelks and direct them over the side. As part of the EU's Common Fisheries Policy they have to be at least 4.5cm shell length.

Pecks and bushels were the traditional way of measuring whelks in Norfolk, later changing to stones and tons. A peck was about a stone, and as everyone over a certain age will remember there are four in a bushel. Whelks were carried in net bags, so fishermen had another measure, 'washes' which referred to netfuls. Retired Bennettt Middleton remembered the Cox brothers landing 200 washes a day. Alan:

'Sonny' Warner braiding a net whelk bag. Wells. (EDP)

A good catch is a ton, or 1½ tons. You can make it pay with a ton. My father and grandfather made a good living from it – they got 1 or 2 tons. We've had 3 or 4 tons. Sometime we'd haul nine or ten shanks of forty pots a day, and they'd be loaded with them! We've had twenty five-stone bags out of forty pots. We would go every day if the weather was fine and the whelks were thick. We measured them into these bags. We used to have a tub on the boat – what we call a bushel. We measure them into a basket now, a five or six peck basket. If you fill that up, it would roughly weigh 35 kilos. We'd put that 35 kilos into a bag, not polythene, but one air can get to – only we can't get these bags now, and they have to go in fish boxes. Last year when the whelks weren't that thick, we'd leave them three or four days and haul the crab pots, one fleet one day, another fleet another day, then go back to the whelk pots when the crabs weren't performing well.

Alan discussed how fishing had changed. On his latest 32½ft boat he has radar, GPS, a fishfinder (indicating the depth of water) and, of course, a hauler. Alan's father had had the hard job of hand-hauling whelk pots, but by the time Alan was fishing on the *Knot*, life was easier:

The hauler we used was an Austin 7 engine with a back axle off an Austin 7 car stuck up in the air, cut off at the bottom! Years ago fishing trips were in daylight hours because we had no lights on the boats, no deck lights, nothing. We had dan buoys, and you couldn't see them in the dark. Say, this time of the year (January), if it was high water say 3 o'clock in the morning, we'd go down and lay outside the harbour for three or four hours, then we'd steam out. We came home when it started to get dark. We used to go with a compass and pocket watch. Say, if we had to go north-east for an hour, we'd look at the watch, say it was 3 o'clock, we'd go up north-east for an hour with the compass, then have a look round and see if we could see our dan buoys. That's how we found them. We didn't have search lights, GPSs, nothing like that!

Now they find them by GPS. These boys nowadays work five-gallon cans (buoys). If they didn't have GPS, they could not work cans, they wouldn't know whose fleet of pots they were. We used to have dan buoys with our own colours on them, red, blue, green, black, so we knew whose was whose. We sometimes still use them – I have just made some up. These days you can go out at night, because we've got GPS, and go straight to them, and put the searchlight on.

Plastic cans are cheap and unlike the old-style dans do not involve work in making them. This is a factor when it comes to replacing destroyed buoys if the gear is steamed over by shipping:

Some of them now crabbing do twenty-four-hour trips. I don't like going at night. I prefer going in daylight, say at dinnertime and come home in the dark, 1, 2 or 3 o'clock in the morning. At least you can have a decent night's sleep. A lot of these young ones go 4 o'clock in the afternoon, go all night and come in next morning. Some of them can sleep on the boats we've got now.

To get back into Wells harbour, 'Once the tide had gone out you had to wait 'til the tide come back in again, that was the trouble. We always used to say, if you get back to the harbour the first hour of the flood that's when you can get in, but after that the sea starts building bigger.'

# Gear

The traditional metal whelk pot (discussed below) was used at Wells and all along the Norfolk coast. Alan:

We stopped using the old type of pot in the 1980s and '90s, though I still have some. We use industrially made pots. These are better, as they don't catch so many hermit crabs. They can't crawl up them, because they're smooth. You don't get the 'rubbish' in them, that's the difference. They last longer because they're plastic, and you've not got to rope them and mend them up, and tar them every year – that's put them in the tar copper and re-tar them.

He mentioned that when the foundry at Walsingham packed up, the cast-iron bases became unobtainable. A trend to use a different type of pot was started in the 1970s by Victor Pells of Brancaster and Ivan Large and Paul Letzer at Wells. They used large plastic flower pots with concrete bottoms to weight them. Ivan told me the pot was turned upside down, and perforated with holes. Iron bars were set into the sides an

*Right:* Alan Cooper with three types of whelk pot. Traditional type behind Alan; modern, reconstructed keg-type on the right; hand-made welded frames bound with rope and car tyre of intermediate period on the left. Wells, 2009.

*Below left:* Traditional whelk pot. Heavy metal base with tarred rope between struts. Horizontal bait bar inside.

*Below right:* Modern 'cut-down' plastic keg with crinny laced at top is essentially similar.

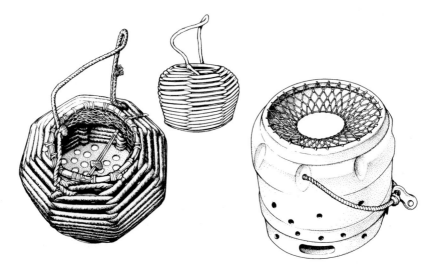

inch from the bottom and some concrete poured onto them. A big hole was cut into the 'top' and a net crinny braided and tied round the hole.

When I visited Alan he showed me stacks of old pots he had made with concrete bases. He had welded the metal frames himself and bound strips of car tyre or rope between the struts. Other homemade pots included heavy-duty buckets and cut-down six-gallon drums. They also had concrete bottoms, or if iron bases from old whelk pots could be found of the right size, these were put inside. Some of Alan's newer pots are cut-down, upside-down kegs originally made to hold liquids. A central section is cut out and discarded. To make the top, a big hole is cut out of the former base of the keg and a crinny laced around its edge. What had been the top of the keg is bolted on to become the bottom of the pot. Alan explained factory-made whelk pots can now be obtained via the internet.

# Processing and selling

Before Alan's time, some of the whelks had been sent by rail to Bridlington and Grimsby for winter long-lining. Alan:

> In my father's and grandfather's time, we boiled the whelks – only some they sent away live for cod bait to Yorkshire and that way, for putting on the hooks. But for human consumption, they always went cooked. My grandfather used to boil whelks in a shed near the Shipwright's pub. We used to have a whelk house by the Quay, Ernie Jarvis owned it – it was knocked down, it's where we call Tug Boat Yard, an open grass area now. To help unload there was a wooden staging with a stand and block-and-tackle which was used to hook onto the bags of whelks and swing them from the boat onto the platform – it's all gone now Now, I have a derrick on the boat to lift the sacks, put a hook in the sacks and pull them up the (Quay) wall.

On the smaller whelk boats of Alan's father's and grandfather's time, it had been possible to unload when the water was down. The Coopers had carried two bags of whelks at a time up to the quayside, using ex-agricultural yokes on their shoulders:

> There were also whelk houses up at the brick yard, past Tug Boat Yard going east, Coxes and that. Some of them are still standing; my father's is still there. My father's was built in 1950. It was quicker for them to unload that end (at the Quay), instead of waiting for the tide to come up here, but we cooked here. These other sheds you see here now, they were built long after that.

An array of fishermen's sheds, where the cooking took place, is situated to the east, away from the main town. When I visited Alan in his whelk shed, I found it used

John Dowsing and 'Diddy' Cooper taking whelks by trolley from the boat (not seen) to the boilery. Wells, 1987. (EDP)

for storing and mending gear. He told me the boilery had only been demolished in recent years. This was a brick compartment housing an old fashioned cast-iron washing copper, which took about two bushels of whelks at a time. It was heated by coal fire, later by diesel burners. Bags of whelks were first washed, then tipped into nets to be cooked. A netful was put into boiling water, brought back to the boil and boiled for a couple of minutes. It was lifted out by pulley. Nets of whelks were plunged in and lifted out in a continuous process. Alan:

> They were tipped out of the nets into one-bushel baskets to cool them off – let them get right cold. Then we had to go back and bag them up. We'd tip two of those baskets into a hessian sack, sew them up, and tie some labels on the sacks with the person's name they're going to. And they'd take them to the train or wherever they're going to. We were doing this until the '70s or '80s. You used to have someone boil for you, so you went home for your dinner for two or three hours, until the whelks got cold. On a cold day they'd stand them outside and get the wind on them, so they cooled quick, so you might go back in an hour and you're done quick. But in summer, it took longer. You couldn't bag them up hot, or they would go off.

In the 1980s, Ivan Large was unusual among the Wells fishermen in boiling his whelks on board. This was in a boiler used for shrimps on his 36ft stern trawler *Remus*. When he got back to Wells he had finished the bulk of the work.

After cooking, the Coopers' whelks would be sent off by lorry or rail:

We didn't need our own transport then. If people wanted whelks they came down
to pick them up themselves. The lorry used to go to Billingsgate, they were Grange's,
a transport business in Wells. Then there was a firm from Fakenham, Duffields. We
used to go to sea on a Thursday and keep the whelks back and go to sea on a Friday,
then they would all go to Billingsgate market to sell. There'd be two great big lorry-
loads going to Billingsgate on a Friday night. On a Friday sometimes we wouldn't
go to sea, there'd been so many whelks! Sometimes if it was not enough whelks,
it was just one lorry-load, or if they were going to Covent Garden they'd put the
whelks on the back and go to whichever drop-off first.

At Billingsgate, that was a market, so you had to take whatever money you got
– no fixed price. Some weeks, it'd go up, some weeks it'd go down. But if you had
your own private customers you had a set price. That's where you would send them
first. They would phone up and say they wanted, say, ten bags of whelks tomorrow
or the next day. That's what we used to do.

For everywhere else – we used to have customers in Nottingham, Birmingham,
Southend, Margate – we used to put them on the train. If you put them on the train
in the morning, they would be there the next morning. People – the fish merchants
– would just go and pick them up from the stations. On the train, they went in the
guard's van. It was a British railways line then. When Wells station was going, it went
to Fakenham, Norwich, and from Norwich I suppose they used to go out from
there. Beeching stopped it, when it went from Wells. If you were sending so many
bags to Joe Bloggs in Birmingham you wrote it down, or eight bags to whoever it
was at Croydon, because it was different prices for different places.

There are two shellfish companies at King's Lynn, Lake's and Williamson's. I was told
that the latter started when EU rules put a stop to the Wells boileries, which were
reckoned not up to European standards. At Williamson's the whelks were processed,
frozen and exported or sent round the country to whelk stalls in seaside places, and
larger outlets in cities, particularly Birmingham and the north:

When the railways finished at Wells there used to be a lorry come down twice a day
from King's Lynn to pick the whelks and everything up – we put them on at the
same time, put them on the back. Then it got down to one a day, then every other
day, then it finished completely.

Alan told me the fishermen did not go to sea on a Sunday, or on a Saturday either
because the lorry did not come through on Saturday to pick them up.

A man called Grick from London had a factory in Wells that processed whelks. It
was where the pub is by the bowling green. We boiled them and took them to him

cooked. His workers pick them out. I think they were frozen, they were for the English market. That was the 70s, early 80s, before we joined the EEC. And years ago Lovelace of Boston used to take the whelks live, but they've finished, and so did Van Smirren, another bloke we used to supply at Boston. I used to supply them cooked to him. He used to pick crabs up (from fishermen along the coast). He'd pick up our whelks, after he'd picked the crabs up.

When we went into the EEC, that stopped us cooking them. It was a lot easier, we just had to bag them up at sea, and when we got alongside the Quay we'd pull them up the quay wall, put them in a lorry – and we'd finished! They would pay so much a ton for them.

Now I take the whelks, live, on my lorry to King's Lynn. They go to Williamson's, the only ones cooking now, Lakes have stopped. Most go to Japan and Korea. They cut the tails off, and only use the heads. They go through cookers, then they're blast frozen – each whelk is frozen separately. Then they go into boxes. Some of them they process and keep for this country, but there are not many whelks sold here – young people go after beef-burgers and things. They used to pick them up, when there were two boats going, the Frarys and us. When Frary finished, years ago when he became cox'n of the lifeboat at Wells, we take them up now.

Alan told me there was no problem keeping whelks live. They would keep two to three days in winter, nearly a week in a chiller. 'They go there in fish boxes. They buy by the kilo now, so when you go to the factory they put them on the scales. It was £460 a ton, but with the Euro now changed I don't know how much they work out at.' Alan told me some fishermen on the South Coast have turned over to whelking. As with most British whelks, these would probably be for the export market.

I asked if any whelks caught off Norfolk are sold locally on the fish stalls. Alan thought it unlikely since cooking them locally, at Wells at least, had stopped. It is now easier for a stallholder to buy a slab of whelks, ready-cooked and frozen, from a processor such as Williamsons, than buy a bag off a boat, employ someone to cook and pick them out, and risk not being able to sell them.

I was curious about earlier 'lost' fishing activity at Wells. Some, like Alan's father and grandfather had gone lining on whelk boats, and before that, on hovellers. His grandfather's generation had gone oystering from Wells. Three dredges like the one displayed in Sheringham Fishermen's Museum, had been dragged from each side at the back of a boat; a small boat had towed one each side. The oyster-dredge was a mat of circular links attached to a metal triangle, with a net to collect the oysters. Oysters would have been brought up on the tide up to the quay as and when wanted and sold.

Alan remembered the Leggetts who came in 1958 from Whitstable with four boats, and later had six, who went mid-water trawling for sprats. Boats also went trawling for skate and cod. He did not recall in his time anyone herring-drifting or lining for cod from Wells as done to the east, but there had been a history of mussel-farming. Mussel lays in the harbour had been worked by Alan's father and grandfather in wintertime, and as a boy Alan had given his father a hand. He later grew mussels at the entrance to the harbour until the sand built up. As the mussel lays in the Quay near where the boats moor have survived, Alan intends to rent one from the harbour Commissioners, the Frary's another one, and put some mussels down. There are still some mussels here in a muddy area from years ago.

The situation now is that a couple of boats which normally go crabbing are trying whelking as well. Alan has sold them some whelk pots. These are two large boats, the *Pathfinder* and the catamaran *Two Brothers*, which are capable of 20 knots, compared with the 7–8 knots of other boats at Wells. They can make twelve-hour or twenty-four-hour trips to way off the Lincolnshire coast.

Now, looking back before he retires from fishing, Alan reckons it has been a good living, having worked hard and put in the hours. His sons have not followed him, although one who is a farm-manager on Holt estate gives him a hand sometimes. Fishermen do not blame the younger generation, as they consider their livelihoods have got harder over the years. Nowadays, buying a new boat could be a risky venture when the returns are uncertain and rules and regulations have become more of an issue.

# Whelking from beach boats

Further along the Norfolk coast to the east of Wells, some fishermen who worked beach-launched boats took to whelking in the winter months. Others went lining instead. This was after the herring season had finished, and it might last until March when crabbing started again. Unlike at Wells where whelking is lingering on, this has now gone.

Sheringham's whelking industry post-war was a shadow of its former self. In the 1970s, when Richard Little of Sheringham went whelking, only two other boats were doing it. Richard told me that although whelks could be caught locally off Sheringham, they were small, so they went to whelk beds 3 miles off Cley, where boats from Wells were also whelking. They worked eastwards off Salthouse, towards Weybourne. It had been a long way to go, and finding good whelks could be hit or miss. With the weather often bad, Richard might only do a dozen trips in a winter. He built a boilery in his garden to cook the whelks, but later took them to 'Downtide' West's boilery behind a fish shop in Cooperative Street, where coppers were hired out to fishermen. 'Downtide' also hired out boats and had contacts for selling on the whelks. Some were picked up by Coles of Lowestoft, who were then paying only 50p for a net of whelks.

I talked to several Cromer fishermen who had gone whelking after the war up until the late 1980s. There was a small revival in the 1970s–80s, following a lull when low returns had not made whelking worthwhile. Like those who had gone

Misty morning at a 'gap' near Bacton, where Cromer fishermen moved their boats to go whelking. Front, Richard Davies's boat *JJ and F.* (Via R. Davies)

lining and herring-catching, most are now retired or approaching retirement age. Some had experienced a good demand for Norfolk whelks, but not always good prices, although things improved if other fishermen along the coast could not get to sea.

## Whelk grounds

Whelks like muddy grounds and are to be found in different areas than crabs. Once located, Richard Davies told me, 'You filled that bit up with pots.' In his grandfather's time, Cromer fishermen had gone westwards to Sheringham Shoal, but whelking from Cromer had not been big like from Sheringham. In his day, post-war, the whelk grounds were to be found the other way, east of Cromer up to 2 miles offshore. These were grounds off Trimingham, Mundesley and Bacton.

Retired fisherman, Dennis Gaff:

When I went to sea there were people with a sail, they used to steam up there for years. Jack Davies had a sail on the *White Rose*. The sail was used for whelking because it's a longer distance to go than for crabbing, to get there and to get home. It'd take the weight off the engine. You'd have the engine running as well, that'd help you.

Bob Cox, also retired, had helped his father during his school holidays. He explained that after the war:

> When we worked from Cromer with my father, we used to use a sail because petrol was rationed. Whelking had not taken off then as it did a few years later. The whelks had died out for a while then restarted in the '50s. That's a good winter's work, providing you've got good weather. But I remember rough weather and pots all tipped up and we got nothing. We baited them up, but they come bad again. We were forever clearing gear and getting nothing out of it! Though sometimes we could do quite well.

Ralph Kirk:

> When I first went, it was with 'Tuna' for three years; we started just off Mundesley and worked 'away' and ended up just off Bacton, that was where all the whelks were at the time. We used to steam from here, Cromer, every day. We only had a little old boat, the *Lewis James*, 'Tuna''s boat, with a petrol engine. First thing in the morning, we'd go down – 'course it'd be frosty because we got frosty days then. The first job was to take the spark plugs out and put them in a handcupful of petrol and set fire to it to warm them up. Then try to get the engine going, because of being petrol there was no self-starters, no putting the key in like they do now. We had a handle in the front like what they used to have on a motor car, that's what we had to start the boat, the boat engines. We'd take turns laying on the engine case to keep warm.

In the 1970–80s whelking became increasingly popular around Bacton and Happisburgh, with fishermen from Cromer steaming there at first daylight. After the North Sea pipeline was laid to come into the gas terminal at Bacton in 1968, this became a particularly good area. John Jonas: 'When we were whelking then, we seemed to get a lot of whelks on the top where the pipeline went ashore. I think the warmth used to draw the whelks to the pipeline – we got some good whelks there, less than a quarter of a mile from the beach.' Even when the pipeline was being built, it was possible to catch whelks near it.

Eventually, boats and tractors were taken to Bacton to be worked from the beach. Dennis Gaff:

> When we went to Bacton, I've seen ten boats up there from Cromer and East Runton. But you couldn't always go to sea, if it was rough. The weather seemed to be rougher than it is now. You got more breezes on your pots then – they'd get knocked about more. Once when I started with six shanks, I got one shank I could use – I'd lost the lot!

Richard Davies added:

> When I started whelking, it was at Bacton. My father didn't bother, he said there wasn't a lot of money in whelking. I'd get a job in wintertime, worm-digging one year, one year I worked as a shepherd, then sprout-picking – I'd not like to go on the dole. Then I rang up Coles of Lowestoft and asked the price of whelks, King's Lynn and somewhere else. It wasn't a bad price, so I told my father I wouldn't mind going. He said, 'You know where the pots are, but I'm not going at my time of life'. So I asked Bob Cox and he said, 'We'll take my boat – got any pots?' So we started whelking, and done alright. Father and them were lining. But we did better, so they came whelking! I finished early to get my gear ready to go back crabbing, but they finished whelking as far as Mundesley and got a nice lot.

Whelks eventually declined at Bacton, and fishermen found the grounds had moved further east, off Sea Palling and Cart Gap. John Jonas last went whelking in 1984, at Sea Palling. Others continued, but by the 1990s whelks became harder to find and eventually whelking was not considered worthwhile. Billy Gaff, who finished in 1990, went even as far as off Waxham, towards Winterton. Some fishermen blamed the decline of the whelks at Bacton on the laying of a new gas pipeline from Holland. John Balls held the view that when the trench had been laid this had chewed up the seabed and the glycol pumped out had produced sediment which had stifled the whelks. Like in a biblical epic, one day the sea had been the colour of milk! Others like Richard Davies reckoned the whelks had been over-fished and the crabs had taken over, eating the spawn. When Ralph Kirk went crabbing towards Bacton, he agreed that the crabs had moved eastwards over the whelk grounds.

Ralph continued:

> Last time I went whelking was with Richard, must have been in the '80s. I went every year, mainly with Richard. That was some of the best times when I went to sea, we had some good laughs. It was hard, though. By the time you got home you got to go and cook them, and bag them up ready to be collected. But it was more of a close-knit lot who went whelking than it was actually on the beach (at Cromer). You had to pick good weather for whelking, and if we didn't go one day, we'd go to the pub at Bacton, knock on the door and he'd let us in – that was way before they thought of twenty-four-hour opening. Sometimes we'd do this at 9 o'clock in the morning!
>
> When we moved to Sea Palling, we drove down every day. In those days there were plenty of whelks about, and five or six boats used to go from there. Sea Palling was a bad beach in those days – it's better now since they had that reef put there. I think there's a brand new ramp at Sea Palling now. It was bad before; sometimes you had to go and get a shovel and shovel some sand to the bottom of the ramp to get the boat down, because the sand would get washed away if there'd been a

tide and a bit of rough weather. Then we moved to Cart Gap, the next one up and worked off there. Cart Gap was a steep one. If it was a frosty morning, we'd get sand and spread it all over the ramp otherwise when you went down with the tractor you'd slide down. I don't think fishermen go from Cart Gap now, though there might be one or two skiffs go off from there.

# Fishing trip

As with crabbing, there was an anchor and dan buoy at each end of a shank. Boats worked typically six shanks of twenty to twenty-five pots. The pots were shot in a line along the sea bed, separated by fifteen fathom tows. A whole shank of pots was hauled into the boat at a time 'dropping with the tide'. Bob Cox:

> The same thing applied to hauling whelk pots as for hauling crab pots. If you had a flood tide, you'd start at the north end. You'd have your engine just ticking over so you stemmed the tide, you might have to make alterations if there's a bit of wind to blow you out. And you'd haul. You couldn't always stop your engine and put it out of gear because the tide'd be running too hard for you to get your pots in. For whelking you never 'underrun'. And you had to be more careful when hauling whelk pots otherwise you would tip them over and spill the whelks out. You shot against the tide when whelking so as to allow a bit of slack on the ropes. If you shot into the tide they'd tighten up and the pot would lay over and you'd not get as many whelks. Its best for them upright and the whelks can go in the top.

Some of the older fishermen remember hand-hauling the pots. A pot weighed about 1½ stone, but when full the weight could double – so pulling up several shanks of these in winter seas was strenuous work. In the days before motor boats, whelking trips must have been even more exhausting. In his first year Richard Davies handhauled, 'Yes it was hard work, but not if it was full – if its 'cauliflowering' – then you're earning something!' Ralph:

> The first time I was hand-hauling with 'Tuna', and I'd haul behind him. When the pot came I'd lift the pot up, pull the crinny out, turn the pot upside down and shake it into a ped (basket). Then give it to the chap baiting up. The last year I went to sea I hauled in front and Brian Lee hauled behind me because he had only just come out of the RAF and he had to learn. Then when I went with Richard, there'd be Richard hauling, I'd shoot and Donny used to bait up. You tried to keep your boat virtually on top of your gear, so you didn't tip your pots over and the whelks all come out. If you couldn't get the throttle running low enough, you used to put a board between the stern post and the pintle. That'd slow her down, and keep her as you wanted.

Whelks find crab very tasty, and can suck all the meat out, leaving just the shell. Crab had once been used as bait by beach fishermen. Later, as at Wells, oddments of herrings bought from the smokehouses at Yarmouth became usual. I was told these were substandard herrings from the bottom of brine pits when emptied out or red herring that had fallen into sawdust at the bottom of the smoke-room. Richard Davies mentioned one agent would buy herring, salt it and send it through to fishermen along the Norfolk coast, although he regarded it as too salty and preferred to get his own bait from Yarmouth. Donny Lawrence:

> We used the Scottish herrings then – you know, the big ones. They had been salted down fresh in barrels, and when they got to Great Yarmouth they were tipped into brine pits for twenty-four hours and taken out and put on poles (speets) in the smokehouse. If the gills were broken and they couldn't smoke them they were chucked to one side and sold to us. When we went we had the herring ban on – but in Scotland they were still doing it, so we got their herring. I think there was the foreign herring at Yarmouth as well.

Cousin Ralph:

> Had a laugh one day, a steam boat came down. He said, 'What you got – have you got some fish?' We said, 'Yes, we got a few fish,' which we had. 'So,' he said, 'Can I have some?' and sent us down a bottle of whiskey and some cigs. We sent up a bucket of red herring. 'O lovely!' he said. Well you *can* eat them, but they're ever so salty! Soaked in salt and dried.

Hermit crabs which are found with whelks are thrown out of the pots when the pots are 'shigged', or emptied. Other than this, there is less sorting by eye on the boat, so some fishermen have said they preferred whelking to crabbing. John Balls described what happened on the boat:

> The pot was upturned and shaken into a measure – a level ped, or basket, which will take four or five stone weight, then you tip that into a net or a sack. The whelks are riddled, the small ones put back. If they are to be sold live, the sack is to be transported. If to be cooked they're shot into a net – then the net had a particular measure in. When you finished hauling, you manhandled the nets one at a time over the side to take the mud off the shells, as you steamed back home. Then they were taken to the shed to be cooked.

The riddling was done with a hand sieve, as at Wells. Riddling became important, particularly when the workers at Van Smirren's factory at Boston complained they were getting too many small whelks and they weren't making enough money. Donny Lawrence, who worked with Richard Davies, remembered riddling whelks on

Cromer promenade and taking bags of small ones back to the whelk grounds the next day to be shot back into the sea. Billy Gaff:

> Anything above fifteen bags was a good day's work. On good days you'd get twenty to thirty bags, perhaps forty. The best trip I had was in the *Sally Elizabeth*, when I had forty-two bags of whelks. That's a lot of weight on a 20ft crab boat! We used to lay the bags in the bottom of the boat and spread the weight about evenly, because the boat could become unstable with a lot of weight in.

Donny Lawrence added:

> The bows of the boat would come up a bit, but it was safe. We'd tie the bags up, lay them on the boards where the man was hauling, jump on top of them to level them out flat – that's how we used to stack them. When we hauled the pots, we'd lay the pots on top of the bags.

Hauling and shooting pots from an open crab boat pitching about in the winter seas was not for the faint-hearted. Ralph described a particularly bad trip when he and Donny had gone with Richard in a small crab boat, only 19ft long:

> We were in the *Young Fisherman*, it had a little old Vedette (engine) which'd go pup-pup-pup, with a hand pump, no bilge pump. We went off one day, and it got bad, started to chip up. We had forty-five bags of whelks, had them spread out all over the boat. And we came to the last shank, and we hauled it. Dick and the others had finished and were on their way home. Got it into the boat, and Richard thought, 'I'll shoot this with the tide', and normally you don't, you shoot against. And we were really ploughing into it! My cousin Donny who was for'ard, he'd chuck the pots over – we couldn't see him half the time the water was coming over, solid green water coming over the bows! And I was on the pump pumping steadily away, all the way to the beach. When we got ashore Dick and them thought we were going to sink. But we had all these whelks, and we were laughing and joking about it all the while.

Donny, who had been baiting up and setting in the pots, added:

> We were about a mile off. Richard was steering the boat, and every time the sea broke over her head I couldn't see Richard for water! All the pots were in front of me – I was picking a pot up and was counting till I was getting near to the tow of the next pot, then I'd just cop it over and hope for the best. Then I'd count to say twenty again and cop the next one over, count to twenty and cop the next one over. Poor Ralph never got a chance to stop pumping; there was that much water coming in! The water was coming through the orrock holes. The weather was so

bad – 'thick'! We shouldn't have gone that day. But when we went next day the pots were chock-a-block full of whelks – it was unbelievable!

Thick fog could descend quickly, making it difficult to find the gear. Ralph Kirk recalled on one occasion he and Richard Davies had set off three times using a pocket watch to time their way to their gear; they had failed each time, and only came across it by chance when giving up and going home. The visibility was so poor they could not find the correct spot on Cromer beach to bring the boat ashore. When they got close to the shore, Ralph had jumped out and shouted to those in the boat where to beach it:

But when I look round they'd gone the *other* way! So I scrambled up the beach, and we had an old Field Marshall tractor, with a big old fly wheel. So I thought I'll get that started and they'll hear that crack out. You're supposed to use a bit of paper, put it in the tube and screw that back in, then swing the handle. But I didn't have any paper, so I used a bit of cigarette end. Bang she went, and they came back! I said 'Are you two deaf?' Richard said it was Donny's fault, 'he'd said *that* way!'

Sometimes fierce winter gales played havoc with the gear, knocking pots about on the seabed. Ralph recalled whole shanks ending up as tangled lumps, which had to be pulled aboard and sorted out.

John Davies, Richard's son, is a full-time crab fisherman today, but had done a spot of whelking in his youth:

I didn't mind whelking, but it wasn't my favourite thing. If you've not been able to get to sea for a while, your pots would get full of blinking mud. And it was *cold*. I remember one day we had to shovel the snow out of the boat before we went! We got off, and cleared a certain amount of gear. Only ourselves and John Jonas was working there. The next thing John Jonas came off, and they were throwing snowballs at us as we went past! On that day they came ashore a lot later than us, and we'd been waiting in the pub for them. They were that cold, shaking like a leaf. We had the last laugh! And we did much better than they did.

## Processing and selling

The whelks caught from beach boats were sold live or cooked. Boiling was small-scale, and as with crabs often carried out in sheds round the backs of houses. This had to take place soon after the fishermen returned. Ralph told me they had once come back from fishing late and left the cooking until the next day. By then some were dead and the smell was so appalling, they had to dump the lot.

Willy Cox and Richard Davies boiled their whelks in sheds at the back of Garden Street in Cromer. If not washed on the way home, they would first be washed in tubs.

Peter Mayes and John'o Lee return from a whelk trip. Cromer, 1954. (EDP)

Billy Davies and Richard Davies hoisting whelks in and out of the boiler. Cromer, 1970. (EDP)

The copper had been lit by Richard's father Jack Davies, who would look out from the cliff top for boat sails so he knew approximately when the boats would return. The Davieses used a large cast-iron cauldron, which had been made to cook up pig swill. It was heated by a coal fire. Other boileries were like those at Wells: coppers set in brick surrounds heated by coal fire or a cast-iron bath heated by oil-fired burner. Later, the boilers were obtained from school kitchens, the same type as used for cooking crabs, and heated by propane gas which made the operation faster. The washed whelks would be boiled in their nets which had been made by the fishermen with a tie at the top. The whelks were then 'stood off' in peds to cool, but not left outside exposed to rain or they would go sour. Donny: 'They were then put in onion or potato sacks and picked up later that day for sale. John Jonas used to help us round at the shed – John and I would eat a whole pail full of whelks, and bigger they were the better – gorgeous!' Donny, who is now retired, still goes round to John's shop to get his weekly supply of whelks, which these days come from the South Coast or Ireland.

As with crabs and fish, Cromer fishermen marketed their whelks independently of each other. Cooked ones were delivered to local fish shops, travelling as far as Norwich and Yarmouth. John Jonas's father Reggie had a local fish round, so could sell direct to the consumer:

Dick Davies and Peter Mayes cooling off whelks after cooking. Cromer, 1954. (EDP)

People would come out of their houses with bowls and saucepans, and father would measure a gallon, some of them would have two gallons, and he'd shoot them in. All the whelks, mussels, etc, years ago, all were measured. Now they weigh them.

Richard Davies, a generation later:

> Mostly I'd be cooking mine and sending them away. My wife Julie used to deliver them, to Norwich (station) with the car and trailer. It was the time of the miniskirt. The old boys would come out and load them for her and put them on the rail. If it had been me, I'd not have seen anyone! My whelks went to King's Lynn or London to Billingsgate market – it was later to King's Lynn, the processing factory. A fellow from London came every weekend and picked a couple of ton up. They were all edible, though we'd sell a few for lining – if 'Shrimp' was lining or Dennis, we'd let them have a few bags.

Richard recalled there was never much money in whelks; in 1970 a large net of whelks would sell in London for 25–30s (£1.25–1.50). Set against this were the investment in time and labour, the costs of fuel for the boat and boilers, the rail fare and making and maintaining the gear.

Several fishermen mentioned that their uncooked whelks were picked up by Van Smirren from Boston, who came at other times to pick up their crabs. Billy Gaff:

> You hoped to sell as many as possible live to different merchants. A chap from Boston, Lovelace, would turn up in the late afternoon after we'd finished, he'd take them live most of the time. He'd take them back to be processed, that's boiled and picked out, and sent them down to London and elsewhere. He bought by weight. I didn't keep any back for bait for lining – if we were whelking, we kept to whelking, and never bothered to go after cod. Whelking was enough to deal with!

Others sent live whelks to the processing factories at Wells or to King's Lynn, where they were picked out and frozen, mostly for the export market One of the fishermen, Andy Roper, transported them over to Belgium for a time. Some fishermen, like Bob Cox, delivered cooked whelks to the agent Cole of Lowestoft.

# Gear

The pots used at this time had iron frames wound round with rope, and heavy perforated metal bases to help sink them to the sea bottom. The pots had to be very durable to withstand a battering in the wintry seas. The design, perhaps adapted from the inkwell type of crab pot, was simple, but it was effective in drawing in the whelks and not letting them escape. Several shanks were a costly investment. I was told the cast-iron bottoms were bought at a foundry at Walsingham or at Tharston on the other side of Norwich, and for Cromer fishermen, blacksmith Andy Wilson at Gresham would weld on the iron bars of the frame and put the ring on the top. Like a crab pot, a whelk pot had a crinny at the entrance and cords which secured the bait with a 'button'. The crinny had a finer mesh than for a crab pot. A big loop of rope attached to the top of the pot rather like a handle was called the strop; this was joined to the tow which linked the pot to the next pot.

In the days before synthetic materials, the rope would only last two or three months, so had to be tarred. Donny described preparing a pot:

> I did the roping. You tied a rope to a first bow, go round and round the pot and hammered it down so it went tight, then went on again so you got to the top, hammer it down again, then finish it off and tied it. Old rope came in handy, old tows from crab pots were used for whelk pots. I have a letter from the council – I was sitting in my shed hammering, and my neighbour complained it made things rattle on his mantlepiece! Then you put in a bait bar, like for a crab pot, but it went lengthways, that far from the bottom of the pot. Then you'd braid a little crinny that length, and tie that round the top ring. Then when that was finished you put a strop on, and the whelk pot is finished. Then you put it in the tar. The pots were tarred, so that whelks could slide up them easier and drop into the pots, and it'd protected the rope which was tied round. In the Davies's shed, we used to do tarring and everything in there. There was a big room where they used to do the pots, but there was a dipping tank for the ropes and all. It was used for dipping the whelk pots, once they were roped up. With a big old glove on, you dunked the pots up and down in the tar. A horrible job. You took them out and you'd hang them, or had a piece of corrugated iron on a slope so the tar would drain and go back into the tank. Then you put them out in the sun; and stacked them in the shed so they were ready for next season. You tarred them every season. Some would get damaged, so then you had to knock the rope off and re-rope them.

The tarring was done in the summer, the hot weather helping to make the tar runny. In the late 1970s or early 1980s, two fishermen had a go at whelking using crab pots off Cromer beach, when the others went off to Bacton. They adapted some crab pots, roping them up like whelk pots. Richard Davies:

> We done alright on one little spot. It took me a couple to three months to find them, and as soon as I hit them everyone else wanted to go. I didn't let Willy get on there much! We disguised it once, so it weren't clear where the whelks were. We put other 'pots' in – only they weren't pots they were just buoys! So when he went there, we just went off and found ours!

Many of the beach fishermen now regard whelking as finished. Richard's son, John Davies tried a few years ago, and got a few whelks, but it is generally believed that

Arthur Coe with beam trawl holding the 'cod end' of the net containing shrimps. Bacton, 1982. (EDP)

crabs have taken over the whelk grounds. In view of the uncertainties, they believe it is best to stick to crabbing.

## Shrimping

Not too far away is the big shrimping industry at King's Lynn, where boats fish in the Wash. In contrast, and cottage-industry style, some North Norfolk fishermen went shrimp trawling in the period when they 'had a go at everything'. This was with a small beam trawl, which had a net with bag-like 'cod end'. Trawling was close to shore on sandy ground, such as at Mundesley and Bacton.

John Davies:

We went shrimping wintertime, autumn – when we weren't so busy. If we were up at Bacton whelking, we'd sometimes take a shrimp trawl. You'd drag a trawl behind you, virtually scraping the beach. It would not get caught up too much, because we went on what's called the Bank, on what we knew we could work on. Father done quite a bit. We've done OK at times when shrimps been there. Yes, we used to cook them, at home. With Father in the *JJ and F*, we had a boiler on board and cooked them on board, gas bottle and a little boiler. I didn't mind that, because you could eat lovely hot shrimps all day. You'd cool them down and bag them up. We'd sell the shrimps to King's Lynn where everybody brought them. Then *they* thought, 'Where you getting these from?' and all the boats from King's Lynn came down there as well, and that cleared it right out, so that finished it for us!

John Jonas, who sells shellfish in his shop, and had once gone shrimping, told me some of the fishermen's shrimps had been sold locally. Demands had changed over the years, from brown shrimps to pink shrimps, and back to brown again. The more flavoursome browns, as once caught here, are now worth more money, and selling well abroad.

Ivan Large recalled shrimping from Wells harbour:

The Wash, that's where we used to catch them. Some off Blakeney Point as well. The *Remus* had a cooker on board. After you had one trawl you were busy all the while until you got home again. Out in the morning, in at night. I'd perhaps boil them when I got in at Wells, but I've got in at 8 o'clock, and still be boiling up at midnight. We had a lorry stand up by the whelk houses, he had a generator going to keep them cool all the while. He'd fill it up with whelks and shrimps, and twice a week go to London, for Billingsgate market. No-one shrimps from Wells now, there's too many pots about. Trawls and whelk pots don't mix.

End note:
1. Some Sheringham fishermen had gone further, to Grimsby to work the Humber fishing grounds. This included the Coxes, a big fishing family with branches along the Norfolk coast.

# CHAPTER 9

# ALIVE, ALIVE O!

## Mussels

Basking at the quays in King's Lynn are large fishing vessels, draped with huge nets and dredges. These are the boats which go off on long fishing trips, shrimping, cockling and musseling in the Wash. Mussels are dredged from the sea bed here on an industrial scale, but to the east of Wells, musseling is very different – it is small-scale and very traditional. It has dwindled considerably over the years, but still going strong is a doughty threesome of fishermen who grow their mussels in Blakeney Harbour. They do their onshore work at Stiffkey Freshes, where the Stiffkey river joins a creek leading to the harbour. The fishermen like the peace and quiet here, away from the 'hurly-burly' of Morston quay, which is a place to embark on boat-trips to see the nearby seal colonies and a magnet for visitors. With only the birds calling, the gentle lapping of the river, and the occasional walker strolling past, the Stiffkey creek is a haven of tranquility. John Webster works here with John Dowsing and Mark Randell, each working independently. It was on a damp and overcast November day that I tramped across a boggy path from Morston to watch them at work.

John was busy riddling and sorting the mussels which had been collected, or 'harvested', earlier. The mussels were spread out in a shallow heap by the riverside and there was another big heap loose in John's small boat. There was quiet banter and joking with the other mussel fishermen. Another local man, John Green, who was leaning on his bicycle, joined in to pass the time of day before setting off with his net-rake to go after winkles. The work at the riverside would go on until dusk, when it became difficult to see. This was typical of most days in the mussel season from September until March. Other days were taken up delivering mussels.

I watched as each net of mussels was emptied into a wire basket – now difficult to get hold of as they have been replaced by plastic ones which are not so good. The basket was put into the river and waggled about and given a bit of a thumping by foot, or 'jamming', as it is called. This is to break up the clumps of mussels and to rub off some of the debris and barnacles. The basket-load was then taken to the 'workbench' standing just clear of the muddy edge of the river. This is two upturned fish-boxes with a mesh scraper at the top, on one side. The mussels were poured into a sieve, and given a few shakes to let the small ones fall through into a fish box. The

A November day at Stiffkey Freshes, John Webster at his workbench. The 'mussel flat' alongside is used to bring mussels back from the lays. 2008.

John riddling mussels at the water's edge.

sieve was then put on the workbench and the mussels sorted by eye – and by ear. The best ones are fat with pointed ends, in other words full of meat. John listens carefully; any giving a hollow sound as they are moved about are removed. Ones with barnacles on are given a quick knock or scrape on the patent mesh scraper. The good ones are put in a bucket, which is also a measure, then 'shot' into bags. One by one net-loads of mussels are jammed, riddled and checked. It is a long day's work, and the fishermen get stuck in.

John Webster has little time to himself, but after making a delivery in Cromer, one cold December day he called round to talk about his work. It was a revelation to me, as I expect it is to most people, to hear of the long hours and often arduous conditions fishermen endure in order that we might tuck into a nice plate of mussels. I have included much of John's account below because of the unusual nature of traditional musseling. It also has a rarity value in the immediate area because several local fishermen who had once worked mussel lays in Blakeney Harbour, bringing them to be sorted on Morston and Blakeney Quays, have either left, or like John's father, died. Their abandoned lays have been brought back to life by John and his associates.

# Riddling

John prefers riddling by hand with a sieve to using a machine:

> It's very traditional by hand. It takes several hours. The tide's up then you go home, but I do forty nets a week, or do ten to fifteen in a day. When you've had enough you go home. It is extremely physical, so you pace yourself as to how many are to be done. When you gather them from the lays, you bring them here loose in the boat. They're thrown out onto the quayside here and spread out thinly like we have in the mussel lays – bearing in mind the tide comes up here twice a day, so they have a drink. So it's a temporary mussel lay. You can drive up close, get out, sort and riddle them, otherwise, if they're down at the mussel lays you can't get at them – only for a two-hour window a day.
>
> When you riddle, you drop some mussels through, then as you tip the riddle up and view them in the riddle – if you hear a 'clocking' noise, that means a mussel with a broken shell and I'll throw it out. A chef might not notice and it'll get on someone's plate of mussels! So quality control you do yourself. The size is up to 1½ to 2½in. Ideally, there is a minimum size, but if you have a 'Several Order' (restricted rights) on your harbour you can sell what size you want, but you'd be foolish if they were too small, you would cut your own throat.

Small mussels might be acceptable abroad, but not to the English customer; they will be returned to the lays to let them grow bigger. The sieves like virtually everything used are hand-made: a circle of marine ply inset with a grid of wires ¾in apart. John has inherited his father's but has stocked up on more from an old boy who lives near the Wash who makes them:

> You *can* gather mussels out of the sea if you've got a big boat and a dredge, but they probably won't be as fat out at sea as in here. In the marsh and the creeks – there's hundreds of them – the seaweed washes up and rots down and filters down all those nutrients from decaying matter up there, makes its way down on the ebb tide, as food for shell fish. You can't create it. It's a natural basin to collect all the organic matter which is coming down here.

I asked John about the riddling machines at Brancaster, a variety of eccentric devices I had seen next to the fishermen's sheds. They are based on the principle of a turning drum with grilles. John:

> The first chap who used one for mussels had seen farm machinery (for sorting carrots). You can buy them now, firms do make them. But years ago, blacksmiths made them. You would go to him and tell him what you want. All the old boys had blacksmiths make them. One chap from Stiffkey, Alan Pells, he did mussels, a very clever chap, there was nothing he couldn't do, he designed his own completely – draw the plans, got the metal and made it. But it depends if you're mechanically minded.

John Dowsing had made a riddler powered by a lawnmower engine which was at his premises, while Mark Randell hand-riddles at present, but was bringing his own home-made machine to the site later.

# Boats

The small boats used to carry the heavy loads back from the lays in Blakeney Harbour are flat bottomed and transom-sterned. John refers to his small GRP boat as a 'mussel flat'; in former times wooden boats with the unlikely name of 'canoes' were used, built by Brett's of Cley. Authors Catling and Malster claim the type goes back to the 1860s or earlier. There seems to have been a tradition of making them oneself. John's mussel flat, the *Lust for Life*, had been made by his father by cutting up a smaller boat in two and extending it in length and width and encasing the whole thing with layers of GRP. John Green's father Philip had also made his own canoe.

Bigger boats were used for taking seed mussels out to the lays in mid-year. The traditional boats used by mussel-men were 'oysters'; one can still be seen at Brancaster. Now they are GRP, made by Hewitts' boatyard not far away. John uses a 17½ft GRP 'oyster', which was moored near to where he riddled.

# Harvesting

From October to March the mussel-fishermen are intensively harvesting and selling the mussels, working long hours. Harvesting is in chest-waders, as the water is up to waist height. When setting out to the lays John walks the *Lust for Life* down the winding river Stiffkey to the deeper water of Blakeney Harbour, where it is punted by oar across a wide channel to the mussel lays. I had occasion to accompany him on a bright and sunny September day and – admittedly, in optimum conditions – was struck by the poetic beauty of the spot. Stiffkey could be seen in strips of pale greens and yellows in the distance, and the fishermen's trucks were just specks three-quarters of a mile away. There was a sense of tranquility and silence only broken by the 'br...nt' murmurings of a flock of brent geese. When we got to a place called Simpool, I could see a carpet of mussels under 2 or 3ft of fast flowing water at the edge of the channel. John has two mussel lays here, close together. One is about 100 yards by 300 yards, the other is smaller.

The implements used to collect the mussels are traditional to the area. John used a 'wim', basically a D-shaped frame with a net at the end of a long pole. This was waggled into the mud to scoop up mussels into the boat, the tide going through the net at the same time. The bar of the 'D' has teeth welded on. These become worn after a while, 'but we are one step ahead now – they're stainless steel!' Years ago the frames were made by a blacksmith, but fishermen with metal-working skills now make them.

A small hand-held version of the wim is used with a rake where mussels are not under water all the time. John might use one to collect seed mussels if they settle in the harbour (see below), but they are mostly used by Brancaster fishermen to the west, and by the 'hand-workers' in the Wash, who sit a boat at low tide in the mud and jump out to gather them. Formerly the D-shaped frame was a curved piece of willow with a length of twine across, now it is a 'D door' from a parlour pot . A net is laced onto this.

John explained about the area where he worked:

> You're not allowed to go in it (Blakeney Harbour) with a boat and dredge. That's a rule laid down by the Several Order and environmental groups, English Nature; it's very strict what you can do. From Kelling right up to the Wash it's a European-designated area of conservation. You can't do what you used to years ago. But I agree with the rules, about not dredging there – some people in the Wash would take everything if they could. But it depends on what life you lead, if you care or just in it for the money and if it's buggered up you can do something else. But I was born and bred into fishing and I would like to see my life out so when someone comes along after me, I've left something there, like most blokes round here. Because it's a fairly traditional way of life.

John using the wim to collect mussels at the lays in Blakeney Harbour. October 2009.

John scooping up the mussels.

John Dowsing demonstrates a mussel rake and D-shaped net for collecting mussels not under water. Bags of mussels have been brought back from the Freshes to go in a purification tank. Stiffkey village, 2008.

I asked if there was an off-season:

> At the end of the harvesting-selling season, end of March, April, you move any heaps which are out of the water, from what's not sold that winter – sort them out a bit, get the lays ready for end of May, June. You're working hard. May, June, July lay your mussels, then there's nothing else you can do. Deep breath. So August, September we're more relaxed.

## The seed

Once I accompanied the mussel fishermen when they were going back and forth to the lays with loads of 'seed', or small, mussels. The boat was well down in the water as it made its way to an area marked with floats. Quickly they shovelled the heap over the side, then returned to get another load.

Getting and laying the seed is a very tense time for John and his fellow fishermen, especially if it comes by road. There is a time limit between collecting and setting it in the lays. John:

Delivery of seed mussels is in May, otherwise June, July, August. It takes eight hours from Wales. You're worrying about it all the while. If the weather turns warm, £2–3,000 worth of seed mussels in the lorry could go bad. You've got one, possibly two days, but they will be dying all the while. They usually bring 23 tons in 1-ton bags on the lorry. We might lose a few kilos if it's hot or there's a breakdown on the way, or we could lose a few ton! But once here, ideally you want to get them laid down in twenty-four hours. The lorry has a small crane and lifts them off. Job's done. Twenty bags sitting there. We have a friend in the village with a JCB digger, we pay him and he spends one or two days lifting them about, otherwise we can't move them. He lifts each bag over the boat, you pull a cord and the mussels fall into the boat. We help one another and get them laid. All hands to the pump!

You're clock-watching all the time. Tide and time wait for no man! If the tide is 6a.m., we can leave the quay at 4 o'clock, so there is a couple of hours until high water, and got more than another hour on the ebb tide, so we've probably got three hours. In June, when there are double tides, at about 6a.m. and in the evening, 11 tons are taken to the lays in the morning, 11 tons in the evening. The job's done, but you certainly know you've done it!

Besides Wales, the seed can also come from the South Coast, or depend on contacts around the country. More conveniently, it comes from the Wash. John:

It's brought in by sea, guys with big boats will dredge them there, and wash them off on deck of the boat with a big hose. It's down to a good skipper, you want mussels in this 'box' marked out with floats, he will come up, nose into the tide, and spray them over the side into this area, go up and down, up and down. They'll settle themselves down, and you'll go down the next day at low tide and make sure they're not too thick in some areas, and using a wim or a fork depending on the depth of water spread them around a bit.

I asked about seed obtained from hand-workers in the Wash. John:

They fill the boat up in 28-kilogram sacks, come alongside the docks at King's Lynn where I drive with my truck and they load their bags on my truck. If they have a surplus of seed they will look to sell it, if not they will keep it for themselves, so then we go elsewhere where there is a surplus. The internet guys advertise seed mussels. Every year – if you miss a year you've had it. It's a continuous growing-on thing.

Up to ten to fifteen years ago the seed could be obtained locally:

You can have an area in Blakeney Harbour which suddenly becomes full of tiny little seed mussels. Mussels spawn but it is a lottery where the spawn goes. More often than not it goes out to sea and we never see it again. But if it settles in the harbour, at low tide you will go down and net-and-rake them, and take your nets to your small dinghy, and fill it up.

I asked how fishermen before him would have got their seed mussels. John thought they got it from the Wash by hoveller, another type of boat:

> If I had the 30ft boat, I would go up to the Wash, providing I had permission from Eastern Sea Fisheries to go there – got to do the paperwork – and dredge mussels or hand-work them, and fill my boat up and go back to sea, and re-lay them in Blakeney Harbour. You have the cost of running the boat, with the licensing that goes with it. I find it easier to buy the seed mussels from someone with a bigger boat. Once I pay them, that's it, I don't have to worry about maintaining the boat and all that goes with it.

## Managing the lays

> If you lay mussels one year you don't sell them from there the next year, but the following year. So you get to have different areas. So when you take a patch out here – mature mussels ready for the table – you then have a clear block which that springtime when you buy the new seed in – that's the area you then fill up again. So it's an ongoing, rotating thing. Ideally the lays are covered in water all the time, so you can produce a good product in a short space of time. If they're out of water they're not growing. There needs to be a hard shingle base. Mussels have a 'beard' which they quickly attach onto the shingle so they're not washed away by the tide. They knit together in clumps on the base.
>
> You have to loosen all this mud that gets underneath them. Each twelve months they're down – they're going to be down two years – they make about 1ft of mud underneath them, detritus, shit, what they filter out. Some will wash away but you need to get in there with a fork to loosen it up, so that on the big tides it scours away and back down to a shingle base again.

The mussel fork is like a potato fork, with tines close together and bobbles on the end, so they do not spear the mussels. It is slightly bent in the middle so that the fisherman can lift a good load of mussels:

> You could take an area out, load it into the dinghy and spread it on a fresh piece of ground. You have to be careful when you start getting them, and distributing these 'mats' of mussels. They're quite tough to pull apart. But you're careful when you're doing this because a big tide might get in amongst them and rip the whole lot away. You could find a mat which might roll back when taking that patch out. If a patch is not that big and you can collect a whole patch in one tide, that's ideally what you

want to do. There's skill and thought have to go in when you gather them. You have to think it through, but you still might get disasters.

As for predators, John told me these were oyster-catchers and gulls. Starfish can decimate a bed of mussels very quickly, but do not come into the harbour. Cold weather does not prevent the fishermen from harvesting. Even with ice in the creeks, riddling goes on as usual:

Snow is not a problem, only if I can't drive to get down there. Whatever the weather I'm down there – three pairs of socks, thick trousers, long johns, quilted anorak, oilskins, chest-waders – almost too hot! Just keep the wind off your hands, you wear gloves.

Danger? Not really. You're out there four to five hours, depending. Different times of the year there are different volumes of water. If it's a small tide not so much water comes in the harbour, but with a big tide it's colossal, it comes in like a torrent. Sometimes only part of the marsh disappears, sometimes the whole lot disappears like it never existed – gone! Spring, January, February it's bad. If you have a small tide which runs quite slowly, if you have a north-west wind and the tide is heading out in a north-westerly direction, on the ebb, it's not so difficult to stop the tide. This wind will eventually stop it from going out. Whereas on a big tide, even if there's a north-westerly wind, there's that much volume of water it will go out regardless. Small tide, it will have an effect. You'll find where the mussel lays are, if that wind, say, is 30 miles an hour, is funnelling in *here,* that bottlenecks the water up here – it will hold it in. We're stuffed then, we can't get in.

Storms can move sand about, can scour it out; its swings and roundabouts. At the moment it's in a dodgy phase, as there is a lot more sand about. My lays are not that stable, sand builds up. In the spring, when there's clear water I'll be able to see what's happening.

# Selling

The North Norfolk mussel fishermen like to sell as directly as possible to the public. For visitors it is a plus being able to buy a bagful of mussels within sight of the sea. All along the Norfolk coast there are small outlets at the side of the road, some in delightful flint cottages like Mr Bean's in Morston. I am told 85–90 per cent of the mussels stay in the region. A gentleman's agreement once a year between John and his two associates seals the selling price.

John has two delivery days a week, when he drives his mussels to Cromer and Sheringham fish shops, and local pubs and restaurants. He also sells to a local shellfish-merchant and to an agent who comes up from Weymouth with fish. Mussels grown in Blakeney Harbour, being under water all the time, have the reputation of being top of the range, big fat mussels. If there are a few days between harvesting and delivering, the mussels are kept under a wet sack or put in a cold store. John told me there is a big demand for mussels in Holland since its mussel-growing areas were turned over to conservation and wildlife. Perhaps selling abroad might be another outlet. He has never been tempted to cook them because of all the regulations that go with it:

> In the old days, mussels were put in hundredweight, or six-peck sacks as they were known then. Some went to local fish and chip shops, and fish shops like Coxes in Cromer or Scotters of Sheringham. Quite a lot of mussels went to the Midlands by rail or lorry other times. A large amount went to Leicester or Nottingham. Billingsgate, no. The Midlands shellfish merchants, they used to come to the harbour, they'd know we had big mussels, and used to outbid anyone else, plus they had the connections. A couple of guys had Seafresh at Cromer, they were processors. They'd buy a lot, cook them and jar them. At Wells, there was a place called Grick's, a processing factory for whelks and mussels – quite a lot were done there once.

In the last ten years it has been required by law that mussels go through a purification process before being put on the market. A purification tank in Stiffkey is used by all three fishermen. They regard the process as unnecessary as the water washing round the mussel lays has tested pure. Premises have to be inspected, and it all makes for more paperwork: 'It's a pain in the backside! It doesn't increase the value, and doing it is labour-intensive. But you just have to bite the bullet and absorb the cost.'

For mussel fishermen in the Wash the last stages of their work are handled by a factory. John admits it would be easier to take the mussels to John Williamson's factory in King's Lynn where they can be purified, packaged and distributed, but like all the fishermen in North Norfolk I have spoken to, he likes to be in control of his product from beginning to end: 'That's the way we are! Better the way it is – a niche market. It's a hassle, but I've got a living and it's interesting and varied.' John speculated that a co-operative would only work if Stiffkey and Brancaster fishermen further along the coast got together to set the prices and controlled their own factory, but was not optimistic this would ever happen.

# Recent past

> Basically it was a free for all until they put a Several Order on – there could be fisticuffs about it! There was no written law. With a Several Order, you lease the land from the Crown Estate – it's all marked on the map what the acreage is. Then you belong to the Blakeney Harbour Mussel Society as well. That's what was done originally. That's when father helped one of the guys, later when the chap died father took it on. But unfortunately a lot of the guys died off, and the mussel industry

took a turn for the worse because it all silted up with sand. Virtually all the mussels'd finished. Originally there must have been eight or nine people then, and various people who'd help at weekends and when they were busy – help riddle and grade them. It was quite a big industry then. That's when they used to send quite a big lorry up to Leicester and Nottingham. They were like the working man's food in those days. When the lays silted up, father had to go back to what he'd done before, which was bait-digging. But there was several years when not much was happening in Blakeney Harbour at all.

John went on to describe how he took up musseling. This was to change from bait-digging which he had done as a youngster to help his father. All the lays in the harbour had silted up, except those of one old fisherman who kept going until he retired. When John got going, he was able to take over his customers:

I remember seeing the lays opened up – not silted up anymore, and I was reading how mussels were up and coming, and pubs going upmarket. As the lays start to open up more, and we got a natural big settlement of seed mussels in the harbour, Major Athill (shellfish merchant) suggested to father we go into it. We started up again. I worked some lays my father used, that is fifteen years before. I gathered local seed and laid it down. It was two years of pretty hard work and money into it for nothing, then once you've got started, it accelerated pretty quickly. But there's only a small area suitable to grow them – so you can't get *more* people on, or expand – there is either moorings in there or more sand. So that regulates what you can do.

So now there is a 'second coming' for Blakeney Harbour! It's due to restaurants and pubs which weren't there years ago. It's *moules mariniere* now! The old boys would have looked at you forty years ago and said, 'What are you on about, boy?!' They had mussels after half a dozen pints of beer with vinegar and pepper and a lump of bread. Since twenty-plus years, people go on holiday, find fancy food and want it here. Have to thank the French for something! That has opened up a new market.

# The future

Away from the hustle and bustle of town life, the work at Freshes Creek – preparing the lays, harvesting and selling – might give an impression of being timeless and hassle-free. But getting the seed mussels every year, together with the threat that the site might silt up or become smothered by sand, are persistent worries. Plus, there are rules and paperwork which earlier fishermen did not even dream of. In his younger days John told me he had 'had words' with officialdom but has since calmed down. Fishermen have had to become increasingly aware of the wider picture and how it might affect their livelihoods. Views might change, for instance, on how the marshes are managed. If it was decided that they should go 'natural' this would threaten mussel-farming, and even samphire-collecting:

> All the way along the coast, it's a European-designated site, you can and can't do
> things – but if oil is found, forget seals and terns, they'll be in there! We'd have
> to throw the towel in. We'd lobby, but they would do it. As you get older, you
> become more aware of the threats. The herring guys thought their jobs were safe,
> then puff!

In addition, there is a belief among some Norfolk fishermen that the Government would prefer to have a few centralised depots to deal with than a lot of 'little people'.

In spite of all this, it is clear John enjoys his way of life:

> Yes, you get a bit crotchety as you get older because you can't do what you used to
> do. This year I've cut down on production. It's very manual. If you do forty nets a
> week, that's OK, if fifty-plus, that's a lot. If twenty, I could do that easily, lovely. Got
> to pace yourself, take your foot off the pedal a little each year!

He and John Dowsing do not have sons to carry on, but he thinks it likely that from among the fishing families along the coast someone will want to take on his lays: 'They know we grow big ones in good water. It might not be someone who lives *here*, can be someone 30 miles away. Before I retire I will put the word around. I have a ready market, so it's a good little number.'

## 'Ducking and diving' around Cley

John went on to tell me about the background to his present work and something of the fishing economy in his area. Like other fishermen, he took on other occupations off-season – 'it's all ducking and diving!' Samphire-picking was one, which runs from July until mid-September. Mark, one of the other mussel-fishermen, does reed-cutting from January to February. When he first left school John had gone bait-digging through the winter months, 'Like everyone else round here!'

John's family came from Cley. His father, Stanley Webster, had been in the merchant navy before turning to fishing. Stanley had gone after cockles, and has the distinction of having an area on the map named after him, 'Stanley's Cockle Bight'. Living on the coast road in Cley he had been in a good position for selling from the door: cockles, samphire and winkles. He would buy mussels from the fishermen who grew them in Blakeney Harbour and sell them on, then began helping one of them and eventually started his own lays.

Stanley was also crabbing off the beach from Cley. John:

In the summer months it was fishing. My father's idea was to fish in Blakeney
Harbour, whitebait and sand eels. Both were niche market, and nobody had done
that round here. He liked traditional ideas, also doing things slightly different.
Everyone else was crabbing, bait-digging and samphire-picking. Whitebait was to
supply restaurants, we had some good ones round here, Gashe's at Weybourne, the
Maid's Head Hotel in Norwich and another one in Brancaster. The sand eels were
for fishing bait. We used to pack them. We bought some freezers, packed them in
small packets and supplied quite a lot of tackle shops, such as in Lowestoft.

Before I left school and worked with him, he used to fish for sea trout. That
would start in spring, through summer right through until the end of September. In
those days sea trout was the Rolls Royce fish of the sea, worth a lot of money. Now
they farm salmon and trout has devalued, but the fish aren't here now anyway. He
made a little barrow about the size of this table with big wheels on, with a handle.
You put your nets, your flask and your gear in there. The two of you would go, you'd
wear wetsuits. At night the fish lose their sense of fear and come close to the shore.

He described beach seine-netting, with a weighted net and floats held up on two
poles. Two men would walk along, one on the beach, the other in the water. John:

You can come round without actually hauling the net. You can walk out to the net
and knock the fish on the head, bring them ashore and put them in the barrow.
You can cover a lot of ground in the night because you're very quick. It wouldn't
be unusual to get a hundred pound of fish in a night. And in those days they might
be worth the equivalent of £5 a pound today, so it was a lot of money when you
hit them. But there were plenty of nights when you got nothing. But that's fishing!

Father'd sell to the Swiss restaurant at Weybourne, a top restaurant round here
for many years – closed now. It was known country-wide, celebrities and stars from
Norwich went there. They sold a massive amount of fish in there, but any surplus
they would sell on to friends in racing and gambling – that's the way *that* would
operate. Then you had hotels in Blakeney, and the George in Cley, Cliftonville and a
select handful of top-class places.

We did it from Holkham Bay, Brancaster, Titchwell and Holme-next-the-Sea, all
along that stretch there. That's where you get the most sea trout coming in, in the
shallow water, and heading west, almost up to Heacham. I went sometimes, but by
the time I left school he more or less packed up doing this. It was a night-time job.
Then nylon (set) nets came in – traditionally it was cotton – people started taking
them in a barrow or a boat, they'd stake them down on the sand and virtually leave
them there. You couldn't do that with a cotton net because after a few weeks it
would rot. Once set or static nets came in, for the guy walking along there was all
these static nets in the way. You couldn't do it, and the job was finished!

Part-timers were going. Father was very bitter about it, because up till then it had
been a lovely way of life – very exciting when the fish hit the net. You'd come home

and they'd all be laid out like bars of silver. They were like people treat sea bass or lobsters now, they were a top class fish. Never any trouble getting rid of them. With set nets the writing was on the wall. Legally, you shouldn't set nets for sea trout because it is almost classed as a game fish, and different rules apply to it. But if they set a net out saying it is for mullet or bass and some sea trout get in there, and the chance is the fish in the net at low tide are dead anyway, what are they going to do – throw it back into the sea? You couldn't regulate that, to make them remove it.

We discussed fishing the native oysters, which had once been an important local resource. John:

Oysters used to be a staple diet years ago, with vinegar and pepper for working people. Now, like mussels they've gone upmarket with wine and garlic. Oysters used to be out here, but there's none now. No one knows why – a disease or dredged out, or other species move in or the seabed change. Once they used to go out of Blakeney Harbour and dredge them from the sea, in old wooden boats, sailing smacks, and bring them into the harbour. If you go down to Blakeney Harbour at low tide you can see areas marked out with big rocks and stones into squares. They were holding pits or lays. They used to bring oysters in from the sea and lay them in there. Still areas now you can find where there were masses of oyster shells where they were once really thick and several died. In Scalp Run and at the end of Freshes Creek there's some there, round and about.

Nowadays, faster-growing Pacific oysters have taken their place in the region. Some are grown in Blakeney Harbour, also to the west, at Brancaster and Thornham. One of the first to try growing Pacific oysters had been Major Athill, in the creeks around Morston. He sold them to classy restaurants in the region until he retired. John told me natural oysters are now being tried again by one or two fishermen in Blakeney Harbour. Ecologically, they tick all the right boxes.

# Bait-digging

Along the North Norfolk coast there were professional bait-diggers and fishermen who dug lug-worms off-season from their normal fishing. From the village of Salthouse, Ivan Large was one of the latter. Ivan spent his early years at Cley, the rest of his life in Salthouse. His father had worked as a roadman for the council, but the family has fishing connections going back generations, and Ivan married into a Cley fishing family. He first went to sea with his fisherman uncle, but worked on a farm when he left school: 'Fishing wasn't very good then, and I went bait-digging at weekends. But I found I could earn as much money doing this as I could on the farm all week, so I went bait-digging full-time. This was winter-time; we used to finish a fortnight before Christmas.'

He became a commercial fisherman in the 1960s with his brother-in-law, and continued bait-digging in wintertime: 'We used to do different things then. If at this time of the year (July) there's any samphire about, we'd pick that. You'd earn a quid wherever you could.' Some fishermen went sprout-picking in wintertime, but he had had enough of this on the farm:

> Bait-digging, we used to go anywhere from Blakeney right round to Heacham for miles, almost to King's Lynn. There were no lugworms here (Salthouse). But we used to dig them out this way – Blakeney was the first place you could get them. Hardly any of them were digging from King's Lynn; they'd be all in the big boats, they'd be musseling all the while. We got there by car, five or six of us, brother-in-law from Cley, Mears from Blakeney. Some of the Sheringham lot as well, Little and Bennett and them, West. It wasn't at all solitary, I had more fun than I did later on, we had a lot of laughs.

From Cromer, several fishermen had also gone, including the Cox brothers, 'Yacker' and Sid Harrison: 'It was dependent on the tides, when the tide was out you went digging. You didn't worry about the weather, you'd put your oilies on.' On very cold days the damp sand would freeze and the fork would not go in, and the fishermen sometimes had to run for it as the tide came in. Ivan was regarded as good at finding pristine places to dig. Retired fisherman David Leeder who went with others from Cromer, remembered Ivan as a superior bait-digger; he would go further off than they did and seemed to get a lot more worms on his fork as he dug. If they finished with 7–800, Ivan had 1,000. Professional bait-diggers who lived near the source of their livelihood would get half as many again. The worms had to be counted as they were dug, because they were then sold by the hundred not by weight. A few extra would be thrown in to compensate for nicked ones. Before the days of decimalisation, the prices would creep yearly from 5s, to 5s 6d, then 6s a hundred. Ivan:

> We sold them all over the country. Used to go up to Whitby, to Lowestoft and down to Dover, down the Thames, Yarmouth, Norwich, North Walsham. They used to go on the train from Sheringham and Holt. Then when the trains stopped – that was Beeching – we had to truck them through, and pay so much a box, and a bloke he'd take them through to Lowestoft. He'd pick them all up from Wells, Stiffkey, Blakeney, Cley, Salthouse. That's all he used to do, take them through every night. They were lining from Lowestoft for cod. That's why there were more bait-diggers in wintertime than any time at all, because of the lining in winter for cod. They went up north to Whitby, where they did a lot of lining there too. And shops used to buy them for anglers.

From Cley, John Webster had gone bait-digging with his father, later for a few years with a 'gang'. This was a time when there were plenty of worms and plenty of orders:

It was merciless. You're on these mudflats. There's no protection whatever weather is coming at you. Get your back into it and get on and dig for bait. You've got to be fairly tough to do that. I was brought up to do that. But it was hard on your back – mussels are bad enough! It was at Blakeney, Salthouse, all along, and in the Wash. One bloke in the gang supplied several tackle shops. They were quite valuable. When you're younger and you have to do it, you stick as many hours as possible. If they stopped imported lugworms from Holland where they dredge commercially, and there was still a demand, it could be revived. All you need is a fork, bucket, a piece of net to wash them in, and a piece of sack to lay them out on. I might do it again for few years before retiring, but not like before when I dug huge amounts. I'd just do it two or three hours, and enjoy it and not break my back! You can have twenty pound or so (carried) on your fork on your shoulder, small-scale, so not a tremendous weight. Two or three chaps who did it fifteen or twenty years ago have now come back to it.

# Cockling

Ivan Large occasionally went cockling 'to earn a shilling' when there was nothing else to fish in the wintertime and bait-digging had dropped off. Although occasionally done by fishermen, cockling was more often done by villagers who lived near the cockle grounds.

Ivan collected 'Stukey blues' from the main cockle grounds at Stiffkey. This was beyond the tracks which wandered north of Greenway lane and the mud flats. The mud here gives the shells a bluish-grey colour and its nutrients impart a good flavour. Another site was at Wells, in an area called West Lake. There are still cockles collected by the locals from Stiffkey and Wells for their own consumption, but I am told hand-working commercially is no longer viable.

Ivan explained commercial cockling by local hand-workers had been a cottage industry. To the west, Brancaster fishermen grow cockles in lays, while in the Wash, cockling is large-scale using boats – 'big boys' with suction dredges, and hand-rakers. It was easier to hand-work on foot, walking out from the marshes, as he had done here, rather than from a boat, where one had to wait until low tide before gathering cockles in the mud around it:

You've got to be out with the tide if you go out by boat, you're out there twelve hours. You have to wait for the tide to come back. But if you walk out you can get a peck of cockles and be home again in two or three hours. I was hand-raking. Put the bicycle in the back of the car, walk out then carry your cockles on the bike back so you didn't have to carry them on your back. It's hard work carrying. I used to riddle them out there, only bring the big stuff back, and put the small stuff back to grow. I had a round thing like a sieve, slats in it half an inch wide, or whatever it is,

and shake the cockles in it. But I never used a machine, though some of them used
a riddle machine.

He explained that areas of dead cockles occur by natural causes:

> They move about, and push one another out when they get big, and the tide washes
> some away, which die in the gulleys. I used to sell them going round houses, to the
> villages, and knock on doors. I put a bath on the back seat of the motor, an Austin
> 12, and fill it up with cockles, and sell them inland. After 3.30 when the women
> were back from work as the kids come back from school, you'd sell your stuff then.
> I never used to cook them, I'd sell them in the shell. But when we went round in
> wintertime selling cockles they wanted crabs, then as soon as the crabs come and
> I went round, they wanted cockles! But I hated going round selling things, I'd rather
> catch the things. Some would give a hard luck story and I'd end up giving to them!

Cockle-picking had been doing well at Stiffkey a generation before Ivan's time, and
earlier still. Frank Buckland, in 1875, had noted a hundred commercial cockle-pickers.
The local women had been a hardy breed of cockle-pickers. One of the few remaining ladies who had gone hand-cockling commercially is Mrs Marjorie Dowsing,
mother of mussel-fisherman John Dowsing. Now in her nineties, she had started
cockling in the 1930s. I went to see her in her pretty cottage in Stiffkey. Mrs Dowsing
is a lively lady with a sense of fun and a good memory. She talked about her experiences, with her son John filling in now and then:

> I came from a fishing family on my father's side, the Greens. They went to sea in
> those days, from Blakeney. They fished oysters then. My father was Nathaniel Green.
> He used to employ women to get the cockles, and he used to go to different vil-
> lages to sell them. My husband was not a fisherman – a builder, but I continued
> cockling after I got married, up to the '60s. I'd be fifty-odd when I stopped. I started
> when I was fourteen. I went with my aunts and cousins, all the family. They were all
> living in Stiffkey, and we all went together. I think it was only people from Stiffkey
> cockling then. There were always five or six people out there. We had some laughs!
> Other families were the Bucks, John Jarvis – there's none of them left now.

Since the latter half of the twentieth century, it has been holiday-makers who have
gone cockling. 'You didn't see anything of holiday-makers in those days. It was only
since the (army) camp that they had holiday-makers and that here. They came later, in
the '60s.' She told me all the cottages in Stiffkey were occupied then by agricultural
or fishing families, and second homes were unheard of:

> We went to different parts, from Greenway. One was The Low, that was a long way
> to walk – 2 miles! And Garborough Creek, and Patch Pit, Black Nock. We had

names for all the patches, and would say, 'Where shall we go today, the Little Hole or the Big Hole?' You got to know the patches, where to get the cockles. Then next day, you'd go somewhere else, another patch. If there had been a gale in the night, it was lovely the next day, they'd be washed into a heap and there'd be perhaps a bushel in one patch! If there had been a good tide there'd be plenty of cockles. You had to carry them on your back. We used to say it was 2 miles there and 2 miles back. I was living two houses down from here then, so it was a long way!

John added:

You'd get Wells people go cockling from Bob Hall's Sands, because it's not that far from Wells. There might be one or two from Wells, like the Frarys, a well-known fishing family, but they went that way and the Stiffkey women went the other way, and they'd meet in the middle. They (the women) had an apron which was back-wards so it was tied at the front. It hung down. They'd load the cockles on in the sack, and it would come up over the shoulders. The idea was you hold the two corners of your apron. Like a knapsack, yes.

Marjorie: 'You got as many as you could carry! We'd help load one another. Six pecks was a nice lot, a hundredweight. You had to be strong to carry six pecks. That's about eight stone! That is how you walked, and you'd be holding the strings like this.' She demonstrated how she would be quite bent over, giving a wriggle to ease her back now and then. She laughed when I expressed amazement at how strong the women must have been:

Well it doesn't seem to have done me any harm! No, I never strained my back, it strengthened my back.

You had to go according to the tides, what we called the morning tides or the afternoon tides. We liked the morning tides – 5 o'clock – because you'd got done and got home quick. It would be dark when we set out, but light when we got there. You'd go at low water. You'd watch and think the tide's gone, and we can go then. We'd be about four hours out there. It wasn't dangerous because you knew when to go and when the tide was coming in. We had tide books to know what time to go.

You had short boots – they were leather. In summertime it would be plimsolls. We wore ordinary clothes, not trousers. We thought trousers were only for men!

She demonstrated how their skirts were turned into pantaloons:

You pulled the back of your skirt through here, and tied round one leg, then the other leg. We wore a headscarf. When it rained, we just put up with it. You took your clothes off and put dry ones on back home. It was all the year round in those days. I wouldn't say every day, but you had to go so many times in the week because

Women cockle-pickers in Mrs Dowsing's time looked little different from these in 1927. Skirts were gathered up between their knees, and reversed aprons were used like knapsacks to carry sacks of cockles. (Norfolk County Library & Information Service)

people bought the cockles. It would have to be very bad if you didn't go. Later on we had bicycles.

The bag was laid over the 'V' of the frame of a lady's bike – not on the handlebars or it could not be steered! 'You had a knife, you'd go like *this*, you had them in your hand. Like that.' She demonstrated a flicking movement:

It wasn't an ordinary knife, but bent over. People used to make them themselves. Then we had a rake, which was better, and a net in the other hand. As you gathered them in the net, you sieved them. You wore gloves or you hurt your hands, they'd be raw with the movement. You went as quick as you could to get the cockles, to keep warm sometimes! The cockles were underneath the surface. You'd see what we called the 'eyes', and you'd think 'there's some here'.

I wouldn't say there were particular *good* years. But there was always several people to get cockles. In war time, you had to wait 'til the guns had finished firing, from Stiffkey camp. If the red flag was flying we weren't allowed to go. The noise would nearly take your head off! They'd let the guns off as we were coming home.

My father would buy the cockles from the Stiffkey women, and go to different villages to sell them, nearly to Norwich, and to Aylsham and all around there. Not the fish shops, he'd take them round the pubs, there were more pubs then. He had a small lorry – a 'tin Lizzie'. He also bought mussels, and would sell these.

John added:

> A horse and cart would come from different villages and pick so many up in the week from people what got them. They'd buy people's six pecks off them. There was Jack Buck, he went round with a horse and cart; he was collecting from the women. My father didn't have a horse and cart, always the truck. They were all bagged up in the vehicle. They were sold by the quarter-peck.

This was a wooden container, bearing a stamp and a crown because it was a legal measure. It was round, steamed to shape, made by a boat-builder for the cockle-sellers. Mrs Dowsing:

> You'd sell them live. But on a Friday my mother used to cook some. They'd be put in jars and my father would take them on the Saturday. She just boiled the cockles in a saucepan, as soon as they're opened they're cooked. You wash them well first. They weren't purified in those days, just washed and boiled. In the jars she put a small amount of vinegar in with the water. But not many were cooked, it was too much trouble – but some people wanted them.

Mrs Dowsing enjoyed her time cockling:

> I wish I could go now! I did not want to do anything else, like cleaning people's houses. And we had some laughs! But I did samphire-picking in samphire time, which lasted a month, but I didn't do anything else. But later on, in the 1960s I did do mussels with Lester. People had mussel lays then.

She had helped her brother and Johnny Bean at the riddling machine out on the marshes.

So ends my trawl around the North Norfolk coast, where I have looked at livelihoods earned from the sea. In living memory, much has either changed or gone. Conservation measures concentrate much on protecting fish stocks in the North Sea, but some fishermen now wonder if they are not endangered species too. Norfolk's coast would be unthinkable without the sights, smells and sounds of boats pulling in and fishermen unloading their catches. Let's hope Willy Cox's comment, 'There will *always* be fishermen at Cromer' will be true for the region as a whole.

# BIBLIOGRAPHY

Ayers, M. *Memoirs of a Shannock: Reminiscences of Sheringham over the last hundred years* (Larks Press, Dereham, 1995)

Barker, B. & D. Lowe. *Norfolk Carrier, Memories of a Family Hauling Business* (David Lowe, Wells-next-the-Sea, 2003)

Bartell, E. *Cromer considered as a watering place* (J. Taylor, 1806)

Brooks, P. *Sheringham: The story of a town* (3rd edn) (Poppyland Publishing, Cromer, 2002)

Brown, C. G. *Norfolk crab investigations 1969–73* (MAFF Laboratory leaflet (new series) no.30, Lowestoft, 1975)

Buckland, F. *Report on the Fisheries of Norfolk especially crabs, lobsters and herring and the Broads* (1875)

Butler, S. & C. Nunn. *Lost Norfolk Landscapes. Paintings by Horace Tuck (1876–1951)* (Halsgrove Press, Tiverton, 2006)

Catling, M. & R. Malster. *North Norfolk Estuary and Beach Boats* (*Norfolk Sailor, No. 13* pp9–20, 1967–9)

Chapelle, H. I. *Boatbuilding, a complete handbook of wooden boat construction* (W. Norton, New York, 1941)

Childs, A. & A. Sampson. *Time & Tide: The story of Sheringham's fishermen and their families* (Mousehold Press, Norwich, 2004)

Cooke, E. W. *Shipping and Craft: A facsimile edition with descriptive notes by R. Frank* (Masthead, London, 2004)

Craske, S. & R. *Sheringham: A century of change* (Poppyland Publishing, North Walsham, 1985)

Daniels, S. *List of crab boats built by W.N. May* (Unpublished ms. held in Cromer Museum, 1999)

Defoe, D. *Tour through the Eastern Counties* (1724, republished 1949, East Anglian Magazine Ltd)

*Eastern Sea Fisheries Joint Committee Reports 2004–7* (King's Lynn, Norfolk)

Emery, M. 'Boat Building in Sheringham' (*Sheringham Shantymen Songbook* pp14–15, Rounce and Wortley, North Walsham, undated)

Emery, R. 'Down to the sea' (1953 BBC interview part-transcribed in *Norfolk Journal*, 14 April 1978)

Festing, S. *Fishermen: A community living from the sea* (David & Charles, Stamford, 1977. Reprinted 1999)

Goodwyn E. A. *Cromer Past* (E.A. Goodwyn, Beccles, 1979)

Heaton, T. *North Norfolk Images* (EDP Publishing, Norwich, 1998)

Lown, J. (ed). *Memories of Old Sheringham*. Sheringham Cameos no.1 (Sheringham History Group, 2003)

MAFF Laboratory leaflet no. 12. *The Norfolk Crab Fishery* (Burnham on Crouch, 1966)

Mr Marten's Diary, 1825 (unpublished ms. held in Norfolk Record Office)

McDonald, B. 'Workaday Classics', pp19–24 (*Classic Boat*, May 1990)

McKee, E. *Working Boats of Britain* (Conway Maritime Press, London, 1983)

March, E. J. *Inshore Craft of Britain Vol. I* (David & Charles, 1970)

Roll, K. *Cromer Crabbers: A Project about the Famous Norfolk Crab Boats* (Unpublished ms. held in Cromer Museum, Lowestoft College dissertation, 1990)

Perkins, G. *Wells-on-Sea, A Town and its People as it once was* (G. Perkins, Wells-next-the-Sea, 1996)

Rye, W. *Cromer, past and present* (Jarrolds, Norwich, 1889)

Sanctuary, A. *Rope, Twine and Net Making.* Shire Albums no. 15 (2$^{nd}$ edn, Shire Books, Princes Risborough, 1988)

Savin, A.C. *Cromer – A Modern History* (Holt 1937, reprinted 1950)

Sinclair, O. *Potter Heigham. The Heart of Broadland* (Poppyland Publishing, North Walsham, 1989)

Simper, R. *Beach Boats of Britain* (Boydell Press, Woodbridge, 1984)

Sparham, M. .*Fishing: The Coastal Tradition* (Batsford, London, 1987)

Stagg, F.N. (ed V. Fiddman). *Salthouse: The Story of a Norfolk Village* (Salthouse History Group, 2003)

Stammers, M. *Norfolk Shipping* (Tempus, Stroud, 2002)

Stibbons, P., K. Lee & M. Warren. *Crabs & Shannocks: The longshore fishermen of North Norfolk* (Poppyland Publishing, North Walsham, 1983)

Storey, N. *Norfolk: A Photographic History 1860–1960* (Sutton Publishing, Stroud, 1996)

Tooke, C. *The Great Yarmouth Herring Industry* (Tempus Publishing, Stroud, 2006)

Unknown. *The Royal Album of Cromer* (engravings by Rock & Co., R.B. & P., London, undated)

Unknown. *Cromer, Norfolk: Gem of the Norfolk Coast. Official Guide* (Cromer Urban District Council, 1954)

Unknown. *Cromer and Sheringham boat listings. July 2002* (Unpublished ms. held in Cromer Museum)

Ward, C. *The Cottage on the Cliff: A Seaside Story* (G. Virtue, Bristol, 1823)

Warren, M. *Cromer: Chronicle of a watering place* (Poppyland Publishing, North Walsham, 1988)

Warren, M. *Around Cromer: Britain in old photographs* (Alan Sutton, Stroud, 1995)

White, E.W. *British Fishing-boats and Coastal Craft. Part 1: Historical Survey* (HMSO, London, 1950. Reprinted 1957)

White, E.W. *British Fishing-boats and Coastal Craft. Part 2: Descriptive Catalogue and the Related Collections* (HMSO, London, 1952)

Worfolk, S. *Whelks and Whelk Fishery at Lynn* (True's Yard Publications, King's Lynn, 1992)

Additional newspaper and magazine articles:

*Cromer and North Norfolk Post,* 16 June, 14 July and 18 July 1894

*Eastern Daily Press / North Norfolk News,* various articles

*The Times,* 25 January 1978

*Norfolk Fair,* May 1972 (R.F. Eastern Ltd, Norwich)

*Whitby Gazette,* 25 November 1876, 'The crab and lobster fisheries. Official inquiries at Whitby and Robin Hood's Bay'

Directories:

*J.G. Harrod and Co's Postal and Commercial Directory of Norfolk and Norwich* (London & Norwich, 1868)

*Kelly's Directory of Norfolk* (Kelly's Directories Ltd, London. 1890, 1896)

*Pigot and Co's National Commecial Directory* (Pigot & Co., London , 1830, 1831)

*The Post Office Directory of Cambridge, Norfolk and Suffolk.* E.R. Kelly (ed) (London, Kelly & Co., 1869, 1875)

*Jarrolds' Directory of Cromer and Neighbourhood* (London, 1896)

*White's Norfolk Directory 1845.* W. White, ed. (David and Charles Reprints, Newton Abbot, Devon, 1969)

Other sources

1841 Census. Norfolk County Council Library and Information Centre.

Norfolk Record Office, Norwich Consistory Court Will Register. 'Aleyn' Folio 34.

# INDEX

Due to the large numbers of times individual fishermen are mentioned in the text, not all their page references have been included in the Index. References to images are shown in bold type.